SALONE ITALIANO

THE TRUE STORY OF AN ITALIAN IMMIGRANT FAMILY'S STRUGGLES IN SOUTHWESTERN COLORADO

BY KAY NIEMANN

WESTERN REFLECTIONS PUBLISHING COMPANY®
Montrose, CO

ISBN-13: 978-1-932738-25-4
ISBN-10: 1-932738-25-8

Library of Congress Control Number: 2005929379

Cover and text design: Laurie Goralka Design

First Edition
Printed in the United States of America

Western Reflections Publishing Company®
219 Main Street
Montrose, CO 81401
www.westernreflectionspub.com

CONTENTS

INTRODUCTION

"Which building was your grandfather's saloon?" my husband asks as we walk along the busy sidewalk near the train depot on Main Avenue in Durango, Colorado.

"I'm not sure," I answer, looking around. I was born and raised in Durango, but now I'm only a visitor, a tourist like the many people crowding the streets.

Durango has changed from the small quiet town I remember as a child, and today it is a bustling place. People gather from all over the world to ride the old coal-fired, steam-powered, narrow gauge train. This railroad system was originally built to transport precious ore out of the remote and rugged San Juan Mountains. It now carries eager tourist-passengers from Durango to Silverton over a treacherous route through a scenic mountain wonderland. When these sightseers arrive in Silverton, they experience and discover a small town that is a relic of the old mining days.

My grandparents were Italian immigrants who settled in Colorado when Durango was in its beginning stages of development and Silverton was a "boomtown" mining community. I experience a feeling of pride knowing that my grandfather built one of these buildings in Durango and that my great-grandfather built the notorious Belleview Saloon in Silverton. But I also feel disturbed that my family history will soon be forgotten, its stories held secret in these buildings.

Then came the letters, landing in my hands as if by grace. I first received an acknowledgement from Angela, a distant Italian-American cousin. She told me of the discovery of letters written from Colorado to family in Italy at the beginning of the last century. Another cousin, Lino Naretto, had found the letters while cleaning out the attic of his parent's home in Italy. Realizing the historical value of the more than 150 letters, written from 1903-1940, he had organized and numbered them in preparation for publication.

Angela and Lino wondered if I would be interested in helping with this project, but I don't think either of them was prepared for the enthusiasm this sparked in me. In my excitement I spread the news of these letters to friends and extended family, hoping that connections could be made, puzzle pieces fit into place, and questions answered. From different parts of the world we bonded together in anticipation. As one Italian-American relative wrote, "The world is small and shaped like a boot."

Progress in deciphering the letters was complicated because they were written in Italian, and it was not often legible. The language was made up of fragments of Piemontese dialect mixed with words from Italian and even from English, with non-existent grammatical structure. They had expressed themselves the best they could, considering some of them were barely literate. Angela agreed to help with translation: Speaking English, Italian, and the Piemontese dialect, she was willing to put forth the effort needed to make these letters comprehensible.

As I read the letters, I discovered the writers to be colorful and the events powerful, so I decided to use the information to tell a story instead of simply having the letters published. As a child I lived in the same house with my grandparents, so I had an understanding of their personal traits, and knowledge of other relatives and family friends as well. With all the facts and information gathered, I decided to use my imagination to bring them to life. I had no need to add fictional characters or to change the facts; therefore, this story is true.

When we are young, we have no past, and we are like sponges absorbing everything that helps to influence our future. Because of this, the letters became a story and extended those precious moments of my youth to another realm of understanding and acceptance. I share stories from these letters, knowing that my ancestors will live again in the words they wrote. They traveled far away from those they loved, but the letters kept them united as a family. Today, the letters magically connect us once again.

EXPLANATION of the DIALECT

I would like to thank Angela Peila Sundquist and Michele (Lino) Naretto for help with the bits of language sprinkled throughout the text. That language is not Italian, but a dialect called Piemontese (of the Italian Piedmont Region). It can also be referred to more precisely as Rivarolese, the language spoken in the town of Rivarolo Canavese. Lino and Angela are first cousins, and natives of this region. They grew up speaking the language, as well as proper Italian, but they both feel a deep pride for the dialect that attaches them to this special area in Italy. For this book, wording was chosen that would have been spoken at the time of the story. As languages are living and ever changing, this dialect is now different from what it was a century ago. Angela laments that with mobility, intermarriage, and immigration from other regions and other countries, dialects are dying out completely.

Readers who are not familiar with dialects must not confuse them with accents, such as we hear in Boston or Houston. Dialects are actual languages, although they may contain similarities in specific regions. It is probable that similarities in dialects will exist the closer the villages are to one another. For example, Favria, a village located just three kilometers away from Rivarolo, has a dialect of its own. Although the dialect is still Piemontese, many words are different from Rivarolese. Actually, the entire Piedmont Region is close to France and the dialects reflect this linguistic influence.

The differences in dialect, according to Lino, are not only in words, but there are differences in grammar as well. Pronunciations of words and verb conjugations may also vary, and dialects are usually a spoken language, not written. I am grateful for all of the caring work in the writing and translating of this fascinating language, because the inserted bits of dialect add much to the expression and feeling of the story.

Silverton, Colorado—
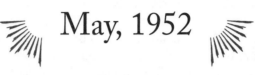 May, 1952

High above the cascading Animas River, our car descends slowly along the narrow two-lane highway into Silverton from Durango. Sitting in the back seat with my grandma, I move closer to her, away from the side of the car nearest the cliff's edge. I look toward the jutting rocks of the steep mountain on one side of the road. Springs of water pour out like little waterfalls, tumbling down the side and onto the road. There are still patches of snow in places, and it is melting in the fresh rays of sunshine as winter retreats slowly in the cool air and high altitude. When we meet another car heading up the mountain, the road is hardly wide enough for the two vehicles to creep past each other. The small town of Silverton can be seen far below as we make our descent, but I find it difficult to look out into the deep, treacherous canyon. It seems that we could easily tumble off this narrow, precarious road where there isn't even a tree to stop us from plummeting into the river.

Nearing the base of the steep mountain, the road finally levels and we leave the highway, approaching the almost vacant town of Silverton. The car moves slowly through the streets to enable pointing and talking about buildings and places. Silverton is considered a ghost town, with quiet streets and buildings that stand as reminders of the boomtown days of the late 1800s. I try to see it as it once was: miners coming into town, horses pulling wagons full of supplies, burro trains loaded with valuable ore, and streets alive with noises from rowdy saloons and dance halls. I recreate a fantasy of the past through the prism of my matinee-movie imagination. At this stage of my life, I have no interest in the lives of the people sitting in the car with me. Perhaps because they are familiar to me, I don't listen seriously. I would later understand that the stories of their days in Silverton rivaled the legends created by Hollywood and portrayed in western movies.

Grandma touches my arm and points to an old structure. I nod my head. It is an old saloon. Her father built it and her family lived there when they came to America from Italy. It had been a grand

Silverton, Colorado. Courtesy P. David Smith.

building in its day. Now it is old but almost unchanged. Everything in Silverton remains much the same as it was. We continue out of town until we come to Hillside Cemetery.

Grandpa and Uncle Phil get out of the car and take shovels and rakes out of the trunk. I reach for the car door to get out, too, but I realize that my grandmother is crying. She reaches into her pocketbook for a hanky and sobs with her head in her hands. I feel a tug of alarm and nervously ask, "What's wrong, Grandma? Aren't we getting out?"

Grandma reaches for my hand and tearfully tries to explain. I struggle to understand as she lets painful memories pour out. A Sartore relative had been accused of being a horse thief, she says, but he was innocent. "What happened to him, Grandma?" She shrinks back suddenly, as if never expecting to be faced with the question.

"They shot him," she says simply. I would find out later that his death in 1906 was shrouded in speculation, but that he had been shot while allegedly stealing horses. Regardless of his guilt or innocence, Angelo Sartore is buried here at Hillside Cemetery in the family burial plot.

Before I could absorb this touching tale, she starts another one. The man in this story, she tells me, was murdered. She then corrects herself. "It was a mining accident," then, "an explosion." She doesn't know how to make this clear to me, but the sorrow and pain that she has kept buried deep within was struggling to surface.

"It was foul play," she reveals through sobs and tears. It was as if the words "foul play" had been rehearsed often or used by others in reference to this story. "Please don't cry, Grandma," I plead, tightly gripping her hand.

She gathers herself quickly as Grandpa and Uncle Phil return to the car. They had cleaned up the family cemetery site in preparation for Memorial Day. Uncle Phil mentions that he will return with Aunt Jennie and Annie to place flowers in a few days.

We then drive to Silverton's main street and stop for ice cream. We sit, relaxed and comfortable at an old table inside a tiny bakery shop, and they converse in Italian with some local people they know. Happy that the disturbing outburst is over, I return to my reverie.

I gaze out the window where there is no view into the future. In Silverton, it is as if time stands still and only the past remains. The old buildings are of another century, and they are here as they were when the mines closed and many of the people left. I like to imagine myself living an adventure in Silverton during those wild "boomtown" days. But looking at my grandmother and remembering her tears, I wonder.

CHAPTER I

Angelina

"Presto, masnè! E sen 'n ritard për 'l treno!" "Children, hurry! We are late for the train."

The New York City train depot was crowded and bursting with confusion as immigrants from Europe con-verged on the city. There was chaos, because no one knew where to go. The discordant, harsh sounds of various languages penetrated the cold morn-ing air as people rushed around in noisy chatter, trying to find the cor-rect train to board. The city was alive with a disordered blend of peo-ple who were now attempting to travel into the heartland of America.

Angelina grabbed the hand of her oldest daughter and struggled forward against the waves of human-ity that surged in different directions. The black engine loomed up ahead, and she glanced down at her ticket once more to check the number the ticket master had circled, because she feared board-ing the wrong train.

Angelina Giordano Sartore,
circa 1895.

When they finally shoved their way clear and boarded the railroad car, they had to scramble to find four seats together. The children quickly plopped themselves onto a bench of seats, making room for their mother. Soon people were standing, sitting in aisles, and crowd-ing three and four people into a seat meant only for two.

Angelina didn't understand American ways or customs and she had no one to help her. She experienced moments of panic, and as the train started moving she sat upright saying quickly, *"A valo tüt ben?"* "Is everything all right?" Were they on the right train? She could not comprehend what the porter was saying, nor did she know if she had paid him enough to handle the huge trunks. Those were special trunks with her family name, GIORDANO, stamped in large letters, a reminder of the loving parents she left behind in Italy. She uttered a prayer that the trunks were safely on the train as she edged forward on her seat with an agitated motion, as if to go and check on them. But Giovanna, her oldest daughter, grabbed her arm and pulled her back into the seat, with the reassurance that everything was all right.

Giovanna, Angelina, Filippo and Caterina Sartore in 1892.

What would life hold for her now that she had left the shelter of her homeland? It wasn't her decision to leave Italy, but the choice of her husband. *"Al diau 'l dì che 'n sù marià!"* "To the devil the day I married him!" she swore under her breath. All this pain and trouble because she had married Louis Sartore!

The children were settling into the rocking, rumbling motion of the railroad car. Giovanna, the oldest at age fifteen, was handing out the bread and sausages they had managed to purchase before boarding the train. Caterina, age fourteen, and her brother, Filippo, age eight, sat quietly eating their lunches, looking weary and fatigued from their three weeks of travel. The hems of the girls' long skirts were soaked with slush and mud from the busy winter streets of New York City, and they all had wet, cold feet.

Conditions on the train were insufferable because of the number of passengers and the weather. It was January, and the train was freezing cold. Because of the bleak, damp weather, the train car now had a soggy, stagnant odor and smelled of garlic. The cigarette smoke was suffocating. Babies cried and most everyone grumbled about the congested conditions. Angelina looked around and realized that she was no different from the hundreds of other displaced persons. She was afraid, and it was difficult to be hopeful about her final destination.

Keeping her fear under control so as not to upset the children was the hardest part. The landscape sped by as she tried to veil her thoughts by staring out the window.

She allowed her mind to float back to brighter days spent in the warm sunshine of the northern Italian countryside. Even though it was deep winter and cold in Italy now, in Angelina's forlorn state of mind it would always remain a warm, safe haven. Her eyes closed as she searched for a fond memory. She was lonely here: The feeling of being cast adrift in a strange place was overwhelming.

She remembered growing up with her two younger sisters and she pictured her parents, simple and loving. Her poor father had endured the task of raising three daughters, never complaining that there were no sons to carry on his family name. Not minding a house full of young women, Domenico Giordano smiled and gloated that he had fathered three very beautiful and brightly spirited girls. He enjoyed a feeling of pride in seeing them together, watching people stare in admiration.

Domenico Giordano was not a wealthy man, but he pointed out that his daughters would not require large dowries. His eyes twinkled as he talked of the many suitors already knocking on the door.

Papa Giordano had expected her to be happy when he told her an agreement had been reached with the Sartore family for her marriage. Recalling her father's excitement, Angelina grimaced in painful memory. Her parents were both pleased that Angelina's future would now be secure, giving no thought to her feelings on the matter. "Marriage is the only future for a young woman," Mama Giordano had preached. "Learn to cook and make a happy home."

Domenico and Caterina Giordano, circa 1895.

Angelina shook her head in disgust, remembering the day of the announcement of her betrothal. Her future was handled like a business arrangement where each family hoped to benefit. She understood that it was customary for the families involved to discuss what was best, but it was cruel and unjust all the same. It was explained to her that this system existed in order to secure a line of legitimate and approved descendants for the inheritance of family property, but why did she have no choice in the matter?

She had screamed, *"A l'é nin giüst!"* "Injustice!" How could they do this? But her parents would not yield or even waver in their decision for her future. Louis Sartore was considered a good choice because his father was educated and the family was respected as prominent landowners. This was important because the patriarchal family was built around the name of the father.

At first, Angelina fought all the forces surrounding her, even Louis himself. She carried on in a rage, with complaints that her parents were unfair in not allowing her to choose her own husband. Her parents were fearful she would frighten Louis away with her belligerent attitude. They warned her that she might upset him.

"Then he'll just have to be upset." Angelina spat out the words. "Perhaps it is the best way to explain to a future husband I will not be complacent nor pushed around by him."

She then softened her approach and asked, "What if I am unhappy and miserable in marriage?"

Her mother offered no words of condolence. "It is a wife's duty to learn to love her husband."

It was obvious that Angelina and Louis were of different natures. Angelina was slow and deliberate, while Louis was quick and anxious to move everything out of his way. The parents reasoned that perhaps these differences would be good and would complement each other. Marriage is a necessity of society, and the forthcoming generation would benefit from this decision. The two families had agreed that this would be a good union and nothing was more important than preserving the family unit.

As the train moved along, Angelina felt her face relax into a smile, remembering that Louis seemed pleased to have her as his bride after a stormy courtship. They didn't know each other well because they were strictly chaperoned before the wedding. Louis was a little older than Angelina, and this was customary. The men were expected to be experienced and wise in the ways of the world, while women were to be innocent about everything in life. It was taught that a young woman must remain chaste, simple, and naïve, as this was the kind of girl that a man would consider best suited to be a wife.

The day a woman married, she ceased to have anything of her own. From that moment on the husband owned everything, her property and all her rights, and he could administer chastisement at a whim. Yet marriage was almost a necessity as a means of support and protection, and from a very early age, young girls were taught that they needed a man to take care of them. Education for a woman was limited, so they had no access to positions of power on their own.

She now thought of a wedding as merely a ceremony to give a young woman one glorious celebration before casting her off into a life of subjection to her husband's will! "Because of my husband, I am on a train on another continent, moving away from my parents and my homeland."

Angelina's early days of marriage had been happy enough. She was shy and submissive at first, qualities that men desire in a wife. But she was cunning, learning that she could win arguments by using her sweetness to manipulate her husband.

Louis was encouraged by the passion in his young bride. He was often brusque and hurried, but Angelina's calm and gentle ways ultimately helped to light a fire in Louis. He was delighted when she announced that she was pregnant with their first child. As the train clicked along, these early days of marriage conjured up fond memories for Angelina, and she felt a rekindling of the closeness and love she had shared with her husband.

Her mind continued to drift as the train moved forward, and she now realized that much of her happiness during those early years had not revolved around Louis. He kept himself busy with his work, leaving her time to spend with her mother and sisters. Italian women were expected to find happiness in the home or with other female family members, while the men went wherever they pleased.

Angelina remembered blooming with joy through her first pregnancy. That is, until her sister, Catterina Antonia, or "Catlina," created havoc in the Giordano household. It was as if war had been declared between the middle daughter and her parents.

Catlina announced her love for Antonio Nigra. This wouldn't have been a problem ordinarily, but both Nigra brothers intended to travel to America. Catlina, madly in love, planned to go with them.

Antonio was as sincere in his intention to marry her as he was determined to emigrate.

The brothers were persuaded to leave Italy by recruiters from the United States, who traveled through Europe in search of workers to help develop companies that mined coal, copper, iron, silver, and gold. The glorious tales they told of wealth and new opportunities were the incentive for many to leave their homes in Europe during this time period.

The Giordanos were firm in their decision to keep Catlina in Italy, saying she was too young and didn't understand what life in a primitive foreign country would be like. She would face poverty and loneliness while her family would be far away, unable to comfort or help her.

Catlina screamed at them, saying she would throw herself onto the ship as it left port if not allowed to marry Antonio. She would run away with him if not given the benefit of a wedding by her parents.

Torturous days of family fights continued, and the parents wept, not knowing how to prevent their second daughter from going across the ocean far away from them. In the end, Catlina prevailed in her wishes, and the Giordanos gave the young couple a suitable wedding.

Because he had taken a wife, Antonio now had the problem of paying for two passages to America. The young couple first had to struggle to save up the necessary amount of money, thus the early days of their marriage were difficult. They lived in a house with a dirt floor, "not much better than a barn," as Mama Giordano described it. They had only one table and a chair, so Catlina had to sit on the windowsill at meal-

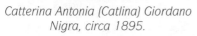

Catterina Antonia (Catlina) Giordano Nigra, circa 1895.

time. The young couple was in love, so these dismal circumstances and the delay in their plans to emigrate didn't seem to matter.

During all this confusion, a pregnant Angelina, in her attempts to console her parents, talked constantly of nothing but a baby boy. She knew things would be perfect if she would produce a son, an heir to the Sartore name and properties. Her mother and youngest sister, Margherita, warned her that she might have a baby girl. Carrying a baby "high" usually meant the baby was a girl. This talk was just silly wives' tales to Angelina.

So, despite the disappointment of giving birth to a girl, it was a happy moment for Angelina as her daughter, "Giovanna," entered this world. The baby was named after Louis' mother, Giovanna Vota. The lovely, healthy little baby was beautiful and the very picture of her father. Louis was passive about the new baby girl, as Angelina had feared he would be. She knew she had displeased him by not giving birth to a son.

Feeling the warmth of that day, remembering the closeness as she clung to her baby, Angelina smiled within herself. Now, as the mother of this precious, beautiful baby girl, she would never feel alone. She wanted to please Louis, but she would also shut him out if he ignored this child. She felt a pang of longing in remembering that bittersweet day, the happiness blending with the disappointment.

Angelina woke momentarily from her reverie to check on the children. *Mè povre cit!* They were all sleeping in awkward positions, as the train rocked and swayed along the tracks. As she looked at her children, it occurred to her that soon her daughters would be old enough to marry. How would she be able to find proper husbands for them in this foreign place? Her lips tightened as she realized that she had been only a little older than Giovanna when she married.

With all the pain and the difficulties relating to this journey, she had been too busy to think about the future and security of her daughters. She had many other things to worry about and, for the moment, she had to put that one aside.

Angelina once again sought the solace of the past and returned to her thoughts, remembering that amidst the upheaval created by Catlina, she remained content with life. She had her baby girl and Louis had a good job. He had finally secured a position as administrator at the local hospital. She realized, however, that Louis and his brother, Joseph, were planning something, and she resented the fact that her husband would not take her into his confidence. It infuriated her when he told her that it had to do only with a man's world.

"Al diau 'dco fina cul dì!" "I curse the day I married!"

She could tell that things were bothering Louis, because he became upset when she pushed him to talk about the subject. Saying that she knew only about household matters and needed to produce babies, he told her to leave him to his business. She felt anger growing inside her and wanted to tell him she was pregnant again, but she held her tongue. It would be a boy this time and this would give her power over her husband. She found it disgusting that a woman had to prove her worth through childbearing.

Those crucial days flashed into Angelina's mind and stirred her anger once again. She remembered her shock as the brothers' plan unfolded. Louis and Joseph were concerned about financial security. For this reason, they were considering going to America, the land of opportunity, where fortunes could be made overnight! All Angelina could do was pray that this would not happen.

Joseph had married Angelina Dighera, and now both brothers had wives named Angelina. Angelina Dighera became pregnant with her first child at the same time as Angelina was expecting her second child. The two women were close friends and spent happy moments preparing for their babies. Both Sartore wives gave birth to baby girls in 1880.

Angelina tried to hide the disillusionment that seemed to flood over her as she gazed down at the face of her second baby girl. She hated this dejected feeling, but she knew Louis felt the same disappointment. Only a boy would satisfy her husband's wishes for a family heir. Sighing deeply, she kissed her newborn infant. They named the baby Caterina after her own mother, Caterina Giordano.

Joseph and Angelina Dighera named their baby girl Maria. Together the Sartore families had three baby girls very close in age. It was hoped they would all grow up together in a strong family unit.

A short time after the birth of his daughter, Joseph Sartore made the decision to leave Italy and find work in America. Angelina tried not to bother herself with worry when he left. "Perhaps your brother will find it undesirable and return to Italy," she said to Louis. However, with the arrival of each letter from Joseph, it was evident that he was working and making a new life for himself in Colorado. He settled in a mining town called Silverton. Two years passed, and although he sent money to support his wife and young daughter, his family became increasingly concerned that Joseph would not return to Italy.

Angelina's now reflected on Antonio Nigra's move to America. It had been a struggle for the Nigras. To earn passage, Antonio first worked driving a delivery cart to Torino, but he later took a better paying job digging tunnels through the mountains toward France. He finally saved enough money for his trip, but by this time they had a young daughter, Frances, and a baby son, Joseph. Catlina stayed behind with the children when Antonio left for America in 1887.

As the train moved along, Angelina felt tears welling up in her eyes as she remembered Catlina's hardships and her own. During this difficult time of tension for them all, she lost two babies. America! She blamed Louis for the two miscarriages she suffered, but she also blamed herself for the weakness that came from the fear that her husband would soon leave Italy and join his brother in America.

She remembered how Louis read every word from his brother with extreme care, as if a secret message would unravel. He looked distant, and his face held a longing she did not want to acknowledge. Angelina knew Louis wanted to join his older brother. With this realization, she tried to swallow the feeling of panic. Appearing calm while cleaning up after the children, she struggled to keep her composure. The two lively little girls were chasing each other around the room. She loved them, but she realized the power a little boy would hold over his father.

"I think I'm pregnant," she told Louis, not stopping her chores while she talked casually. "This time it will be a boy."

Angelina remembered Louis' half-acknowledged awareness of her announcement and how he gave his full attention to the letter. She knew he was thinking that he had much to do in making plans to travel to this land called Colorado, but he would not discuss it with her. She would have no choice in this decision anyway, and she knew he didn't want to bother with her tears and heart-felt pleas.

The world grew dark for Angelina as Louis finally prepared for his forthcoming trip. Amidst this feeling of gloom, she fulfilled her prophecy and delivered a healthy son. They named the baby Filippo, after Louis' father, with the middle name of Joseph, to honor his brother.

The day before Filippo's christening, a major blow was delivered. Joseph sent money for his wife and daughter to join him in Silverton. The family was being torn apart, and this was a sign that Joseph planned to stay in Colorado. They were all afraid that none of them would or could return to Italy once they settled in America. Angelina saw this as a door opening for Louis, while in her life a door was closing.

Not long after this, an intently eager Louis left his wife and three young children, promising to send money as soon as he found employment in Silverton. With both Louis and Joseph gone, there would be no income and Angelina would have to depend on whatever money Louis sent them for survival.

She smiled arrogantly within herself now, recalling the pride she demonstrated that day. She did not allow herself to cry or plead with him to change his mind. As a man, he was free to find adventure or to seek success wherever he desired. She had three children and her aging parents to care for. As Louis left that day, Angelina cursed him under her breath.

Yes, he sent a bit of money to his family in Italy from time to time, very little money. *A basta nin.* Angelina fought to swallow back the anger that this thought brought out in her. She heard the rumors that both Louis and Joseph kept prostitutes in "cribs" in Silverton. What would she find when she got there? She didn't understand or like this new direction in which life was taking her. She didn't know her husband anymore, and she didn't want to go to Silverton! *"E vöj nin 'ndar!"*

Angelina's mind wandered to Catlina again, remembering that by 1890 Antonio had saved enough money to bring his family to America. So Catlina, Frances, and Joseph finally followed Antonio to the "new world." They had only a few belongings but Catlina lovingly retained her prized possession—a wool mattress. Catlina settled with her husband in the copper mining area of Calumet, Michigan. Antonio worked different shifts in the mines as a timberman, while she operated their home as a boarding house.

The Giordanos were grief stricken, wondering if they would ever see their daughter and grandchildren again.

The rocking of the train lulled Angelina as she recalled the years after Louis' departure. The Giordano family was hit with another blow, this one from their youngest daughter, Margherita. Now Angelina had to face up to the realization of what had happened to her youngest sister.

Margherita was the victim of a contradictory society. One side told of love and romance in stories and songs, while the other side expressed strict religious values that forbade these feelings. Opera was a passion for Italians, and this was a time when the operas of Giuseppe Verdi were gaining popularity and were considered to express the "soul" of Italy. The stories in these operas, such as *La Traviata,* were often based on illicit love affairs and were vaguely explained to young children with sighs of disapproval. While Italy held to the strict moral teachings of the Catholic Church, it also resounded with Verdi's beautiful music.

Margherita fell in love with a traveling musician. She wasn't to blame. The smile of that handsome young man would have melted the heart of any maiden. He was tall, with flowing blond hair, and had an open, warm personality and a tenor voice that resonated with passion when he sang.

She found it impossible to treat him like air and look right through him. He seemed to single her out in the audience, giving her his full attention as he sang heartfelt romantic arias from all the popular operas. She began to wait for him after each performance and they would stroll

Margherita Giordano, circa 1895.

together along the river. She would listen attentively to his dreams of becoming a great opera star. Margherita was soon attending every performance and delighted in being asked to pass the tin cup for gratuity from the crowd.

Angelina was fearful and protective of her sister, but she thought it beautiful watching Margherita blossom in her love for this inappropriate man. The girls had been brought up with their mother's words hammering in their heads: "Don't forget, a man is not yours until you marry." But in her youthful innocence, Margherita was blind to everything except the happiness flowing through her with this special love.

Unfortunately, Margherita was soon to suffer fear and humiliation. She stood there, stunned and confused when she realized her lover had left town, and that she might be pregnant. Her first thoughts were of sin, because she had been taught that a mortal sin like this would send her soul straight to hell. She knelt in the church, fervently in prayer, before the statue of the blessed Mother Mary, begging the statue to grant her salvation. As she stared at the statue, she studied the baby Jesus held by his mother. Now her worries about her own tortured soul were replaced with agony of concern for her unborn babe.

Her fervent praying and the tears streaming down her face caught the attention of a young and understanding priest. He gently coaxed her into talking and convinced her to be brave, saying God would grant her forgiveness through her confession. She explained to him that she was afraid to have a baby out of wedlock. But the priest talked lovingly about God's ways, persuading her to have faith that God already loved the baby growing inside of her. With a renewed sense of direction and hope, Margherita decided to face her family.

Angelina now remembered the horror and pain she experienced when Margherita came crying to her with this problem. In a moment of shared trepidation, they had clung to each other and cried anguished tears. Angelina had finally come to her senses, promising her sister that together they would find a way to mend this situation. Hope in Margherita's wounded heart seemed to be growing as Angelina reassured her that having a baby was a beautiful thing and that God, being merciful, would not condemn her for it. However, they both feared that Margherita would now be looked upon as a "used" woman, unworthy of ever having a proper marriage.

With encouragement from the young priest and Angelina for support, Margherita finally explained the degrading tale to her parents, crying for understanding and a solution. Her parents were at first stricken with the enormity of the problem, but being gentle and loving, they were soon crying and consoling their daughter. Margherita expressed heartfelt sorrow for the shame this would bring to her family. Her parents forgave her weakness, and with tearful affirmations they now focused on hiding this disgrace from the community.

The Giordanos concluded that because Catlina was living far away from the eyes of the Italian community, the solution would be for them to somehow appropriate funds and provide Margherita passage to America. Under the pretense of "going for a visit to help Catlina," Margherita could live with her sister until after the baby was born. This would save the dignity of the family. They would have to hurry with the plans before anyone realized Margherita was pregnant.

Sadness enveloped Angelina as she remembered her sister's hasty departure to America in 1891. She had wondered then if she would ever see either of her sisters again. At that time, it hadn't occurred to her that she might be traveling to America herself one day.

It was, again, a bittersweet moment when the letter arrived from Michigan announcing that Margherita had given birth to a beautiful baby boy, naming him Tony. There was also news that Margherita would soon marry Giovanni Boggio, an Italian miner living at the boarding house where Margherita had taken a job. Boggio had fallen in love with Margherita and had no qualms about adopting baby Tony as his own. Angelina sighed with these memories, thinking that perhaps things would work out well for Margherita after all.

Angelina returned to the present and thought of her two sisters, both living in Calumet, Michigan, a place Angelina could not even imagine. At least they had each other for consolation, while she was alone. Angelina longed to see them again. She was thrilled with the news that Margherita had given birth to a second child, naming the baby girl Maddelena. The family already referred to the new child as "Maudie." Angelina said a little prayer in hopes that her sister had now found peace of mind and happiness.

Angelina felt drained and exhausted with all that had transpired with her family and her own life. Now all three sisters were in America and the poor, aging Giordano parents were left all alone in Italy.

Angelina never wanted to leave Italy, but what choice did she have in the matter? *Le fumne a polan mai dir gnente.* Women are not allowed to voice an opinion. If she refused to join her husband, perhaps he would stop sending money, and the family would starve. She would forever live with her poor parents, and in order to survive, she would be forced to take in washing, or to sell her body as a prostitute. *Brüte crin! 'L diau ch'a s'je porto tute 'nsema!* Pigs all of them! Curse all the men of the world!

There were many questions posed to Angelina, as her friends clutched her hands, begging her to stay in Italy. "Why do you go when you want to stay here? You should stay here where you are happy!"

Refusing to leave Italy meant abandoning her husband. Perhaps Louis would then use that opportunity to find a wife in America. This kind of thing did happen. There were many wives left behind in Italy, and they never saw or heard from their husbands again. Without a man to provide for them, a woman was lucky to survive.

With the contemplation of these irreversible facts, Angelina felt overwhelmed and was not aware of the tears streaming down her face. She was once again brought back to the present, this time by her daughter, Caterina. *"Piansej nin, mare!"* "Mama, don't cry!"

Angelina pulled Caterina near her and they hugged warmly. Then together, they gazed out the window, following the landscape that was new and foreign. The wheels of the locomotive were speeding along into the unknown world that awaited them in Silverton, Colorado.

CHAPTER II

Louis Sartore

"A l'é tüt prunt. A l'é bele ura!" "Everything is ready. It is almost time!" Louis Sartore impatiently paced about the room, because waiting in any form was difficult for him. He was ready, and it was almost time to meet the train arriving from Durango. The snowfall during the week had delayed the train from reaching Silverton day after day, but today the news from Durango was good. The tracks had been cleared and the train was expected to make it over the mountain passes.

"It is enough to drive a person crazy," Louis was nervously spouting to himself. *"Che fola!"* "How dumb! Why did Angelina wait until winter to make this trip? It is like living in hell getting around in Silverton in January with all this snow piling up. *Veramènt l'infern a l'é 'n pò 'd pì caud.* Of course, hell is much hotter!" At this thought, he smiled at his own joke.

Louis hoped that nothing would delay the train from making it all the way into Silverton today. He was happy his family would soon

Louis Sartore, circa 1895.

arrive, but he had another reason. He needed supplies. The bar was running low on liquor, and that was not good for his saloon business. Because Silverton was remote, they all needed to keep well stocked with food and commodities. They could go months without out the train bringing supplies during the winter. He was sick of eating polenta, a type of cornmeal that could easily be stored in barrels for these times of emergency, and a new supply of food would be welcomed. There were no roads into Silverton, only dirt trails, impassable in the winter. Only the narrow gauge railroad kept Silverton from complete isolation.

He swore to himself as he continued to pace, still fuming as to why Angelina waited until winter to travel. Things were bad during the winter months in the deeply remote high mountains, but he admitted to himself that spring was not much better. Avalanches were a threat at either time, and they came as quickly as the blink of an eye, without warning, with a sudden, loud rumbling announcing the movement of colossal amounts of snow. Rolling down the mountainside, they changed the landscape with their immense power, snapping trees and sending huge boulders to the bottom along with the icy mass of snow. People were killed every year, surprised by the roar of an unexpected snowslide.

Louis felt a chill run down his spine as he allowed his mind to relive the times he had watched helplessly as mine workers and friends were caught in avalanches. They would try to keep on top, to ride the slide to the end, but most were sucked into a certain death, or terribly mangled from the horrible plunge. Some stood on mine trestles trying to grab hold of something solid, but in most cases, it buried them instantly. Avalanches were powerful enough to carry a train into the canyon below. He shook his head to remove these thoughts, but it was natural to worry about the safety of his family.

Not wanting to arrive at the railroad depot too early and wait, standing out in the freezing air, Louis continued to pace the room, uneasy about seeing his family. Would his children remember him? He had spent seven long years away from them.

He wanted them to see the success he had achieved with his business enterprises. He was a well-respected member of the Silverton community and he enjoyed a prominent position. Because he had established many business ventures, he could entrust his mining interests to partners, so he no longer worked in the mines. He and his brother, Joseph, had a saloon, livery, and cribs for prostitutes. These types of businesses, he reasoned, were better than gold or silver mines for making money in Silverton, especially since the price of silver was unstable after the Great Silver Panic of 1893.

During those first years in Silverton, he had worked in the dark, musty mine tunnels, and he hated it! Closing his eyes, he remembered the sensations of terror he felt when he, as a newly arrived immigrant, first walked into a dark mine shaft. Desperate for adventure and anxious for the money to roll in, he didn't anticipate the fear he would experience. Inside a mine tunnel it was unnervingly quiet, and in the darkness all you could hear was the drip, drip of water along the walls. He shuddered as thoughts of those early days returned, causing his eyes to narrow. "A mine tunnel, cut deep into the side of a mountain, is darker than a tomb, and the feeling of fright on entering into the darkness is so immense that I feel it yet today."

He had a choking sensation in his throat as he tried to fight back the memories of healthy men, crushed and injured in mining accidents deep inside the tunnels. They were taken to the mine entrance and sometimes left until the shift changed. Doctors were often far away and the trip into town could be fatal. Most had no family to tend to them, so they simply died or were maimed for life. If they survived the accidents, there was always the possibility they might end up with miner's consumption. This disease was caused from the dust created as miners cut into the rock. Sharp particles of rock dust would eat away at their lungs. Louis felt his body tremble as he realized that digging into the bowels of the earth, into hard rock, changed a man forever.

"Now I know what hell must be like," he mused, letting his mind run freely. "It is not a fiery hot inferno, but a completely dark mine shaft, winding deep into the earth. In an endless black hole, it is natural to be claustrophobic, with a feeling that the mountain is riding just above your shoulders, waiting to fall and crush you." He had been told a man could go crazy in the dark long before he died of thirst. "If a soul is left there alone to wander forever in darkness, trying aimlessly to dig a way out, that is truly hell! When you are buried alive, darkness can seem to be a living thing, with a presence that is soundless and yet overwhelming to everything it touches." He went even further into thought. "The light keeps blowing out from downdrafts and it is dark all the time. The sounds of men screaming and the rumble of shored timbers failing as a mountain caves in, make it even more of a hell!" Louis swallowed hard as these thoughts turned over in his mind.

There were many things in Silverton that Louis could relate to hell. He often watched the endless pack trains of burros and mules as they lumbered, heavily loaded, up the mountains and then back down in never-ending sequence. These patient animals were often mistreated, overpacked and cruelly overworked as a necessary means of moving ore down from the mountains and supplies up to the mines. Louis sometimes wondered if they represented souls in hell, or maybe those working off their sins in purgatory.

However, one of the most powerful miseries in Silverton was that of being alone, and Louis recognized loneliness on the faces of every patron who walked inside his saloon. Yes, he saw hell in many facets of life. He wasn't religious in the way of attending Mass or services, but the fear of eternal damnation caused him to make large donations to the small Catholic parish of St. Patrick's. He viewed this as a precaution. It was his thought that in doing his share of giving, he might be pulled from the clutches of the devil on Judgment Day and lifted into heaven.

Hating mine work forced Louis to save every penny. He wasn't foolish, and neither was his brother, Joseph. They didn't drink at the saloons and end up broke after payday. They saved and planned and worked extra time when it was needed.

Angelina complained in letters that he was not sending enough money to support his family, but he strained and stretched every penny to the limit, and he expected her to do the same. She would see now that it had all been worthwhile. Life would be better for all of them.

Louis left thoughts of the past for a moment. His eyes held a flicker of excitement as he contemplated his future plans. There were opportunities in Silverton, and Louis could envision that his ideas would soon materialize. At present, he and Joseph ran a saloon on Greene Street, but Louis was making plans to build his own saloon, and he wanted it to be impressive. He had already purchased property on Blair Street and planned to name his saloon the Belleview. His name would be on the sign for all to see. He would put trees in front of the building, following the example of the fancy businesses in town. These trees weren't planted, but simply cut down and placed in the ground as decorations. The trees were easily removed when they were dead and replaced with fresh ones.

His grand saloon would have a boarding house on the second floor, and this would be the biggest financial winner. There weren't enough rooms available for all the miners who came to live in Silverton, and many lived in tents at the edge of town. Yes, there was need for good boarding houses in this mining town.

Louis envisioned a family living quarters at the rear of the saloon on the first level. However, in the meantime, as he developed plans for the new building, he had purchased a home for Angelina and his family. He wanted their introduction to this "new world" to be happy and positive.

To Louis, it was clearly apparent what a boomtown like Silverton needed, since it was overflowing with miners seeking their fortunes. These men were here without families. They looked for comfort, companionship, and entertainment. After a few weeks of hard labor inside a dark mine, men needed to kick up their heels and celebrate by drinking, gambling, and raising hell.

He and Joseph decided on Blair Street to build their new businesses. There were saloons on Greene Street, but this was developing into the main street for proper business. The immigrant Italian community preferred Blair, which was evolving as the red light district. This area later developed a reputation for being the rougher and wilder side of town.

On the northwest corner of Twelfth and Blair Streets, Joseph Sartore and a distant cousin, Ludovico "Ludwig" Vota, owned a notorious dance hall. Ludwig took over management of the property and it became known as Ludwig's Dance Hall. This scandalous building was the scene of brawling miners, threats, gunfights, shootings, and even suicides. If there were wild times in town, it was usually at this dance hall. Joseph, Louis, and Ludwig also owned cribs, which were rooms in buildings where prostitutes received customers. Louis found himself wondering what Angelina would think of all this.

His mind drifted back to the last days he had spent with his family before he left Italy to come to Silverton. Leaving had been an easy decision to make, except for Angelina's silly antics. He reasoned that women draw conclusions based on emotions, and she thought to control him with sentiment as a weapon.

"I think I am pregnant," she had told him. *"Stavota a l'é 'n cit."* "This time it will be a boy."

Louis had ignored this announcement. He felt the tension between them, but he had much to do before he could leave; however, a son would please him after the birth of two baby girls. Not wanting to discuss any of this with his wife, he let the silence hang awkwardly between them and said nothing.

He had decided to join his brother in the mountains of Colorado, but he would wait until Angelina gave birth to their third child. *A j'avija già decidü 'd partir.* He would leave, eventually.

Louis was proud of his Italian homeland and hadn't planned to live out his life on another continent. He had even tried his luck in 1881 when he went over the Italian border into France and operated a boarding house for miners in a place called Aiguebelette. He returned to Italy after a short year, discouraged with the drudgery of the hard work and lack of financial success. But he was still drawn to America, where everything was new and uncharted. In America, it was said that a man could rise above his station in life if he worked hard. Louis wanted nothing more out of life than to be successful. He loved Italy, but the lure to find a life of prosperity was pulling him away.

Louis was born in 1853 in Rivarolo Canavese, a *citta* (town) outside the city of Torino in northern Italy. Pasquaro is a rural center near Rivarolo Canavese, and it was in Pasquaro that Louis had spent many of his formative years.

Not far from the home of his parents, Louis had purchased a large farmhouse where Angelina and the children had spent those seven years without him. Angelina was thrilled with this house. It was large with a livestock barn on the first floor beneath the living quarters. The structure was divided into two sections for living areas, one for the family and one for the farm workers. Louis had written with instructions for Angelina to sell this house before coming to join him in America. She argued against this decision, claiming that her parents had nowhere else to live. Angelina had moved the Giordanos into the house with her and the children when Louis left for America. The house held happy memories for Angelina and she refused to sell it.

Sartore farmhouse in Pasquaro near Rivarolo Canavese, Italy, circa 1960.

Louis recognized that Angelina's mind was set on keeping it with hopes of returning there one day. He decided to wait until another time to work out this problem.

Louis now let his mind wander back to Italy, recalling the beauty of the landscape. He followed Italian politics and knew much about the history of his homeland. He came from a rural area in the northern province of Italy called "The Piedmont," or Piemonte Region, meaning, "Where the plain lies at the foot of the mountains." It is a land-locked area, surrounded by the Alps, and includes the upper Po Valley, an area rich with rivers, lakes, and beautiful hills.

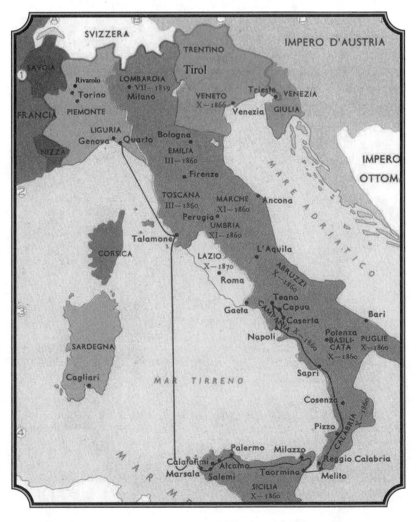

The history and landscape of the Piemonte Region are similar to that of the nearer parts of France. Even the language is a dialect that reflects the French influence. It borders France and Switzerland, and the Piedmont grows substantial amounts of food products, including grapes, which are the source of the finest wines of Italy. Rivarolo Canavese and the tiny village of Pasquaro, where some of his family still lived, are both located a short distance northeast of the major city of Torino, or "Turin."

Louis was proud of Italy's history. He had lived through the difficult wars with Austria as a child, but by 1866, the Italian people had suffered enough and had started rebuilding the economy. In 1870 Italy was finally at peace, having driven back Austria's hope to dominate the continent. Victor Emmanuel II was officially recognized as king, and Italy was unified into one nation under a constitutional monarchy. By 1878, Italy's diplomatic status was on the rise. The unification helped make a previously fourth- or fifth-rate power become a second-rate power.

However, by 1882 Italy still consisted mainly of rural areas. For many generations, these farming communities had endured domestic economic hardships. The industrial revolution should have helped the economy by putting the population to work with the transition from hand industry to the application of power-driven machinery, but the progress was slow. The country's backward economy was reinforced by the reluctance of the rural society to accept change, and by their lack of education. So its economic development didn't create enough employment to overcome the profuse supply of unskilled labor. Skilled workers were required in Italy, while the United States wanted unskilled labor for the mines and railroads.

The excitement of a free world where a man could become rich pulled at the spirit of the Sartore brothers. There were still more workers than jobs in Italy, so the prospects of a better life in a new land was promising. It was Joseph who decided to take the first steps and go to America. If all went well then Louis would follow.

Joseph Sartore kissed his sobbing relatives good-bye and left for America in 1883. During the months that followed, they all waited anxiously for news and letters from him. These were slow in coming at first, so the family searched for news from the disheartened Italians returning from America.

Not everyone who left Italy remained in the new world. Those who returned had stories to tell their countrymen about the life of hard work in the gold and silver mines, the copper and the coal mines. Some had worked to build the railroads that stretched into the vast frontier of the West. These pilgrims talked of the hardships and long hours of heavy labor, made more painful without any family for support. They saved their hard-earned wages and returned to Italy.

"Joseph was all right when we saw him," some had responded. *"Quand ch'e l'an vist a stasìa ben."* "When we met up with Joseph, he was heading for Colorado."

When Joseph had been gone for two years, his family became increasingly concerned that he would not return to Italy. Louis read every word his brother wrote in letters. He was envious and felt frustrated that he was not there to share in this adventure.

Remembering back to when Joseph had first left for America, Louis recalled the look of alarm on Angelina's face as she realized that he wanted to join his older brother. She grew despondent and depressed, but Louis resisted the urge to comfort her with lies. He would not back down on this decision. It was during this time of tension that Angelina had two miscarriages. He knew she was struggling with the stress of his leaving, and he was surprised: He thought Angelina to be stronger than that.

Louis was elated when Angelina had given birth to a healthy son in August of 1886. Now his family was complete. This day would have been pleasing in every way, except for the agitation that the impending trip stirred up in Angelina. If she thought she could keep him from leaving, she was naïve and emotionally fragile. He did not think her to be either, but he recognized the fact that she was not happy with his decision and he chose to ignore it.

With fondness, Louis ruminated over the christening day of his young son, so small and precious. His heart had been full with the anticipation of the forthcoming trip, but the joy of having a baby son elevated him even further. Everyone had gathered at the church for the baptism and then moved on to his home. A feast that had been in preparation for many days was set out for everyone to enjoy. The day was filled with happy festivities until Joseph's wife, Angelina Dighera, arrived. Her face was streaked with tears and she held tightly onto the hand of her young daughter, Mary, as she moved to join the other family members.

Her voice was shaking when she announced, "We have to go to America," and as she blurted out these words, friends and relatives rushed to her side. Everyone gathered around her as she struggled through her tears to read the letter from Joseph.

"Enclosed you will find the necessary amount of money to buy passage to America for you and Mary. Soon you will join me in Silverton, Colorado, where I am making a good life for us."

Now it became a day of mixed emotions. Everyone deemed it unlikely that Joseph would ever come back to Italy, and now his family would also be taken away from their homeland. To those present, traveling to America was the same as a trip to the moon, because it was so unknown and far away. Only Louis kept the spirit of the day with cheerfulness. He raised his young son up in the air and whispered to the child, *"Ncö a l'é na bela giurnà."* "It is a new day, a good day."

Louis didn't wait much longer. In early 1887, a short time after the departure of Joseph's family, Louis left his three young children and his wife, Angelina, behind. She did not cry or plead to change his mind, but the look she gave shot through him like a bullet. Louis gave thought to consoling her as she stood there holding his baby son, with two little girls pressed against her skirts, but instead he turned away with stubborn determination. As he did so, he heard her cursing him through whispered breath. At this memory, he remembered thinking it doubtful that his wife would actually ever join him in another country.

As Louis pictured Angelina with eyes that sparkled under heavy lids, and cheeks that flushed with the glow of color, he felt his heartbeat quicken. She was tall and stately, with gentle, slow-moving expressions. He had seen the soft look in her eyes turn to fire in an instant, and it was the fire in her that was perplexing. It mystified him. These thoughts stirred a longing deep inside, and he had the feeling that he would enjoy having his wife with him again. It had been too long. Now he couldn't recall if he ever told her that he cared for her. Maybe he should tell her.

Louis was interrupted from his reverie when he heard footsteps approaching, crunching in the snow outside. He eagerly opened the door and greeted his brother, Joseph, pulling him inside and shutting out the icy cold air.

"Bôn dì!" "Hello, my brother! Did you get the horses and wagon-sled?" Louis looked outside as Joseph shook his head and, half laughing, pointed to the contraption that had been rigged up by the blacksmith to accommodate the family and the large trunks that would be arriving by train. Two big black horses stood in front of a buckboard and snorted puffs of condensed vapor in the cold air.

The wheels of the wagon had been removed and in their stead were sled runners.

"A va ben!" "Good, good!" Louis replied nervously, rubbing his hands together against the cold air. "Thank you, my brother." Louis grabbed Joseph's arm in gratitude. Joseph smiled, turned, and walked once more into the snow. Waving at Louis, he called back, "We will be waiting for you to bring your family to the house. *A l'é na bela giurnà, a l'é 'n dì 'd festa. E dsì 'n pò e saràn turna tüte 'nsema.* It is a new and happy day and we will soon all be together again."

CHAPTER III

Silverton, Colorado,

1895

"*E sen 'ncur nin rivà?*" "Are we there yet?" Filippo asked. Angelina shook her head, but said nothing. They were almost there. Silverton was just across those mighty and majestic Rocky Mountains. Forty-five miles of narrow gauge track was all that was left of their journey, a trip that had lasted three weeks and had taken them across two continents and one ocean. They were exhausted, and the January air continued to be cold and biting.

As they prepared to board the small train in Durango, Colorado, Filippo's face wore a wide grin. He commented that the locomotive looked like a toy train after the larger wide-gauge ones they had been riding. "*Me ch'a l'é cit! A smija quase na dimura.*" The train and the tracks were built smaller than standard gauge to accommodate the sharp curves and the rugged mountain terrain. Narrow gauge track is

This resembles the train that transported ore and passengers from Silverton to Durango and back. The Denver & Rio Grande Railway Company (D&RG) was incorporated in the Territories of Colorado and New Mexico in 1870, to build a railroad from Denver south to El Paso, Texas.

laid at a width of three feet, whereas standard gauge track is four feet, eight-and-a-half inches.

Standing outside in the cold at the Durango depot, Filippo watched as a sudden burst of steam made the engine hiss like a huge monster. The coal-fueled engine was fired up and ready to move forward. Black smoke, soot, and cinders poured out of the stack and the whistle blew. The conductor gave the call, "All Aboooard," and the young boy scrambled to climb into a passenger car, waving for his mother and sisters to join him.

Young Filippo (Phil) Sartore, circa 1895.

"We can't be certain that the train will make it all the way into Silverton in this weather," the man at the ticket stand had been telling everyone. "If there is a blockade of snow, the train will go as far as possible and a pack train of mules or burros will be used to bring the supplies and the mail the rest of the way into Silverton. The people will have to walk in."

Angelina stood back, shaking her head in disbelief that she had come this far to this uncivilized and primitive place where she might be stuck in the snow. An Italian man at the depot had explained the circumstances of snow possibly blocking the tracks, and because of this, she hesitated, mumbling, *"Que ch'e fu belesì?"* "What am I doing in this place?" With trepidation she finally boarded the train, ready to cross the dangerous and steep passes into the San Juan Mountains. She was nervous, and her face was etched in self restraint to hide her fears from the children.

They were all silent for the first part of the trip. Fear of the final destination plagued each one of them. Watching out the window at the remote scenes of the Colorado Rockies, white with the snow of January, they marveled at the beauty of the untamed, rugged mountains that surrounded Durango. As the train pulled out of the depot, they could see the peaks of the La Plata Mountains in the background to the northwest and Perins Peak on the western skyline. Snow was piled everywhere, but the sun shone brightly against the blue Colorado sky. The air was so clear that objects were visible at great distances. It was a beautiful sight.

Soon they were out of town and the little train clickity-clacked in a steady rhythm. It rocked and swayed over the steel rails as metal ground against metal. The coal was stoked and the steam engine hissed them on their way.

The children sighed, "Ah," as they sighted herds of elk, because this was something they had never seen before. The scenery along the Animas Valley was stunning, with the sparkling river cutting through the ice and snow, and trees hanging heavy with white against a bril-liant blue sky. They mar-veled at the colors of the red cliffs along the river and passed waterfalls almost completely frozen in the bitter temperatures of January. Pristine blan-kets of snow, unbroken by footprints of man or animal, covered wide mountain meadows. Mountain streams were only a trickle of water escaping through the ice as the train crossed over bridges and trestles. There were murmuring sounds of worry from many of the passengers as the engineer slowed the train around a narrow gorge. Below, they could see a narrow chasm that carried the river cascad-ing its way deep into the canyon. The train carefully maneuvered along the narrow shelf of solid rock, causing passengers to gasp in fear, and they leaned to one side, attempting to help the train cling to the side of the rock cliff wall.

The view was both awe inspiring and frightening as the train moved over the steel rails, crossing bridges suspended over canyons, between peaks, and on the sides of very narrow cliffs. Filippo leaned to look over the dangerous edge into the deep canyon, with the intention of teasing his sisters. They pulled him back, complaining that he might upset the balance and thus topple the train into the Animas River below!

Angelina's breath caught in her throat at the sight of the vistas of sharp, jagged peaks looming ahead. These were portions of the San Juan Mountains, including the Needle Mountains. The train moved into the heart of the rugged mountains now, with layer upon layer of rocks that hugged the canyons and jutted from the ground.

They all admired the landscape covered with beautiful trees. The quaking aspen and willows appeared graceful even without leaves, and some lovely blue spruce stood vibrant against the white of the winter day. The boughs of the ponderosa pine bent low under their weight of snow, and the dark outline of lodgepole pines seemed to stretch in an attempt to reach straight up to the sky.

Because water was needed to create the steam to power the little locomotive, water tanks were placed along the tracks at strategic locations. The train stopped to take on water at Needleton. Angelina looked at the sparsely populated community that consisted of little more than a post office. At this time of year it was almost buried in snow, and this train was the only source of civilization for the few people living here and in nearby mines. She shook her head and wondered how people could survive in such desolation.

Underway once again, they started passing mines with their wood-framed structures, called "tipples," hanging down the side of the mountains. The open mouths of tunnels scarred hillsides dotted with small cabins. Miners waved enthusiastically as the train moved slowly along the narrow track. The children opened a window to wave back to the miners and thick black smoke from the train poured in, causing everyone to cough and choke. They quickly closed the window, but continued to look at the sights, realizing they must be getting close to Silverton.

The train chugged along and Filippo made a comment that now they were almost on the same level as the Animas River, which rambled slowly through the ice and snow next to the tracks. It was pointed out by another passenger that there were signs of snowslides and avalanches in certain places along this area. Angelina clutched the seat tightly, and her eyes clouded with worry that such a thing as a snowslide might happen at any moment.

They noticed that the river and the rocks around it appeared rusty, yellow, and brown. It was explained to them that iron minerals from dumps and drains were carried along by the river and deposited on the rocks. Now there were mines in sight everywhere along the steep mountains. Wooden structures hung all around as if suspended. "How do people get up to these mines?" was Filippo's question. Angelina had no answers as she looked into the apprehensive faces of her children. It was plain to see they were all experiencing some

Double engines are pushing through the snow on the outskirts of Silverton, circa 1900. Photo from the files of the San Juan County Historical Society Collection.

fear, wondering what life held for them in the small mining town ahead.

Finally, they chugged into Silverton and slowly made their way into the small snow-covered depot. The children were smiling and murmured small expressions of gratitude, cheering for the accomplishment of the little train. Angelina gave a sigh of relief but wondered, *"Que ch'aj capiterà adés?"* "We are finally here, but now what?"

Caterina shook the black soot from her long skirts as she climbed down from the smoking train. She turned to help Filippo so he wouldn't stumble and fall down the steep steps. The young boy looked dirty and tousled and Caterina knew she looked much the same. He was tired and whining about the cold air, so she pulled his wool hat down around his ears. They had worn warm clothing but were not prepared for the bitter cold temperatures. She picked up her long skirts to keep from dragging them in the snow and ice as she walked.

"Me ch'a và che sen 'gnü 'nt 'n post parèj brüt?" "Why have we come to this awful place?" she heard her mother whisper.

It was late afternoon and clouds hovered low over the town; everything around them looked grey and bleak. When they opened their mouths to speak, they could see their breath. The high altitude made them gasp and the dry air seemed to crackle with tiny ice particles. They were finding it more difficult to breathe. The dark, towering mountains loomed in the background and everything was covered in snow and ice. It was somehow a lonely feeling knowing that this formidable place, so frightening and foreign, would be their new home.

Giovanna, as the oldest, took the positive approach and happily pointed to the fast-moving figure coming toward them. Louis Sartore was there to greet his family. *"Varda, a jé papa!"* "Look, it is Papa!"

Louis hugged and patted each one of them, with reassurance that things would be better now. *"Aura a 'ndrà mej."* Angelina responded with indifference, not looking directly into the face of her husband. Louis had been away from his family for seven years, so did he expect that she would greet him warmly?

Louis paid the baggage handler and they all followed him to the open buckboard with the sled rails. Vapor poured from the nostrils of the two horses as they moved around restlessly trying to keep warm. The bags and trunks were loaded and the family was soon on their way. Louis headed the team in the direction of the home he had purchased. The children would soon see that their father had done well in Silverton.

Angelina looked around as the horses pulled the sled through the town of Silverton. On the streets were signs of prosperity, with false-fronted stores, several saloons, restaurants, and hotels. Her jaw dropped open at the sight of the lavish Grand Imperial Hotel, a sign that Silverton prospered in many ways. As they moved into the residential areas, she could see that those who made this town their home took pride in their Victorian style houses. But never had she seen such snow. It was piled high everywhere!

When they arrived at the house, Angelina raised her eyebrows and nodded to herself that it looked sufficient. Waiting inside to welcome them was Louis' brother Joseph, his wife, Angelina Dighera, their daughter, Mary, and baby Phillip Amerigo. The baby boy was

Silverton deep in snow on Greene Street, circa 1900.
San Juan County Historical Society Collection

born in America, and it was a delight for all of them to see this new addition to the family. Uncertainty was forgotten as they saw familiar faces and heard the welcoming voices. *"Finalment e sej sì! A l'é 'n bel pò che vë spetan. E sen parèj cuntent d' vesve!"* "Welcome, we have been waiting for you. We are so happy to see you!"

Hugging and kissing amidst tears and laughter brought them all joyfully inside the house. Food had been prepared and the aroma of recognizable dishes was heartening, bringing a feeling of familiarity to the otherwise foreign circumstances. Plates full of golden fried polenta and steaming spareribs were placed on the table while the warmth from the wood-burning stove made the atmosphere comforting and inviting. The warm ambience surrounded them like a cocoon, because now the contentment of being once again with family was heartening. Amid the noise of questions about relatives in Italy and hugs of elation, a festive atmosphere soon pervaded the small parlor where they gathered.

A loud knock at the front door disturbed this cheerful celebration, and they all turned to see a large, gregarious woman enter with a flourish of enthusiasm, her arms open to embrace anyone and everyone. Maestra, "the teacher," was followed into the room by her quiet husband, Alex Perino. Shrieks of delight prevailed as they were all reunited once again.

Louis smiled slightly as his cousin, Domenica Vota Perino, entered the room and became the center of attention. She was always called "Maestra" because she had been a teacher in Italy. She was better educated than the others, meaning that her education exceeded that of the fourth grade. Maestra was interested in matters of the intellect and also in social graces, but it was her gentle nature and kind heart that drew people to her. She loved to share her knowledge of American ways because she had lived in Silverton for the past few years. Maestra was already assuring them all that now she would be there to help them adjust to the new language and customs.

When Louis paused to look at Alex Perino, he realized that time would be short for her instructions. The couple was planning to travel home to Italy soon, hoping for an improvement in Alex's health. Alex was suffering with miner's consumption.

Now in the soft glow of kerosene lamps, amid the noise of chatter, they all filled their plates with delicious food. Mary quietly directed the girls, Giovanna and Caterina, to a corner away from the noisy adults. Mary was fifteen, the same age as Caterina, and only a year younger than Giovanna. Her lovely young face wore a vibrant expression as she began to tell stories, painting a colorful portrayal of what awaited them in Silverton.

Silverton's Greene Street piled high in winter, circa 1900.
San Juan County Historical Society

The young cousins, straight from a restricted life in Italy, opened their eyes wide with interest and curiosity as Mary explained life in this remote mining community. It was an intimidating but intriguing fact that there were many men and few women in Silverton, so there were strict rules. Proper women did not walk the streets alone and decent women did not ever walk on the streets where there were saloons and gambling, especially Blair Street. This is where the lewd women and drunken men caroused.

Both Giovanna and Caterina looked at each other with uncertainty as Mary told them of gunfights, feuds between groups of Italians, and other scandalous stories about miners and the wild sides of life in Silverton. "These men are starved for female company since they work up in the mountains for months," Mary was saying. "When they come to town, they get drunk and make trouble. That is the way of life here.

"There are 'sporting women' available in dance halls and bordellos," Mary added. Caterina and Giovanna looked at each other, and Mary realized they didn't understand. Mary whispered and motioned for them to put their heads close to hers while she explained about prostitutes. Caterina appeared dazed by all this new talk, and Giovanna put her hand to her lips to stifle a giggle.

"This crazy town keeps going day and night, but there are also decent and fun things to do," Mary told them. "Dancing is a popular form of socializing. Sometimes my parents take me to dances in some of the nearby mining communities so they can visit with friends. At these dances a young woman is never without a partner."

"O Nusgnùr!" "Oh, my goodness," the two girls chorused. They were aware just how dull and repetitive life had been up to now. Mary assured them there was much to learn besides that which Maestra intended to teach them.

Filippo sat on the floor playing with his young cousin, Phillip Amerigo, who was born in Silverton in 1894 and was only a few months old. Both of the young boys were named for their grandfather, Filippo Sartore. From this time forward, young Filippo and Phillip Amerigo would be known as Big Phil and Little Phil.

As the evening lengthened into darkness, it was time for Joseph and Louis to go to work in the saloon. As Joseph and his family headed toward the door to leave, Angelina Dighera took the hand of her sister-in-law, telling her to be brave, that they would be there to help. *"Et daràn na man gnèt."* "Maestra and I will return tomorrow. It is important that you all learn to speak English and learn the customs of this land," she confided. *"A venta che t'ënpare me ch'as fa belesì."* "Life here is difficult enough, so you must learn the new ways."

The house seemed foreign and quiet after the others left. Angelina, her heart heavy, did not feel up to the task of unpacking and settling into her new home. She solemnly instructed the girls to clean up the kitchen while she took Filippo to a small room and helped him into bed.

The girls chatted softly as they worked. There was much to think about, and they repeated and discussed the things Mary had said. Fear was mingled with excitement as they spoke about the unknown boomtown around them. In a matter of hours, Italy had become part of another lifetime that had passed. Their eyes were bright with the wonder and spirit of youthful adventure as they pondered and discussed this new situation. *"Me ch'a sarà aura?"* "What would this strange community bring to their future?"

While the girls looked ahead, their mother sat alone in her room, clinging to the past, refusing to accept this new life and what it might hold for her. She let tears fall and cursed the fate that brought her to Silverton.

Louis and Joseph worked behind the bar of the saloon where smoke filled the room and the aroma of cigars and spilled whiskey soured the air. The late night roar of boasting, laughing, and chattering of drunken men made it difficult to converse. Louis was trying to convey to his brother how happy he was to have his family here. *"Nchö e su cuntent."* "Today I am a happy man."

The girls were especially pleasing to him. They had been mere babies when he left Italy, and he had not prepared himself for the budding young ladies they had become. Giovanna, soon to be sixteen, was a lovely young woman, and it was easy to see the potential of Caterina's beauty. His thoughts of pride were paternal, but he also considered their usefulness in the work at the boarding house. Boarding houses suffered for the lack of women to do the cleaning, for as soon as any young woman was hired to work as a maid, she would decide to marry. Any decent girl was easily pursued and persuaded into marriage in a town where men greatly outnumbered women. Now, with the arrival of his daughters, Louis was assured of having maid service for his new boarding house.

"Hey, Sartore," one of the customers at the bar hollered out. "I saw your two young daughters arrive today. *"A sen prope bele."* "They are quite beautiful!"

Until now it hadn't occurred to Louis that men would be interested in his daughters, and his brow furrowed with this disturbing thought. It suddenly reverberated blatantly through his brain that men would lust after his daughters. They would soon flock like bees to honey! He contemplated this new and unnerving dilemma thinking, *"A va nin susì, a fa scör!"* "This is not good. It is disgusting!"

Giovanna (Jennie) and Caterina (Katie) Sartore in 1899.

As Blair Street was Silverton's red light district, dotted with many saloons and brothels, it was marked as being established mostly by Italian immigrants. Many of these Italians, like the Sartore family, were from the Piemonte region of Italy. There were also many immigrants from the Tyrol, an area northeast of the Italian border near Austria.

These "Austrian-Italians" came from a region often disputed in border conflicts and, to some, represented the oppressive wars between Italy and Austria. In Silverton, there was considerable friction between these two segments of immigrants, and it was simply because they originated from different regions.

Silverton's Twelfth Street marked the dividing line for the separate factions. The Piemontesi lived north of Twelfth Street and ran their businesses there, while the Tyroleans stayed south of Twelfth Street. There were often clashes as these two groups harassed each other over ancient prejudices, and hostilities became volatile. This is where Louis Sartore planned to build his new saloon and boarding house, at Twelfth and Blair. This is where he proposed to bring his family to live.

As winter became spring, Louis watched the beginnings of his dream become a reality as the foundation for the new saloon was dug out to make the basement. Right from the beginning, he had plans for a tunnel to go from the basement to the other side of the street, and he started work on that immediately. The tunnel was a narrow passageway, just wide enough for one person, and almost five feet overhead. The ceiling was boarded with wide planking and the walls of the tunnel were rock and mortar. The tunnel was meant to be an escape route, or an alternate way of leaving the building, because patrons often needed to get away without being seen or identified. He also worked on a plan to connect his saloon with the Grand Imperial Hotel. Gentlemen, wanting to gamble and revel on Blair Street, would not want to be seen making their way to this more licentious side of town. They could use this tunnel as a convenient passageway. So, Louis made two connections for his tunnel from his saloon. One came out in the middle of the block across the street near a popular whore house, and the other connected his saloon to the Grand Imperial Hotel.

Louis also arranged for a coal chute to be located directly below the front of the building. The boardwalk would cover the entrance of the chute, with access readily available to delivery wagons. Coal, for heating, would be stored in the basement.

It soon became evident that Louis would not have enough funds to complete the building. Since the Great Silver Panic of 1893, silver prices had become unstable, and Louis was steadily losing money on his mining investments. Without telling Angelina or the children, he sold the house they were living in and prepared to set up a family living quarters in the newly finished basement of the building in progress.

Angelina greeted this new living arrangement with utter shock. It wasn't enough that she had to live in this uncivilized frontier town; now she and her family would have to burrow in the ground beneath a partly built saloon. Giovanna sobbed that it was like "living in a cave" and cried at having to leave the lovely bedroom that she shared with Caterina. Angelina fumed that they would never have a place of any prominence in this town if they were forced to live like animals.

Louis then shrewdly gave Angelina a choice: She could allow him to sell the house and property in Italy, or she could quietly resign herself to temporarily moving into the basement apartment. Angelina stared at Louis with hatred in her eyes. He knew she would never agree to sell the house in Italy.

At times when life seemed miserable at best, it was a welcome sound to hear the cheerful voice of Maestra. She brought her light-hearted attitude into their lives and made things tolerable. Louis was fond of his cousin, but he grumbled when she interrupted the work schedule. Through it all, Maestra taught them new and proper ways to conduct themselves so people wouldn't laugh at their old country ways. "It is important," she told the children, "that we Americanize your names. You will now be called Jennie, Katie, and Phil."

It saddened all of them when Maestra and Alex went back to Italy in September of 1896 in hopes he would recover from consumption in a warmer climate. Alex died a short time later. But Silverton had become home to Maestra and she returned to Colorado with her mother.

With the family newly moved into the basement, constructing the new saloon, cooking, and washing clothes became monstrous tasks. They were dreaded chores under the best of conditions, but now they entailed extra labor. Amidst the confusion of the building construction, the two young girls were expected to do the family washing, which happened approximately once a week.

So, while hammers banged and wooden beams were set into place, Katie and Jennie would begin by building a fire to heat the kettle of water in the middle of the backyard area. They pumped and carried water to fill the copper-bottomed tubs that fit on the coal cook stove. It was necessary to prepare two tubs with heated water, one for rinsing and one for scrubbing. They learned to set the tubs so the smoke and saw-dust wouldn't blow into the water or on the clean clothes.

Next they shaved one whole cake of lye soap into the boiling water and made starch by stirring flour into cold water. Sorting the clothes into piles of whites, colored, and work clothes, they next rubbed the dirty spots on the scrub board. The hardest part was poking down the billow of bedding and other things that floated up, then lifting the heavy, steaming wad, one item at a time, from the boiling water. They waited for it to drain and then swung it over into the rinse water. Happily, they did have a wringer, otherwise that would have had to been done by hand. After the clothes had been hung out on a line to dry, the girls were expected to scrub the cement floor of the basement with the soapy wash water and rub it dry with newspaper.

Doing the family laundry was a day-long chore that had to be fitted into a whole myriad of other household tasks. At times like this, Phil often used his mischief to annoy his sisters. When he saw them setting up the washing tubs he went into action, gathering some of his friends to have a little sport, assuring them they would soon have coins jingling in their pockets.

Blair Street was actually only two blocks long and consisted of mostly bars and brothels. Miners came to Blair Street to find entertainment of the lowest sort. However, watching a couple of lovely young women hang out their undergarments might be worth the pennies the boys required to view this scene. The wooden structure was still a skeleton as the frame of the building took shape. It offered no obstruction, so the crowd gathered as the news spread. Dirty urchin faces peered around the corner of the adjacent building where the girls were laboring with the weekly wash.

"Hey, Jennie, show us your dirty laundry!" one of them called out to add some amusement to the show.

Jennie muttered to Katie as they prepared to hang up the wash to dry. "Why are Phil and those boys here every wash day?"

Phil on the right with his friend, "Pinot." Circa 1899.

Katie nudged her sister and together they glanced behind them at the lineup in the alley. There were more than a few men milling around and gawking in awkward fashion. Hammers were quiet as even the builders were watching the eye-catching scene.

Jennie appeared to continue with the chore as she picked up a bucket and scooped out some grey water from the rinsing tub. As she raced over to the entrance of the yard, she shouted, "I'll teach you kids to have some respect!"

The contents of the bucket went flying, launched by her strong right arm. The boys let out squeals of surprise and disgust as the water drenched them. Miners scattered in all directions when she went to load up another bucket. The two young women had little time to laugh and enjoy the moment before their father appeared and scolded them for playing around instead of working. With the appearance of Louis Sartore, the crowd dispersed and hammers sounded once again.

Clothing dried quickly in the dry mountain air, and then came the ironing. Everything *had* to be ironed, even the bed linens. Two irons were used: One was heating on the stove while the other was in use. The girls were also expected to help Angelina with the constant rounds of cooking, baking, sewing, cleaning, and mending. Louis made it clear that they could not afford to hire someone to do these chores, saying the girls had nothing better to do anyway.

Louis made no excuses, tightening his mouth into a hard line, ignoring the wails of despair and protests as they all complained about the work and the living conditions. All he would say was that they all had to make sacrifices in order to be successful. It would only be for a short time, then the new saloon and boarding house would be finished. He repeated over and over that "The Belleview" would be magnificent, and he enjoyed explaining in detail the proposed grandeur of this new building.

A welcomed break in the routine occurred when, on June 11, 1898, everyone traveled to Durango for the celebration of a double wedding ceremony. The beloved Maestra married Peter Rudellat, and her former sister-in-law, Teresa Perino, married John Motto at the same service. Maestra longed for a child and she and Peter both expressed the desire to have a family. She worried that she was not young enough, and would not be able to have children.

As time moved on, Louis finally moved his family to the new living quarters attached to the rear of the saloon. Stairs leading up to the boarding house were outside the building. The upper level had a long hallway with rooms on either side, and at the end of the hall was a door that opened out to Blair Street. The door was decorated with lovely stained glass and was opened when they needed to shake out the small carpets. The front of the building was used as a sitting room for boarders and a work area for the girls and maids. On one side was a pigeon roost where eggs were gathered from inside, and "pigeon on toast" became a popular meal during the winter when supplies were short.

When the Belleview Saloon and Boarding House opened for business in 1899, Louis became even more of a taskmaster. His tirades

Belleview Saloon in 1899. Angelina, Phil and Louis Sartore stand in front.

drove Angelina to distraction as he constantly stirred things up, keeping them all in a state of exhaustion with hard work assignments. Being strict and intolerant, he expected unquestioned obedience from all members of the family, including his wife.

Phil was the most difficult for Louis to control, using his obstinate nature to defy his father whenever possible. He liked to hang around the saloon and play with the new dog, Bismarck, a large mongrel Louis acquired to keep the drunker patrons from leaving the saloon without paying. The big, lanky animal loved the children, but Bismarck's job was to deal with the customers. The dog would fiercely stand between the saloon door and the astonished, intoxicated client until payment was procured. The family was proud of the wonderful dog, but they had cause to worry. There were so many dogs on the streets of Silverton that some people saw them as an annoyance. It wasn't unusual that a dog might be poisoned or that someone would throw lye on the poor unsuspecting animal.

Phil avoided school as much as possible and hung around the saloon with a distant cousin, Angelo Sartore. He was older than Phil, the same age as Jennie, and he liked teasing and taunting the Sartore girls. Phil would quietly laugh and follow Angelo, who served as protection when other children chased Phil, calling him "saloon boy!"

Phil and Angelo did odd jobs around the saloon to help Louis, or rather, Louis put them to work whenever possible. "Polish the brass on the bar rails! Empty and shine the spittoons! Sweep up the floors beside the bar. Add new sawdust to the floor. Shovel the snow! Bring in more firewood! Go to the ponds and chop ice! Meet the train and pick up the liquor order." The chores were endless.

Louis sometimes paid Angelo a little for his work, but chores were expected of Phil. He often experienced the wrath and temper of his father and felt pain where the heavy belt left welts on his backside. However, this never deterred Phil from shirking his duties, and he would find his friend Pinot, or Angelo, and sneak across the railroad tracks to spend the afternoon fishing in the river.

The girls were expected to cook for the family and the boarders, clean the many rooms, change the beds, do the wash, and iron the linens. They cleaned the lamps and lanterns, trimming wicks and refilling reservoirs with acrid kerosene. At times they found young women to work as maids and help with some of the chores, but it was difficult to rely on them for any length of time. There was a saying out West that "Women are as scarce as cow eggs." A single woman was snatched up and directed to other working arrangements or into marriage. Some answered the seemingly lucrative call of prostitution.

Clothes were, for the most part, made by hand, with the help of the pedal sewing machine. It was considered recreation for the girls to sit and crochet lace for decorations on sleeves or add lace to towels and bed linens. It was discovered that Jennie was an artist with needle and

Belleview Saloon left to right: Katie, Angelina, Louis, and Bismarck the dog, with Phil and bar patrons, 1899.

thread. She was considered old enough to handle a job, and it was decided she would become a seamstress.

As she set up her sewing business, Jennie accepted this as a decision that wasn't hers to make. Her argument was that she was now part of the adult world, but only as far as work was concerned. The money she earned was considered to belong to her parents. She was allowed little freedom of dating or mixing with friends, and this was the issue that outraged her the most.

"You keep Katie and me as prisoners, while Phil goes wherever he pleases," Jennie would plead her case. Angelina would lose her temper, reminding her that she was a girl and needed her family to protect her.

Angelina's message was, "We only want what is best for you!"

Jennie would argue in an obstinate manner. "I never get to go anywhere. It's unfair!"

Angelina would continue to scold her, and Jennie would fume at the unbending ways of her parents. Their methods seemed old fashioned and unjust. She was young, with a restless spirit, aided by a voluptuous figure that seldom went unnoticed. Bold in her determination, Jennie flirted shamelessly, and it was easy for her to catch the eye of admiring miners. She had no qualms about sneaking off to meet a young man whenever possible.

Katie shuddered with fear at the thought of Jennie's rendezvous being discovered by their parents, so she covered for her sister, telling lies when necessary.

Angelina was aware of some of Jennie's activities and tried to discourage them quietly. If Louis found out, there would be hell to pay! She wondered at the differences between her two daughters. Katie was sweet and gentle, always trying to please, while Jennie rebelled and caused problems with her impudence and wild conduct. Angelina could see that something needed to be done to curtail Jennie's activities.

Winters became springs and life continued, despite Angelina's desire that this nightmare disappear. She wanted, more than anything, to return to Italy. She continued to complain, even though she realized the children appeared to have forgotten their homeland. They had adjusted to life, as it was, in Silverton. "It is the adaptability of youth," she said to herself sadly. "They conform because they don't know any better. *E sun sula 'nt se brüte muntagne!* I am alone in these ugly mountains."

The Sartore family, left to right: Louis, Katie, Jennie, Angelina, and Phil, circa 1899.

CHAPTER IV

The Belleview Saloon

 ## and Boarding House

Katie stood in the kitchen laboring over the scorching hot, wood-burning range, where pots simmered and the aroma of fresh bread permeated the back area of the saloon. She pushed back a lock of hair from her face, exposing beads of sweat forming at her temples as she worked to prepare supper.

"Nte ch'a l'é tua surela?" "Where is your sister?" Louis bellowed as he entered the kitchen, grabbing nineteen-year-old Katie by the shoulders and shouting in her face.

"She went to get more firewood for the range, Papa," Katie stammered, not looking directly into her father's face. Louis was flushed and irritated as he stared intently at his youngest daughter. He finally shoved her aside and took long strides towards the back door.

"A j'é gnente, papà!" "Nothing is wrong, Papa!" Katie yelled after him, the crack in her voice giving away her apprehension. It was not in her nature to upset anyone, especially her father.

Louis looked around the back area of the small yard, and at first he contemplated retracing his steps, because Jennie was nowhere to be seen. Then with a jerk he pulled open the doors to the woodshed, and immediately all hell broke loose as he stared at his oldest daughter in the throws of a passionate embrace with a young miner.

"Que ch'e 't fè scundüa si 'ndrinta? 'l diau ch'a 't porto!" "What are you doing, hiding in there? Go to the devil!"

Screaming threats and profanity, Louis chased the man away, hurling sticks of wood at him. Jennie tried to stop her father by pulling on his shoulder. It was the wrong thing to do when Louis' temper was flaring, and in a blinding rage, he turned to deal with his daughter. Swearing and calling her indignant names, his anger boiled over and he started hitting Jennie, slapping her face and shaking her, finally throwing her to the ground. Angelina appeared, begging him to stop and be rational. Katie cowered back inside the doorway, afraid to breathe.

"You are never to leave this building!" Louis shouted, shaking his fist, his face red with rage. "*Stà 'ndrinta e travaja! E ch'a basto!*" "Stay inside and do your work! That's all!"

Jennie looked downcast, her eyes averted from her father's livid glare. She swallowed a throat full of protests and clenched her hands defiantly, wanting to lash out at her father and call him a tyrant and an oppressor. He continually made life miserable for all of them. She couldn't stand it that he treated her as if she were a naughty child, but she held her tongue. Angelina had often preached that Louis held power over all of them and could "throw them out into the street, if he so desired."

Angelina looked at Jennie and Louis together and sighed. There would be no peace with these two constantly at odds. It was obvious to all, except Louis, that Jennie, at age twenty, was now a young woman. She enjoyed being noticed and having men smile at her, and there was no lack of masculine attention in Silverton. Both Jennie and Katie were the focus of male interest wherever they went, and Angelina could see that this was just the beginning of many problems to come. Her daughters were lovely at ages nineteen and twenty, and they were not little girls any more.

"*Fala star 'ndrinta!*" "Make her stay inside!" Louis bellowed at Angelina; then he turned and stomped back into the saloon.

Jennie's reputation as a seamstress proved to create another problem, and Angelina was in for a surprise one day when she was cleaning the bar. It was around noon and no customers were around. She looked up from her scrubbing to see three colorful "ladies of the evening" enter the front door of the Belleview. They wore gaudy hats, dangling earrings, short skirts, and high-heeled shoes, and each struck a provocative pose as they stood before Angelina.

"Get out!" Angelina shouted briskly, wondering what was going on. "This is a respectable place of business. You can't come in here!"

One of the "ladies" put her hand up to stop Angelina from chasing them out, using her other hand to adjust one of her falling shoulder straps. "We don't mean to upset anyone," she said as the other two sauntered closer and stood beside her, eyeing Angelina. "We've come to see the seamstress."

These ladies from the bordellos wanted to make appointments with Jennie, because she had been recommended as "the best seamstress around." They wanted her to make them new working outfits. These "fallen women" or "sporting ladies," as they were called, wanted elegant outfits, made just right to show off their bodies.

The lure of prostitution was everywhere in Silverton. The boomtown atmosphere created a place with many men who needed booze, gambling, and whores on their times down from the mountains. These "soiled doves" made a good living from the miners. Now, here they were, strutting into the Belleview to consult the dressmaker. These "ladies" wanted and could afford the best in fancy finery.

The lifestyle of these women appeared to be easy on the surface, but it was not unusual for a prostitute to come to a violent end. This way of life was simply the only alternative for many women, as some had few choices for survival. A young girl without a family to care for her could try to support herself working at a laundry or as a maid, but the pay was minimal and it was heavy drudgery and endless toil.

Instead, work as a prostitute promised easy money. One survey found that the average age of these women was 23.1 years, and very few were over the age of thirty. Despite the legendary success of a few women, prostitution was neither an attractive nor a rewarding occupation. Many committed suicide, died of disease or alcoholism, drifted away into other occupations or, among the more fortunate, found a husband or protector.

Now, here they were, facing Angelina, these fallen angels, wanting to order fancy outfits with bangles, feathers, sequins, and velvet. They requested that their bodices be cut low, wanting "peek-a-boo" lingerie and sheer frilly peignoirs. Angelina looked at them closely, noticing that they were brazen about their bodies, wearing tight corsets that pushed their breasts to overflowing the satin cups. Angelina wasn't sure what to do, but she decided to call for Jennie.

Angelina worried at the interest and curiosity in Jennie's face as she measured these women for a correct fitting.

"Aj piasan parèj a j'oman!" "So this is what men like!" Jennie thought to herself.

"Que che pös far?" "What am I to do?" Angelina shook her head in dismay as she watched her daughter at work. Jennie was eyeing her customers shyly as she moved around them with her measuring tape. Jennie lifted her eyebrows in wonder as she took notice of the painted lips and cheeks, the powdered faces, and the short skirts revealing

black silk stockings. The prostitutes teased and bantered with Jennie and, after a fashion, the young seamstress felt comfortable and was making jokes right along with her racy clients.

Katie peered silently from the kitchen, not believing the scene. *"Susì aj piasrà nin a papà!"* "Father will not like this!" she whispered to herself as she tried to size up the situation, "Unless Jennie makes lots of money with her sewing."

Louis wore a serious expression as he pondered the question, but in his final decision, Katie was right in her prediction. He decided to allow Jennie to continue with her lucrative business of sewing for the prostitutes. He often collected her wages himself, not allowing Jennie to pocket any of her own money. It was the same for Katie. Now much of the boarding house work fell on her shoulders, but she didn't collect pay or even an allowance for the work she did. Louis considered it all joint income for the good of the family.

Both parents were aware of the distinct differences between the two sisters. Jennie knew how to flirt, and shamelessly flaunted this talent, while Katie was more passive and demure. Katie was tall and thin and more moderately endowed than Jennie. Men flocked around Jennie: Those who approached Katie did so with careful respect, knowing she would rebuff any attempt at frivolous or insincere attention.

Seeing the differences in his daughters, Louis did not feel the need to restrict Katie as he did Jennie. He delighted in taking his younger daughter with him on trips to deliver liquor to some of the mining areas, and Katie looked forward to this. She wanted nothing more than to visit with some of the women living at these remote camps and perhaps exchange news or have someone instruct her in new embroidery or crochet stitches.

The towering Rockies loomed majestically in every direction on these trips to the remote mines. The loaded wagon would move slowly over the narrow, rutted road. At an elevation of more than 9,000 or 10,000 feet, summer days could be cool even with the sun shining. But the trips away from town were peaceful, with the mountains offering a freedom from noise and clutter. At times, Louis would stop the wagon after a steep incline to let the horses rest. In the quiet of the mountains, they would listen to the sounds of the wind moving through the trees and the quivering of the aspens. However, the mining camps would be a noisy contrast to this peacefulness, as gulches and entire hillsides resounded with a steady rhythm of pumps and pounding of sledges.

Katie enjoyed talking with her father as they slowly moved along, finding these to be special moments to experience his gentler side. They would discuss the news of the day, local gossip, or Louis' passion with opera. Louis followed news from La Scala Opera House in Milan, considering this to be the lifeline that connected him to Italy. Katie would share in a light-hearted moment as her father tried to sing some of the arias he played constantly on the gramophone. Louis would smile, feeling certain that this daughter would never cause any trouble for the family. *"Katie, e tsé na brava cita!"* "Katie, you are a good girl!"

On one of these trips, Louis stopped in Howardsville on the way home to pick up feed for the horses. Katie remained seated on the buckboard while her father went inside to place the order.

"How are you today, Miss Sartore?"

Hearing a masculine voice, Katie turned to see a young man with a heavy feed bag over his shoulder. He unloaded the heavy bundle onto the back of the wagon and then casually placed his foot on the wagon wheel. Looking up at her he asked, "Do you remember me? We met at a dance in the hall here in Howardsville a few weeks ago. My name is Pietro Dallapiccola, but everyone calls me Peter."

"Yes, of course," Katie replied shyly. She did indeed remember him. She hadn't danced with him, but he was handsome enough to turn every girl's head, with that broad smile and wavy brown hair. On that occasion, many young ladies were vying for his attention, but it was not in her nature to approach him in a forward or flirtatious manner. Even now she could feel color rushing to her face as he stared up at her smiling visage, and she clasped her own trembling hands together.

"I thought you worked in the mines," she said, her mouth suddenly feeling dry. She had to concentrate on her breathing so she wouldn't choke on a quick intake of breath.

"I worked in the Silver Lake Basin until a few weeks ago, but I have been saving money for the past three years and hope to buy into a business soon. I am working here temporarily," he said, never taking his eyes from her. "I want a better life than working in the mines."

Seeing her father walking toward the wagon, Katie smiled tensely. Peter turned to glance at Louis Sartore, but quickly added, "Will you come to the dance here next weekend?"

Before she could answer, her father yelled, "Haven't you finished loading the feed? Hurry it up!"

Peter brought two more bags, placing them in the bed of the wagon. Katie sat with her father, not looking at anything or saying a word. When Peter indicated all was loaded, her father quickly moved the horses forward. Peter tipped his hat as they pulled away.

Katie struggled to sit there calmly and tried to curb her emotions, but with an overwhelming desire to see if it had all been a dream, she looked over her shoulder. Peter stood there and waved his hand when he saw her turn. Katie felt a tingle go through her entire body, creating a warm glow that she radiated in all the way home. She barely heard her father's words warning of the dangers in talking to men she didn't know.

As time moved on, it became more obvious that something needed to be done to stop Jennie's conduct where men were concerned. She was becoming outwardly bold in her rendezvous with young men, and her parents knew they could not keep ignoring this problem. The girls were old enough to have suitors, but their parents continued to restrict their social lives.

"Our family is very old fashioned." Jennie said to Katie. *"E pudràn mai viver nostra vita!"* "We will never have a life of our own!"

Katie nodded in agreement adding, "We will be lonely old spinsters!" Then Katie asked solemnly, "Do you think they will let us go to the dance on Saturday?"

"Why do you want to go to Howardsville?" Jennie said, looking at Katie with a suspicious grin. "Have you got a secret beau?"

Jennie then proceeded to provoke her younger sister until they were both rolling with laughter. Katie had a "feeling in her heart" for the very first time. Jennie was delighted that her prudish sister was now smitten with someone. Perhaps together they would be able to put pressure on their parents to have more freedom in socializing with young men.

"Who is it?" Jennie teased, insistent that her sister tell all. "I am your sister, and you can confide anything in me."

Katie sat still, her brown eyes twinkling, but she hesitated to let the secret leave her heart for fear that once it was out, it would cease to exist. She moved around uncomfortably, studying Jennie's mocking, teasing face. Struggling to find words, she suddenly felt a need to tell someone of the wonderful feelings she experienced upon meeting

Peter. Fidgeting with the folds in her dress as she tried to compose herself, she began to tell Jennie about him. Katie's face held a wistful expression as she explained that he had only flirted with her for a fleeting moment, but she related how her heart was pounding when he spoke to her.

Jennie had found this all amusing at first, but she frowned when Katie mentioned his name. She remembered meeting him, too, trying all evening to get him to notice her. She played the same coquettish games with other young men, and it usually worked. Now she was particularly annoyed with the thought that Peter would be interested in her sister. Jennie bristled, and disguising her feelings of jealousy, jumped into Katie's romantic chatter.

"Dear sister, I don't want you to be taken in by a scoundrel. Peter Dalla is well known for playing young girls for fools. He is only toying with your heart to see how far he can get with you. When you are crazy in love with him, he will drop you like a hot potato!"

Katie stammered, stopping in mid-sentence. The twinkle left her eyes and she hesitated, staring at her sister with a look of vagueness and doubt. She looked down at her hands, fiddling with them in her lap. "Oh, I don't think so, Jennie. He was just being nice and showing an interest."

"You are naïve and innocent as a dove, and men will take advantage of you," Jennie scolded. "Listen to me and stay away from men like that!"

Katie wrinkled her brow in the uncertainty of her sister's words, trying not to show disappointment. She had been so happy in her warm, romantic glow. Was it wrong to feel that way? Now she felt despondent, but she was not completely convinced that Jennie knew what she was talking about. Perhaps her sister's harsh words were intended for her own good, but something deep inside was telling her to ignore them.

"Perhaps," Katie muttered to herself, "I am not as meek and docile as everyone thinks! I am strong and stubborn enough to follow my own heart!"

The family continued to live behind the Belleview but kept the girls away from the saloon area. Angelina kept them out of the bar, even though she worked her own way into this "forbidden world," where proper females were not allowed.

Angelina was cunning in how she handled her husband, and she slowly talked Louis into letting her assist him in the bar. She liked the activity and enjoyed talking with the men. She was a good listener, and to the many lonely miners she represented a maternal image. Many of them asked about her daughters, because most were very much aware of the two beautiful Sartore sisters. Angelina ignored some of these questions and encouraged others.

While Jennie and Katie were kept out of sight of the barroom, their brother Phil, being male, had free run of the place. Both Louis and Angelina were strict in this discipline with their daughters in hopes they would be brought up as respectable and decent. However, they thought it reasonable that Phil be raised with a different standard. Phil grew up seeing and experiencing all the bawdiness that goes along with life in a saloon. He always watched things going on around him, but never said much.

Jennie's "social activities" continued to be a problem, and Louis was perplexed when hearing the gossip around the bar. He complained of this constantly to Angelina, expecting her to handle the problem.

"Perhaps it is time Jennie married." Angelina said casually one evening to her husband. Louis whipped his head around in surprise at this comment. It was something he had not considered, because to a father, a daughter is never old enough for marriage. Besides, he needed her to work and help the family.

"Whoever would she marry?" was his reply.

Angelina, knowing that she had his attention, used the opportunity to put her plan into action and replied, *"Chi ch 'e decidan gnèt."* "Anyone we want her to marry."

Louis was quiet as he considered this new idea. He pictured many of the young men hanging around waiting to see Jennie. *"A van nin ben!"* "They would not do!" he thought.

Angelina was fond of a group of young Piemontesi Italian men who frequented the Belleview and gathered around her, patronizing her and giving her flattering attention. She would suggest that one of these young men marry Jennie. She decided to wait to break this news to Louis, knowing that he needed time to adjust and think about this idea of marriage for his daughter.

Late the next morning, while Angelina was doing her usual cleaning behind the bar, Louis came in with a friend and seemed in unusually good humor. *"Angelina, A l'é decidü."* "It is decided." Our friend Bonavida has agreed to marry Jennie!" Louis beamed with the excitement of this news. Louis Bonavida stood with her husband, and they were both playfully shaking hands and slapping each other on the back.

Angelina felt a shock run through her body. Trying to conceal her surprise as she forced a smile, she found she could not utter a word. Louis had not consulted her but had decided on his own. She fought back her anger, deciding she would now have to deal with this problem in another way. Bonavida was not suitable for Jennie. He was fourteen years her senior, and, worst of all, he was Tyrolean, an Austrian. Yes, he was a friend and had lived as a boarder at the Belleview, but she did not want him as part of the family. What was Louis thinking, asking him to marry Jennie?

All through the long day, Angelina pondered the problem of Bonavida. She could not go against the wishes of her husband, and to disagree with him would just make him angry. She suddenly realized that Jennie was a strong-willed young woman and would probably solve this problem by herself if Angelina played her cards right. Jennie would hate the idea of marriage to one of her father's friends: She would not agree to marry Bonavida, and then Angelina could mention her idea of a young Piemontese as a solution. She would be patient and wait to witness her daughter's reaction.

"Angelina," Louis called out, rushing into the bar area in his usual brisk manner. He irritated her at this moment and she had to force herself to act civilly toward him. She thought, "He drives us all crazy, moving like a devil, always prodding us with a hot poker." *"An fa 'gnir tüjt nervùs!"* "He makes us nervous!"

"Angelina," Louis said, repeating her name with sharper tones this time. "You must tell Jennie about her betrothal to Bonavida. We want to announce this news soon. She will then settle down to more mature matters and stop running around on the streets."

Angelina gave him one of her half smiles and assured him that she would do this. She quietly said to herself, *"E vesràn co ch'aj sücéd!"* "Now we will see what happens!"

CHAPTER V

The Wedding

Angelina waited until late that evening to talk to Jennie. All day she rehearsed, invoking a dramatic masquerade in preparation for the moment when she would present the circumstances to her daughter. In doing so, she wished to portray an image of complete despair when she brought up the matter of the fateful marriage to Bonavida—as though Jennie was destined for the gallows. She was determined to prevent Jennie's marriage to Louis Bonavida. *"A va nin ben e an pias nin."* "It is not right and I don't want it to happen."

Her plan was to upset Jennie, making her angry enough to fight against her father's wishes. Angelina lifted her chin, taking a deep breath before walking the distance from the saloon to the back of the living quarters, where her daughters shared a room.

Angelina stopped at the bedroom door, hearing muffled sounds of giggles and laughter. She shook her head knowing that her girls were in a mindless mood of nonsense. As she walked into the room, the girls looked up, startled at the appearance of their mother. The look on Angelina's face made them suddenly aware that their mother carried some message of doom. Angelina had a look of greyness, remaining stoic and downcast, ignoring the jovial mood apparent in the room.

Jennie and Katie struggled to gain serious composure. They were still flushed from laughing over their imitation of one of Jennie's colorful customers. Both were wearing only a chemise, their corset laces open, and they were lying on the bed in disarray. Only moments before, they had been tightening their corsets in hopes of achieving the same "overflowing bosom" effect one of Jennie's customers had displayed earlier that afternoon at a fitting.

Angelina kept focused on the matter at hand. She turned her attention to Jennie and, covering her face with her hands, she started to cry. *"Mia povra cita! Mia bela cita!"* "My poor beautiful girl! For what your father has planned, he should burn forever in hell!"

Both Jennie and Katie looked at each other with their eyes round in fear and confusion. *"Que ch'a jé, Mama?"* "What is it, Mama?" Jennie asked softly. *"A 'n manda via papa?"* "Is Papa sending me away?"

"It is much worse," Angelina spoke each word with passion, shaking her hands for emphasis. *"A ja decidü ch'e 't marie."* "He has planned for you to marry."

"A ja sernü' queidün për mi?" "Has he chosen someone for me?" Jennie asked cautiously.

"He has done more than chosen someone for you. He has sealed it with the person of his choice without even consulting you. He did not even ask me!" Angelina ranted on. *"A l'é 'l padrùn!"* "We have no choice, as he is the mighty one and makes all the rules."

Katie's eyes were wide open and full of fright as she realized the magnitude of this problem. They were allowing Jennie to marry, but it was not to be to someone of her choosing. Would her sister have to marry someone horrible? Would this soon be her fate as well? All these thoughts passed quickly through her mind in a flash. Their mother would not be so upset if this was not a terrible tragedy.

"Cun chi che duvrìs mariame?" "Who am I to marry?" Jennie asked urgently, feeling trapped and uncomfortable.

"One of your father's friends. He is too old for you, and I don't know what your father is thinking. The man is at least fourteen years older than you! I want you to have a happy life with a handsome young man." Angelina sighed heavily amidst the tears and dabbing at her eyes, she said, *"A l'é gnanca italian, a lé n'austriaco!"* "He is not even Italian: he is Austrian!"

Chi ch'a l'é, Mama? Dimlo!" "Who is it Mama? Tell me! I can't stand it any longer!" Jennie rose and went to sit beside her mother. "Tell me who it is that I am to marry."

Angelina lowered her head and in a sad voice, said, "Your father demands that you marry Louis Bonavida."

Katie's head came up with a start. "Bonavida is a nice man, Mama. *Me ch'a và che t' ënrabie parèj?* Why are you so upset?"

"Caterina, e t'é fola a pensar parèj." "You are a stupid girl, Caterina, to think that way." Angelina angrily spat out the words as she jumped to her feet. "Picture your sister married to that old man, Bonavida. It is not the life for a young, beautiful girl like Jennie. She should have a nice Piemontese man, not this Tyrolean!"

Both girls shrank back with fear at the furious, irate tone of their mother's voice. They knew when she meant business, and no more was said on this issue. For moments, silence hung in the air as if waiting to fall and crash to the ground. Angelina took steps to leave the room but stopped at the doorway. She turned and, shaking her finger, said in a voice that shook with venom, *"A l'é la tua vita për sempre!"* "You are both too young and not smart enough to realize that marriage is your future and means forever!" With these words of parting, she left the girls alone.

Jennie moved slowly to shut the bedroom door, her mood somber in the wake of her mother's words. The girls prepared quietly for bed, but there would be little sleep for them. The world seemed to spin in every direction. Whispers filled the night as they talked of the decision that Jennie would have to make. Her father wanted one thing and apparently her mother wanted another. There would be no way to please them both.

"Neither Mama nor Papa see us as grown-ups and we never have any freedom. I'm not surprised that a husband has been chosen for me. Our parents will never allow us the privilege of choice," Jennie said with bitterness.

"The alternative is to stay here with our parents forever and be spinsters," Katie responded. Some of these words were uttered over and over throughout the long night.

"A l'é la mia vita!" "It is my life!" Jennie finally decided, speaking to no one in particular, since Katie had drifted off to sleep. Angelina had been correct in assuming that her daughter would make up her own mind. Jennie was not about to let anyone control her destiny! But she couldn't sleep, so she lay awake with her mind racing wildly. She was still bewildered about the decision she must make. What would happen if she refused to marry the man her father had chosen?

Jennie left the room just after dawn while Katie was still asleep. She had determined a resolution to the problem and prepared herself for a confrontation with her parents. She would first tell her father, and she wondered how her decision would affect him. He knew how contrary she could be. Would he be surprised?

She smiled, remembering the talk with Katie last night. As they discussed each of Silverton's prospective candidates for a husband, none of them came out ahead of Bonavida. Both Jennie and Katie were fond of him. With the innocence of youth, they both completely agreed that Bonavida was a handsome and desirable man, and the choice for a husband could have been much worse.

Bonavida was a good man and respected in the community. Yes, he was older, and considering him as a suitor would never have occurred to Jennie. He was a family friend and he often spent time with her father. She let her imagination direct her feelings as she entertained the idea of being Bonavida's wife. At this thought she smiled and felt sensations that caused her skin to tingle. She lifted her chin with confidence in her decision: She was ready to marry, and she would agree to marry Bonavida. She went to the kitchen to prepare a big breakfast for the family. This was a day to celebrate the beginning of her new life!

Angelina took the news with quiet resignation, knowing that she could not go against the decision they both had made. Louis was jubilant, promising his daughter *na bela festa,* a grand wedding, the likes of which the town had never seen. Much to Angelina's chagrin, Jennie and Bonavida seemed enchanted with the situation and with each other. As they stood together before Louis, both of them eagerly consented to the proposal.

It was soon noticed that in light of all this, Jennie's demeanor immediately changed. As if by magic, she now appeared more gracious and reserved, especially in the company of her fiancé. This improvement in his daughter's manner pleased Louis, and he gave credit to Angelina for recognizing that marriage was a solution. As he expressed this, Angelina stared at her husband as if her eyes were sightless, but she gave him no sign of disagreement. "He might be happy," she thought to herself, "but I am not at all pleased."

Angelina remained silent when it was decided that the date for the wedding would be set for February. They were deep into summer now, so it would give them a few months to plan. The winter months were a slow time in Silverton. Because of the difficulty of heavy snow and cold in the high country, some of the mines closed and many people left Silverton. Louis and Jennie agreed that the quiet month of February would be the perfect time for a grand wedding celebration!

"We will have a feast with all the trimmings on Sunday for the entire family and special friends," Louis proclaimed. "We will announce this engagement in style!"

Katie tried not to show her disappointment as Saturday turned into a day of preparation for Sunday's feast and celebration. She would not be able to attend the dance at Howardsville and would miss the opportunity to see Peter.

It took everyone's help and support to make the specialties Louis requested, so the women congregated to prepare the feast. Men might consider women to be weak and foolish, but cooking was an entirely different matter. The favorite recipes indigenous to the Piemonte Region had to be made from scratch and took time and skill.

Preparing food for these occasions was a celebration in itself, a time when stories were shared as the women arranged food into works of art. The warm summer days had provided a wonderful vegetable harvest, so they would create a menu with an antipasto of roasted peppers doused in bagna cauda with anchovies, salami, and prosciutto, thinly sliced, and stuffed tomatoes. *Frittura dolce* or "fried mush," green beans, and zucchini with sauce would accompany the ravioli and veal scaloppine, along with cheese and bread. Wines from the barrels of many of the guests would be served, because Italian men followed in the proud tradition of making their own wine. At the end of the meal would come the Macedonia, a salad of fresh fruit all chopped together, dressed with white wine or some sweet liquor. This would be served along with a generous amount of zabaglione, made with egg yolks and Marsala wine.

In this happy confusion of bustling about the kitchen, Katie wondered if she would ever have the chance to see Peter Dalla again. She knew her thoughts were selfish: She should be rejoicing in her sister's upcoming nuptials. But Jennie was acting like a royal princess, basking in all the attention, and actually seemed pleased that Katie would be unable to further pursue her interest in Peter. This clouded Katie's mind while she tried to laugh and carry on with the others in the kitchen.

Angelina sat with Maestra and other friends who gathered around the table. It had been only a few weeks since Maestra had lost her young son at only six months of age. The baby had suffered poor health in the past four weeks, and everything possible had been done to save him. The funeral had been held at St. Patrick's Catholic church with many sympathizing friends and relatives in attendance. With sorrow still fresh in the hearts of the grief-stricken parents, Angelina and many others had coaxed Maestra away from her mourning in hopes of putting life back together for the beloved "teacher."

Some of the women chattered boisterously as they cleaned the green beans freshly picked from the garden. Others were exuberant as they took part in the noisy conversation while preparing the zucchini and making the stuffing for the tomatoes. Because the summer weather had been good for the wild mushrooms that grow in the mountains at high altitude, many had been gathered and were being cleaned. Some were being set out in the sun for drying and would be stored for later use. The larger mushrooms would be sliced and used for the dinner, adding flavor to various dishes.

Tables were brought in and set up in the barroom as delicious aromas floated outside, where more tables were placed near the bocce court. The warmth of late summer lingered in the air and Angelina felt a sharp flash of nostalgia, remembering her own wedding festivities. These small rituals were meant to create lasting memories, but Angelina could not abandon the argument or keep up with the happy banter of the women around her. Jennie was engaged to marry an Austrian! There seemed to be no justice in the way of life in Silverton!

Suddenly Angelina's ear caught a few words between Katie and Mary as they rolled out the dough for the ravioli. Katie was expressing a desire to go to a dance. Angelina's spirits rose a little, realizing that she would soon have another daughter ready for marriage. She intended to have more control over this one.

She turned to Katie with words intended to draw her into a plan that was taking form. "You have no need to worry about suitors, as I know many men wanting to court you. What about that nice Piemontese, Barney Fiori? He always asks about you!"

Katie's response to her mother's words was a scowl. She bitterly disagreed with her mother's selection but said nothing, giving her full attention to the careful working of the dough and the sprinkling of flour. This was no time to argue with her mother, but Barney Fiori would never be her choice!

The Sunday announcement was a happy celebration, and it seemed that everyone but Angelina was joyous over the fact that Jennie would marry Louis Bonavida. Soon the adults gathered outside the saloon where accordions and mandolins played familiar strains of Italian music. These Old Country melodies pulled everyone together in song. With the cheerful sounds of singing, dancing, and happy laughter in the background, Mary pulled Jennie aside where they could talk. Mary was jubilant that Jennie would marry soon, noting, "Next it will be my turn." Mary was anxious to be lavished with all this attention and to be honored with parties and gifts. The two young women stood together whispering and laughing as if they shared a private secret. Katie walked over to join them after the dinner had been served and enjoyed. All too soon it would be time to clean up all the dirty dishes. She needed just a little time for herself.

The talk in the corner was of boyfriends, as Katie expected it would be. She had missed the part where Jennie disclosed some of her earlier dalliances with a menagerie of young miners. Now Mary was drawing them closer, talking softly, not to be overheard, telling of her infatuation. Everyone knew that Mary was enamored with her father's business partner, Ludwig Vota.

Mary quietly whispered, "One time I was home alone when Ludwig came over. We were talking and he kissed me."

Jennie squealed with excitement, taking hold of Mary's hands. "Tell us more!"

"It felt very nice and warm as he held me close," Mary continued. "He told me I was beautiful. My mother came into the house through the back door and we heard her, so nothing more happened. Ever since that time, Ludwig smiles at me in a special way." All three girls were certain there would be no objections to Ludwig courting Mary, since he was already close to the family as her father's business partner.

Jennie then added her similar feelings toward Bonavida. As this talk continued, Katie felt left out of the conversation. She had no special relationship and could not share in the parley of romantic feelings. Mary and Jennie now seemed to glow in a shared spotlight.

"It would have been terrible if your parents had chosen someone you didn't like," Mary added. "Who do you think they will choose for you, Katie?"

The question created a shocked silence as they looked into Katie's bewildered and stunned face. Katie felt heat rise to her cheeks, and she had nothing to say in answer to this question. She was the same age as Mary; both were only one year younger than Jennie. Yes, it would soon be time for her to marry.

Suddenly, to escape any more questions, Katie dismissed herself, saying she must start clearing the tables. Both Jennie and Mary looked cautiously at each other as Katie quickly moved away. They both followed in an attempt to continue the subject of finding a future husband for her. As the three girls joined in the process of cleaning up, the prospect of finding Katie a suitable marriage partner was suddenly an exciting topic.

"If they attempt to have me marry someone like Barney Fiori, I will run away from home," Katie shouted. Her voice was laced with anger and her face red. She scrubbed harshly at the pots and pans as the three young women worked together in the kitchen washing the dishes. "Mama has already mentioned his name to me," she added grimly.

In an attempt to console her, Mary added, "This is a new world, and most girls have a say in whomever it is they choose to marry. I'm sure your parents won't force you to marry someone you don't like."

Katie ignored this comment and continued to work in a furious fashion. Her bad mood deepened as she remembered again that she had missed the dance at Howardsville. This entire conversation was making her feel unsettled and fearful!

As Katie lay in her bed at the end of this long and difficult day, she wondered what it would be like to have feelings for one man and be told she must marry another. She prayed this would never happen to her!

Angelina sighed and tried to show some interest as Jennie chattered away, happily sewing a trousseau for her new life with Bonavida. In the months that followed the engagement celebration, Katie and Mary often clustered around Jennie, discussing love and the fantasies surrounding a wedding day. The young women's hands were always busy, putting embroidery and crocheted lace around bed linens and towels, or sewing buttons on new garments. There was much discussion about the elaborate wedding dress, and they all helped work on the special design. Angelina did add some lace to a couple of pillowcases, but she kept as remote as possible from these daily festivities. Her heart was cheerless. Why had fate brought her to this land where such a marriage would be permitted? In Italy, Jennie would marry one of her own kind, not a Tyrolean. The situation was out of her control, and she felt powerless to alter the chain of events.

Angelina had nothing personal against the man her husband had chosen to be a son-in-law. Louis Bonavida was known to be one of the most energetic and active mining men in Silverton. His special project was a quartz mine called The Silver Ledge. Bonavida hoped he would be successful with this mine and that someday it would produce rich amounts of silver and gold. He worked hard to acquire investors and business partners. This was necessary so that he could purchase machinery for the power to dig ore out of the mountain.

Bonavida had been a boarder at the Belleview and was close to the Sartore family. Louis Sartore respected him, feeling that it was of no importance that he was Tyrolean. *"E sen 'n Merica!"* "This is America!" Louis would say, *"A l'é divers belesì."* "Things are different here. We left the old problems in the old world."

Bonavida felt it an honor that he had been chosen to marry one of the lovely Sartore sisters. Being fond of both girls, he was delighted with his betrothal to the high-spirited Jennie.

There were many days of preparation in the busy weeks that preceded the wedding. It was exciting that expensive materials for their gowns had to be ordered from Denver and sent by train to Silverton. It seemed there was no end to the amount of money Louis would spend to make this wedding elaborate and special.

It was a glorious time for Jennie, who relished the attention. Katie and Mary shared in her happiness, anxious for their turn at having all these favors directed toward them. With stars in their eyes, they enjoyed talking of romantic dreams.

Engagement photo of Louis Bonavida and Jennie Sartore in 1900.

It seemed to Katie that she would never have a life of her own because everything revolved around her sister's wedding. Finally, a few weeks after the engagement was announced, the girls were allowed to go to the Saturday night dance at Howardsville. It was decided that all three of the girls would go, with Bonavida acting as chaperone.

At first, Jennie looked a little ill at ease as she sat beside her fiancé while the others danced and flirted. Missing out on this fun disturbed Jennie, and she felt a tug of jealousy at not being "belle of the ball." There was some compensation as friends gathered to see her ring and give congratulatory wishes. She soon basked in this attention and seemed to glow with happiness when Bonavida took her hand in his.

Mary was dancing, taking turns with many young men. She knew Ludwig wouldn't be present at the dance because he was working at the saloon, but that didn't matter to Mary. She knew their relationship would come to be in time, and she was content to wait and enjoy herself with this lively social activity.

Katie was dancing every dance, but her eyes were always watching the doorway. It was getting late, and Peter Dalla had not yet made an appearance. "He probably isn't coming," she admitted sadly to herself, trying not to let disappointment show. But she suddenly knew he was there, even before she saw him. He had just walked in. Katie tried to listen to the talk around her over the loud drumming of her heartbeat. Finally spotting her, Peter made his way to her side just in time for the orchestra to begin playing *"Varsouvienne."*

"Would you please dance with me, Miss Sartore?"

Katie smiled, trying to act surprised that he was there. As she put her hand in his she felt tremors, and the warm tingle in her arm spread throughout her body as they moved together on the dance floor.

"I didn't know if you would be here tonight," he managed to say as they danced.

"I wanted to come last time," she found herself confessing as she felt pleasure at being with him.

"Would you like to go for a drive tomorrow?" he asked, looking directly into her face. "I can borrow a horse and buggy, and we could meet at the corner by the Catholic Church at 2:00."

"I can try to come," Katie stammered, not knowing what her parents would allow.

When the music stopped, Katie and Peter were still lost in talking, oblivious of things around them. The trouble began as Barney Fiori pushed Peter away from Katie, demanding the next dance. Katie was flustered and backed away, knowing a fight would ensue. Fiori was shouting that a Tyrolean should know his place and dance with his own kind. He tried to take Katie's hand, but Bonavida intervened, leading Katie off the dance floor. Peter would not fight with Fiori, saying he didn't want to embarrass Katie. He would leave rather than upset her. He turned and walked away.

Barney Fiori then boasted that the Tyrolean was afraid to fight, and he walked over to Katie and once again tried to dance with her. She pushed him away. This brought laughter from many in the dance hall, and Fiori backed off. Bonavida led the young women away from the crowd that had gathered and proceeded to take all three Sartore girls home.

As the horse and buggy made its way the short distance back to Silverton, excitement sparkled like electricity in the evening air. Jennie and Mary chattered away, energized with the confrontation that had stirred things up at the dance. Their voices were high pitched and animated. Two men had been ready to fight over Katie!

"There were many Tyroleans there to back him up in a fight," explained Bonavida.

"Yes, and many Piemontesi to help Fiori," Jennie remarked.

"It would have been a big fight if he hadn't been a gentleman," Mary said, turning to Katie with questions. "Do you like him, Katie? What is he like, and what is his name?"

"A 'm pias prope." "I like him very much." Katie answered with her voice wavering, still a little shocked over what had happened. She waited for any negative reaction from Jennie, but her sister moved closer to Bonavida, distracted and seemingly disinterested.

"His name is Peter Dalla," Katie continued. She radiated with enthusiasm as she explained, "He is saving money, hoping to buy into the new saloon right across the street from the Belleview. He wants to see me again."

This brought squeals of delight from inside the buggy, and Mary gave Katie a hug as they all basked in the romantic mood of the evening.

Back at the Belleview, the news of the incident at Howardsville reached Angelina, and she muttered under her breath. Now Katie would be the subject of local gossip. She was a stupid girl to be caught in the middle of an argument between two men. *A l'é na cita fola.*

Angelina had much to think about with the wedding of one daughter; now the other one was creating a problem. Angelina was especially fond of Barney Fiori and had encouraged him to play up to Katie. Her scheme to have Katie paired off with a Piemontese suitor had been bungled by another Tyrolean. Other plans would have to be made before this situation got out of control. She gave little thought to what Katie might want, thinking only that this second daughter was docile and would be easier to control. She would intervene now, before Katie got any ideas in her head!

Angelina looked up and smiled warmly as her favorite group of young Piemontesi walked into the Belleview Saloon and greeted her with stories of the evening.

Sunday morning, following the dance at Howardsville, brought tense moments for Katie. She doubted very much that her parents would allow her to go for a buggy ride with Peter. That morning she prayed fervently in church, asking for a miracle. Later, she worked harder than usual in the kitchen, preparing Sunday dinner for the boarders and her family. In her nervousness she kept picturing Peter, waiting for her at the corner by the church. She hurried to clear the dishes away.

It was well after two o'clock when she could stand the strain no longer. Not having the courage to confront her parents with the truth, she blurted out that she was going over to Mary's. To her surprise and chagrin, no one seemed to care where she was going. Her parents were absorbed with wedding plans, still hovering around the table discussing arrangements with Jennie.

Katie darted out the door, heading first in the direction of Mary's house, in case her parents or sister were suspicious and watching. She looked back toward the Belleview, not believing that this could be so simple.

Concerned that Peter might give up and not wait, she hurried, almost running up the street. Her soft brown hair came loose in wisps around her face and in her haste she grew short of breath. Her heart almost stopped when she saw that he was actually there by the church, waiting. Peter stood near the buggy, smiling, and he quickly walked forward to meet her.

"I am so happy you could come," he said warmly, their faces almost touching as he grasped her hands in his. "It is a beautiful autumn day and perfect for a ride in the mountains."

The wedding of Jennie Sartore and Louis Bonavida was a grand affair, and both Angelina and Louis were exhausted as they sat watching their guests at the ball following the day's events. Jennie and her new husband danced and radiated happiness as the center of attention. Louis Sartore beamed at the scene before him, watching the happy couple and his friends dance and celebrate at the ball. He was proud that he could afford to show off his success. Angelina was happy that the ordeal was almost over; she just felt very tired. *"A 'm va tüt për travès!"* "Things are not going right for me!" she thought, still wondering why fate had been so cruel as to place her in this harsh frontier town.

Angelina set her jaw as she looked solemnly at her younger daughter dancing with a guest. Next it would be Katie's turn to marry.

She looked around for Phil but assumed he was outside with Angelo and the other younger guests. Phil's future bride had been decided when he was born. Angelina smiled proudly, visualizing her son dressed for his own wedding and pledging himself to his first cousin, Mary Sartore. Angelina and Mary's mother had already discussed this in Italy, when the two were just children. What did it matter that Mary was six years older than Phil? "Keep the good Piemonte blood in the family," Angelina and her sister-in-law had agreed. Phil had balked, almost gagging at the idea of marriage to his older cousin, but what did he know at age fourteen? Angelina knew things would change, when Phil grew older and wiser about women.

Now she had to concentrate on Katie, and she had to put her plan into action quickly. She would start to work on this project before Louis had time to ruin it. She would tell Katie that it was time she married, and the perfect choice would be a nice Piemontese man, like Barney Fiori.

A few days later, the excitement of the wedding was starting to wind down. Angelina sat looking at the extensive array of photos, choosing special ones to send to Italy. She looked at the newspaper and smiled at the description of the wedding. She would translate it, the best she could, from English into Italian, and send it to them. No matter how much she hated being in Silverton, she wanted her family and friends in Italy to see that she was doing well. Life must appear glamorous, and they must imagine she had money to spend lavishly. *The Silverton Weekly Miner* wrote the following, and Angelina translated it into her letter:

BONAVIDA— SARTORE WEDDING— Monday, February 4, 1901 at 11:00 a.m. Louis Bonavida and Miss Giovanina Sartore were joined in the holy bonds of Matrimony at St. Patrick's Catholic Church, Father O'Rourke officiating.

About forty invited guests attended. After the marriage a grand celebration occurred which lasted until 2:00 the next morning. The program started with an elegant repast which was served at the popular restaurant of Mrs. N. W. Savage, where all the good things were had and champagne had its way as it never had before in Silverton. After the dinner the merry party participated in a sleigh ride and the event wound up with a grand ball at Gerow's Hall, where everybody was made happy.

The bride wore white mouslin de soi over white satin and her magnificent physique was covered with American Beauty roses. The bridesmaids, Misses Katie and Mary Sartore, were attired in white satin and wore white roses. The best men were Messrs. Esa (Jess) Bonavida and Ludwig Vota. The newly married couple left

Tuesday morning on their honeymoon trip to Denver and other points throughout the state.

The wedding was the most elaborate ever given in this city and was the first young Austrian couple ever married in Silverton. [Angelina decided not to write this part into her letter, as, to her, it was distasteful to think of them as an Austrian couple.] *Mr. and Mrs. Louis Sartore, parents of the bride, spared neither pains nor money to make this affair the event of the season.*

The new couple starts out well in life, being the recipients of many handsome and valuable presents. Following is list of presents:

    Louis Sartore, father of the bride: beautiful 3-mirror dresser
    Mrs. Louis Sartore, mother of the bride: fine linen table set
    Miss Katie and Philip Sartore, sister and brother of the bride: China dinner set
    Mr. And Mrs. Joseph Sartore, uncle and aunt of the bride: parlor suite
    Miss Mary Sartore, cousin of the bride: embroidered sofa pillow
    Philip A. Sartore: cousin of the bride: bouquet of flowers
    Mr. And Mrs. J. Boggio of Calumet, Michigan: lace window curtains

Angelina finished her letter and put it with several photos of the wedding, sealing them into the large envelope. She smiled, knowing that this would be the talk of both villages in Italy, Rivarolo Canavese and Pasquaro.

Louis and Jennie Bonavida, 1901.

Back row left to right: Angelo Sartore, Ludwig Vota, Mary Sartore, Katie Sartore, Jess Bonavida, the next three are unknown. Front row left to right: The first two are unknown. Jennie Bonavida, Louis Bonavida, Angelina Sartore, Louis Sartore, and Joseph Sartore, 1901.

Back row left to right: Peter Rudellat and his wife, Maestra, Ludwig Vota, Mary Sartore, Katie Sartore, Jess Bonavida: the others are unknown. Front row left to right: Angelina Dighera Sartore, "Little Phil" Sartore with his father, Joseph Sartore, Jennie and Louis Bonavida, Angelina, Phil, and Louis Sartore: The next man is unknown. Photo taken in 1901.

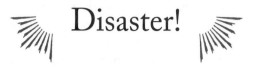

CHAPTER VI

Disaster!

Winter was slowly retreating, being replaced by the uncertainty of spring in the high mountains of Silverton. Tiny slivers of warm sunshine struggled against the wind-chilled air to thaw the frozen mining community. Patches of brown grass peeked through half-melted banks of snow. The creek that ran through town was a rush of energy as snow receded in the high country. It was April, and things were settling back to normal after the excitement of February's grand wedding. The newlyweds had returned from their honeymoon travels and moved into a small house near the Belleview.

Life soon fell into a routine, with Bonavida going to work at his mine for weeks at a time. He was mining quartz because a large amount of gold or silver had yet to be found. Quartz was used to make glass and other products, making it moderately valuable. When veins of quartz surfaced, it was usually a sign that gold was hidden in the rocks nearby. Bonavida and his partners continued to be hopeful that they would make a discovery of a more profitable ore.

Drawing of a typical mine of the Silverton area.

Jennie continued with her sewing business but was lonely and bored when Bonavida was away. Angelina spent many afternoons talking with her while Jennie worked sewing costumes with needle and thread. Angelina was upset when she learned that Jennie was making plans to spend the summer in a tiny cabin at the Silver Ledge with her husband. She planned to help Bonavida by cooking for the miners working there.

Angelina protested. *"A l'é nin 'n post për ti!* It is no place for you! You won't even be able to take a bath. You won't see other people. I didn't raise you to live like an animal!"

Jennie would only shrug her shoulders, as if to say, "He is my husband, so I will go there with him."

"Do you have to keep fetching that sauerkraut for your husband? It is shameful to see you go to the Tyroleans to buy it," Angelina complained. "Everyone sees you collecting that Austrian food. *A l'é 'nbarassant për la nostra gent!* It is an embarrassment to your own people!"

These afternoon visits became a time for Angelina and Jennie to argue, but they were also building a close relationship. They enjoyed exchanging stories and sharing the gossip of Silverton. Jennie often took advantage of the opportunity to include her sister as a topic for discussion, since Katie had always been considered the "good" one in the family. Jennie wanted to make certain that Angelina knew everything Katie was doing, especially the time she was spending with Peter Dalla.

"E t' ël savìe che la Katie a ià 'n murùs austriaco?" "Did you know that Katie has an Austrian boyfriend?" Angelina's head came up with a start at this news, and Jennie held her undivided attention as she continued. "The young Austrian over at the Todeschi saloon has been trying to get close to Katie," Jennie told her mother. "He wants to get rich the easy way. He plans to marry Katie and take over the Belleview. *E 'l veso già bele fèt!* I can see it happening!"

"A vènta nin pensar na cosa parèj!" "Such nonsense! He is no good to think such a thing!" Angelina shouted. "The Belleview will belong to Phil in time, and your father won't let anything like that happen. Don't worry! There won't be another Austrian in this family. *E t' l'ën-prometto mi!* I promise you that!"

Angelina's tirade was interrupted by the arrival of Jennie's clients from the brothels as they stumbled into the room in disheveled disorder. It was almost two in the afternoon by the clock on the wall, but these "ladies of the evening" worked all night, so it was the crack of dawn from their point of view.

Winter had been a difficult time for Katie as there had been little opportunity for her to have much contact with Peter. They were kept apart by the rules inflicted by their Italian society, so she was lucky if she occasionally caught a glimpse of him across the street at the Rock Saloon. Peter had become a business partner with Mrs. Todeschi, and it was common knowledge that only Tyroleans patronized the Rock Saloon. The Belleview was a Piemontesi saloon, and because of this rigid feud between the young Italians of Silverton, there seemed to be an impossible barrier between Katie and Peter. The two saloons were on opposite sides of the street, but there was an invisible line of bigotry keeping them apart.

Yes, Peter was right across the street, but he might as well have been a million miles away. He was not allowed to enter the Belleview because it was on the Piemontesi side of the street, and it was not proper for a young lady to be seen in any saloon, least of all a Tyrolean one. This was a mighty dilemma, until Bonavida intervened.

Louis Bonavida did not share his wife's feelings regarding Peter Dalla. The young Tyrolean was a fellow countryman and was reliable and likable in every way. In Peter, Bonavida saw himself at that youthful age, and he could see that Peter worked hard and was sincere and honest. Bonavida was aware of the many forces and circumstances keeping Katie and Peter apart and, realizing that they were desperately in love, he started relaying messages between them whenever possible.

Therefore, it was not by accident that Katie ran into Peter while she was shopping one day. She smiled, blushing and lowering her eyes in the act of surprise, and greeted him happily. He asked to carry her basket and other bundles as they both openly relished the opportunity to be together.

"I tried to enter the Belleview to see you," he told her as they slowly walked down the street. "But before I could do anything, a group of rough Piemontesi pushed me and told me to get out. *Hanno detto che agli austriaci non è permesso di entrare al Belleview.* They said Austrians were not welcome at the Belleview."

Katie was not surprised to hear this, but she said her father did not feel that way about Austrians or anyone else, and that she would talk to him.

"I would ask your father's permission to call on you. *Va bene così?* Would that be all right?" He asked this, regarding her with tenderness, anticipation sparkling in his eyes.

The smile that broke over her face charmed him thoroughly, as she softly said *"Sì!"* and the expression of love, along with the color rising to her pretty face, held all the answer he needed. She didn't try to conceal it, and her eyes were shining with the enthusiasm gathered from his words. She would have loved to reach for him, kiss him warmly in the happiness of the moment, but she knew she had to be discreet out in the open. There were watchful eyes everywhere in this small town. He understood and smiled with satisfaction at her response. He continued walking her home, carrying the baskets and groceries. A cool April breeze stirred around them, putting a chill in the air. There was still snow on the ground, but the sun was shining, taking possession of the day. The clear crisp dry air had an invigorating effect on the young couple. They walked through the melting slush and mud, oblivious to the noise, the busy streets full of people, and the wagons and burros loaded for trips to the mines. They walked slowly, talking and savoring this time together. Avoiding Blair Street, they came up behind the Belleview through the alley.

As she reached to take the groceries from him, their hands touched. Gallantly keeping a firm hold on the parcels, he leaned forward and gently kissed her. She felt a little flustered, but he stood there calmly, a smile covering his handsome face. She looked cautiously at the Belleview, and whispered. *"E' meglio che io vada. Ti vedrò presto?"* "I'd better go. Will I see you again soon?" He nodded, still smiling, and he tipped his hat as she disappeared into the back entrance of the saloon into the kitchen.

The rest of the day was a blur for Katie. She kept touching her lips, remembering how it felt to have his mouth touching hers. She couldn't concentrate on any of her cooking tasks, and she burned the bread she was baking. She tried to find a time to discuss the matter of Peter with her father, but Louis was busy and agitated about something. She hesitated, wanting to catch him at a time when he might be in good humor. Wringing her hands nervously, she tried to think of how she would approach her father with this topic and realized that the discussion would have to wait for another time.

By late evening she had fed the boarders and finished cleaning up the kitchen. She started in the direction of her room, feeling the loneliness of Jennie's absence. She would love to tell someone about today. It seemed magical for her to be with Peter, and she repeated his name and stood for a moment as if in a trance. She could hear the noise from the inside of the saloon, and the smell of smoke from cigars and cigarettes crept into the back area and into the kitchen. The sounds of gambling reached her as the roulette wheel turned. This was followed by either shouts of triumph or moans when the dice or the wheel failed them.

She decided that sleep was impossible at this point and found herself outside behind the saloon, climbing the stairs to the second level where the boarders stayed. She entered the boarding house and walked down the hall to the front section where the windows faced Blair Street. Pushing open a window, she sat on the window ledge and looked across at the Rock Saloon. *"A jé Peter."* "Peter is there." She said this to herself as she sat gazing at the building across the street.

Then, as if sensing her presence, the door of the Rock Saloon opened and Peter walked out into the night. Katie's heart pounded madly in her chest and she waved to get his attention. Because he was staring at the Belleview with similar thoughts and intentions, he saw her. She could see his magnificent smile in the moonlight as he started walking toward her. But just then the door of the Belleview opened and boisterous confusion poured out in the form of Barney Fiori and his wild group of Italian companions.

"Hey, Tyrolean," Fiori shouted. "Stay on your own side of the street!" Just then someone noticed Katie at the window of the Belleview. This drew anger from the crowd, to think that this Austrian would dare to seek out a Piemontese woman. They advanced toward Peter Dalla shouting threats. The noise was an alarm alerting the patrons of the Rock Saloon. Doors flew open, sending many Tyroleans into the street to back up one of their own. Fists flew and the two groups of Italians slammed into each other with enraged and malicious vengeance. Katie muffled a scream as Peter was jabbed in the stomach and sent rolling. He came up hard against the horse trough, but he was back on his feet in a heartbeat.

Katie stood there at the window as if frozen, unable to look away with both her hands pressed against her face. It had all exploded into this nightmare in a very short time. After what seemed like an eternity, the sheriff arrived, breaking up the disturbance, and the two groups moved apart, breathing hard and still angry. Angelina walked out in time to see the fight disperse. She happened to glance up at the windows and saw Katie's face. Somehow she knew and read the circumstances.

"Nostra fia a l'é diventà na slandra. E su pi nin que far." "Our daughter has become a harlot, and I don't know how to deal with it," Angelina said to Louis, hoping to involve him in deterring the Tyrolean. But Louis replied that her worries were nonsense, and the two unruly groups of Italians were just testing their territories.

"A paserà." "It will all pass over. They will somehow have to learn to live together," Louis said, but Angelina was deep in her own thoughts. She did not want Katie involved with a Tyrolean and was afraid that Louis would be tolerant, allowing another Austrian into the family.

"You should control your daughter," Louis suddenly said to Angelina. "Look at Jennie now. She is settled and happy. You let her run wild and loose and the same thing is happening to Katie. She is your daughter! *A l'é ti che 't deve cuntrulala!* You should control her!"

Angelina felt the anger rising in her chest: She could not respond, with the fury that was building inside her. How dare he criticize her as a mother!

The warm April weather brought something more serious for Angelina to think about. Everyone told Louis not to go to the ponds for ice that day. They were slowly melting and were becoming dangerous. "My husband is impossible when he gets an idea in his head," she said to herself. *"Lasa che 'l mengiàr ' a vajo a mal!* Let the food rot! Getting ice to preserve a little food should not be a matter of life and death!"

Louis was angered that no one was willing to help and went by himself to cut and to pull ice from the ponds. He struggled with a large piece of ice and slipped into the freezing water.

Angelina rolled her eyes when her husband was carried dripping wet and freezing into the Belleview. "You can't tell Louis anything," she said, apologizing for her husband's stupidity. She then tried to feed Louis the soup that Katie prepared to help warm him, but he did not respond.

Days later Angelina was still cursing the stubborn ways of her husband, mostly in jest, thinking that this situation was not serious. When pneumonia set in, Angelina felt panic, but the doctor assured her that Louis was doing well and would recover. She returned to her work behind the bar of the Belleview with Katie and Phil keeping watch over their very sick father.

After a few days, Louis seemed to be feeling better and even sat up in bed, but the coughing and choking returned and the doctor was again summoned. His illness had advanced and become gangrene of the left lung. With this news from the doctor, the distressed family knew there was no hope for recovery. Louis Sartore died on April 17, 1901, at age forty-eight, with his family around him, only two months after Jennie's lavish wedding.

As the wedding was grand, so was his funeral. The procession was one of the largest witnessed in Silverton. Considered to be an upright and honorable man, Louis Sartore would be sorely missed by the community of Silverton.

Angelina went into shock and most of the arrangements for the funeral had to be handled by Jennie and Louis' brother, Joseph. Jennie signed the death certificate and Joseph wrote out the obituary for the newspaper. Katie and Phil wept constantly, kept on the emotional edge by the despair of their mother.

Angelina realized that the feelings she had for her husband were those of respect, and that was a type of love. He had worked to create a good life for his family, and though his tactics were not always easy to live with, he had built economic security. Would it last? What was ahead for all of them now that Louis was gone?

Angelina could not get out of bed to attend the funeral. She was dazed, paralyzed, as if her body had gone, vanished. Her spirit was so low that she could not feel or think. She always considered herself strong and in control, but now she could not find the strength to lift her head from the pillow.

Angelina later listened as Phil told her about the funeral—how the members of Silverton Hook and Ladder Company and the Fraternal Order of Foresters of America were carrying the United States flag. Many Silverton citizens were assembled and, in marching order, were followed by the hearse and pallbearers. The relatives and friends in carriages were at the end of this procession. Angelina patted Phil's hand as he described this sad but imposing spectacle making its way to Hillside Cemetery.

The funeral of Louis Sartore: Phil, Katie, and Jennie are behind the casket at the center of the photo.

"E 't vesrè ch'a 'ndrà tüt ben, Mama." "Things will be okay, Mama," Phil said to her reassuringly.

"Aura e t 'é tì l'oman d'la famija." "You are not yet fifteen years old, Phil," she said to him sharply, "and you are now the man of the family."

They each sat staring into the face of the other, both deep in thought of what had been spoken. *"Nté ch'a l'é la Katie?"* "Where is Katie?" Angelina asked suddenly.

Phil answered that she was in the kitchen talking to someone.

"Chi ch'a jé aura?" "Who is here now?" Angelina asked.

"That Tyrolean man from across the street," Phil answered directly, not expecting the response he received.

Angelina threw back the covers, grabbing a robe to put over her nightgown. Phil moved away, not knowing what to think. Muttering to herself, Angelina stalked out of her room and, moving quickly, she angrily flung herself into the kitchen. There she saw Katie, sitting at the table in quiet conversation with the Tyrolean man from the Rock Saloon, Peter Dalla.

Katie rose to greet her, starting to introduce the young man, but Angelina gave her no chance. Shaking her fist, Angelina shouted at him to get out of her house and to never again set foot inside her door.

Embarrassed and confused, Katie stood there shaking, as Peter slowly rose and tried to explain. Angelina was yelling, her face red with rage, so Peter awkwardly left by the back entrance.

"*Ch'a intro mai pì 'nt sa ca!*" "Never again is he to enter this house!" Angelina shouted. "The dirt is still damp on your father's grave, and you can't wait to be flirting and throwing yourself at a man."

"Mama," Katie sobbed, "Peter was expressing his condolences and offering to help in the bar." Katie had more to explain, but Angelina interrupted her, shaking her hands in the air.

"I will have no Tyrolean in the bar! He is a gold digger and a moneygrubbing opportunist! You are too stupid to see that. He wants to take over the Belleview now that your father is gone. Oh, yes, he thinks it will be easy to do that, as he has only to talk nicely to my daughter! I will not allow this, Caterina. Stay away from that man! Besides, we are now in mourning for your father. *E 't capistö?* Do you understand that?"

With those words, Angelina started sobbing and fell into a chair at the table. She let loose the tears she had been holding back for several days. Katie was stunned to see her mother so distraught and in such pain. Katie rushed to her side, hugging her mother, sharing in her grief. They each felt the loss of a strong family figurehead, and both felt fear of what life would bring without Louis.

Katie was crying for the death of her father, but the actions of her mother had caught her off guard, leaving her with new reservations about the future. She reasoned that her mother was suffering and would soon be more rational, hoping that the outrage had possibly been brought about by grief. Her mother could not have meant what she said, could she?

Angelina was crying for the emptiness created by the death of her husband. Yes, she would miss him, but her tears were also for the fears and new responsibilities she would be forced to face in her own life. How would she cope with the business problems? How would she, a woman, be able to keep things going? Many attempts would be made to take over Louis' mine interests as well as other businesses of which she had no knowledge. What about the prostitute cribs she had heard about? How would she handle these confusing problems? What would become of her and her family if she failed? How would she face tomorrow?

She was overcome with despair as Katie gently helped her back into bed. Angelina said no more and Katie left her alone. Making a vow that no one would take advantage of her, Angelina felt stronger and her mind was active as she lay there working out a plan. She knew how to run the saloon, and Katie could handle the boarding house. Perhaps Phil could manage the livery. He spent much of his time there anyway.

She had to keep things going until Phil was old enough to inherit what legally belonged to the Sartore name. She would not take any help, especially from a Tyrolean who wanted this business empire for himself.

With these feelings of determination running through her tired veins, she slept restlessly, waking to the noisy sounds of drunks on Blair Street. *"La vita a va avanti."* "Life continues," she dismally muttered to herself.

CHAPTER VII

Giovanni Baudino

Angelina had been right about the photos of Jennie's wedding: They made a memorable impression on the two communities in Italy. Everyone in the rural areas of Rivarolo Canavese and the outlying area of Pasquaro was talking about the Sartore wedding in America, but the news of the death of Louis Sartore had not yet reached Italy.

One young man, hearing of the grandeur of the American wedding, was anxious to see the photos for himself. He planned to emigrate to this "land of opportunity" soon and had been saving money for some time. However, working in the fields didn't pay much, and

Street scene, Rivarolo Canavese, Italy, 1900 (copy of a painting by Giuseppe Naretto).

there was always a need for the money at home. Things had been difficult since the passing of his parents.

Giovanni (John) Grato Baudino was born in Rivarolo Canavese in the Piemonte Region of Italy, on December 16, 1876. John was the youngest of six children born to Giovanni senior and his wife, Francesca Merlo. Those who knew him well called him "Neto."

The Baudinos were a close, hard-working family. Young Neto followed his father into the fields to work at a very early age, learning the art of tending the grapevines and watching them grow into thick, black grapes for making wine.

The education provided to the children of the field workers was minimal, and it was often the case that younger children were taught by older students. Domenica, Neto's older sister, taught reading and writing and helped these younger children, including Neto, work with numbers. For a brief period of time, Neto received education from the nuns at the Catholic church. For the rest of his life, he would remember the pain inflicted from a ruler being whacked over his knuckles when he didn't answer correctly. As soon as the children were about ten years old, they were taught to care for the farm animals, and the days of formal learning were over. Neto tended the cows, watching them graze on the pasture grass, reading a book whenever one was available.

His mother, Francesca, would prepare a small bundle of lunch for each of her six children as they went off to work or school. Neto would grimace at the thought of another day of eating *pan melia*, or corn bread. It was dark, ugly, coarse, and heavy and was all they had to eat day after day. Of course, his mother would remind him that it was better than having nothing at all to eat. But the young boy longed for the day when he would have better fare.

As soon as he was considered old enough, Neto went to work harvesting grapes. He was small in stature, but he hefted the heavy baskets of grapes on his shoulders, keeping up with his taller and stronger, older brothers, Carlo and Antonio.

In 1899, when Neto was 22, his mother unexpectedly died from an illness. The following February, his father, Giovanni, was hit and

Washing day at the river near Rivarolo (copy of a painting by Giuseppe Naretto).

killed by a train when his shoe became trapped in a railroad track. The shock of this incident and the death of both parents plunged the entire Baudino family into grief. Now in 1901, Neto wanted a new chance at life. In the depths of his soul he wanted to be more than a field worker.

The rural area of Pasquaro, where the fields were located, was very close to the larger city of Rivarolo. Pasquaro had a population of only about one hundred people at that time. Because the local inhabitants of both the Rivarolo and Pasquaro communities were well acquainted, it was a thrilling pastime to follow the news of those who bravely took on the adventure of going to America. Neto had watched both Joseph and Louis Sartore leave, and now he loved hearing news and listening to their success stories. He reasoned that if the Sartores could work in the mines of Colorado and earn enough to build grand saloons, why couldn't he do the same? He wanted that opportunity

Giovanni Grato Baudino (John or "Neto") in 1901.

and was working long hours in the fields to earn his passage. To fuel his hopes, Neto longed to see the photos of the wedding that Angelina Sartore had sent to her parents, the Giordanos, but he felt himself too humble, as a field worker, to knock on their door.

After work one day, John heard these words: "Neto, we want to give you this." The owner of the vineyards handed him extra money on payday, rendering John speechless. Looking at the large amount of cash in his hand, his face held a look of disbelief, and he deemed it a miracle that this was happening to him. Because his desire to emigrate to America was well known, he had been handed the extra money he needed.

Coming to his senses, with gratitude shining in his eyes, Neto made a promise, assuring his employer that no matter what he had to do, he would pay back every penny of this debt. He would always remember the generosity bestowed on him.

Giovanni "Neto" Baudino was a simple man, but he always carried himself with dignity. He showed proper respect for others and took pride in his work. His integrity and admirable attitude had not gone unnoticed. The owner of the vineyard slapped him on the back when he kept uttering his thanks. "You are a hard worker, Neto, a good and honest man, and we are happy to help you. *Buna furtüna!* Good luck to you!"

"Aura e pös 'ndar a far furtüna." "Now I can go to try my luck." He said to himself over and over as he made his way home that evening. He felt something stir deep inside him, something he had kept buried. It was excitement, the thrill of seeking something that, until now, had not been immediately attainable. He suddenly had the confidence to stop at the Sartore home, where the older Giordanos lived. He would tell them of his good news and ask to see the photos of the Sartore wedding.

Caterina Giordano was bent and wrinkled but greeted him warmly as she answered the door. *"Ven 'ndrinta, Neto."* "Come inside, Neto," and I will show you the wonderful photos from America. Oh, what a beautiful wedding it must have been! My Angelina has a good life in the new country and they must be very wealthy. Look, just look at these photos." She handed him the pictures of the lavish wedding, her face brimming with pride. These photos testified to the success of her son-in-law, Louis Sartore.

"I will go to visit the Sartore family," Neto remarked, never daring to imagine this prospect before.

"E t' vètö 'dco tì 'n Merica?" "You go to the new country, too?" Dominic Giordano entered the room, shuffling his feet in well-worn slippers. Neto greeted the older man and they talked for a few moments about traveling to America. Neto then turned his attention back to the photos, admiring the well-dressed people at the wedding in a world far away. The finery they wore made him painfully aware that his own clothes were old and dirty from heavy work, and far from stylish.

The Giordanos were elated at the idea that Neto would visit the Sartores, and they asked him to take a package to Angelina when he was ready to leave for America. "They live in Silverton, Colorado," the Giordanos continued to explain, both talking eagerly. "It is a small mining town, but a very profitable place to work. They are all doing well." The old couple talked on, portraying a wonderful vision of the good life in the new world. Tears formed in their eyes as they related stories from Angelina's letters, and they expressed over and over how much they missed their daughters and grandchildren. All three of the Giordano girls were now living far away in America, two of them in Calumet, Michigan.

"But the photos cannot lie," the old woman shook her head and pointed. *"E t'ël vese 'dco tì me ch'a stan ben."* "See for yourself that they are all doing very well."

Neto looked at the photo and expressed admiration for the three lovely Sartore girls. He studied Jennie as a bride and then searched for her sister, Katie. He remembered them from six years earlier when they left Italy to join their father. Because Mary had left Italy as a small child, he had trouble remembering her.

"Che bele fije!" "Beautiful girls!" he said to the Giordanos, watching their eyes light up with pride. "Any man would be proud to have a Sartore woman for a wife."

The old lady chuckled at the looks of veneration Neto wore as he studied the photos. Teasing him good naturedly, she said, *"La Katie a l'é nin marià."* "Katie is not married. Perhaps you still have time." He blushed openly and awkwardly returned the photos. He then hastened to leave, feeling ill at ease. He could not imagine that he would ever be considered a suitor for someone as special as Katie Sartore. Thanking them for their cordiality, he promised to return to collect the package before his departure for America.

Left to right, Ludwig Vota, Jess Bonavida, Luigi Bonavida, Jennie Sartore Bonavida, Katie Sartore, Mary Sartore in 1901.

Neto was a new man as he purchased his ticket to travel to America, and now he had a plan. He would follow in the steps of Louis Sartore. With this inspiration as his guide, he would work his way to a prosperous and successful life. Because of the rigid class system in Italy, he would always be considered a peasant, finding work only in the fields. He had heard that working in the mines was far worse, and very dangerous, but he wanted the chance to make something of his life. He would take the risk.

Four members of the Baudino family in 1900. Left to right, Giovanni, Carlo, Antonio, and Camilla. The older sister, Domenica, is not pictured.

Perhaps he would become someone worthy of Katie Sartore. He smiled at the jest of this, but new hope allowed him to imagine a very different life for himself. He had grown tired of thoughts of the future that only locked him into the role of observer. Elation pumped in his veins and he suddenly felt confident to acknowledge dreams of his own.

Neto's sisters and brothers understood his desire to leave home, and they encouraged his plans for a better future. They agreed that it was in his best interest, even though they were fearful of this adventure into the unknown.

Neto's oldest sister, Domenica, had married Michele Naretto, a saddle maker, and they now had two little boys whom he loved dearly. Seeing their Uncle Neto approaching, young Peppino (Giuseppe) and little Giovanni would squeal with joy, running to meet him, begging for his attention. Uncle Neto would spend time twirling them around and carrying them on his back. His brother, Antonio or "Tony," would laugh and tease, saying that Neto was a short man because of all the time he spent with nephews on his back.

Tony and Neto were as close as brothers could be. Tony was the tallest in the family, with a gregarious, relaxed sense of humor, while Neto was younger, short in stature, and serious about everything in life. Somehow this created a balance, and they depended on each other in good times and bad. Tony also wanted to try his luck in America, and the younger brother promised to help him financially. Neto planned to work in the mines, sending money so his brother could join him in Colorado.

The Naretto family, left to right: little Giovanni, Michele, Giuseppe and Domenica Baudino Naretto, circa 1902.

Their oldest brother, Carlo, and sister, Camilla, were both unmarried and decided to stay in Italy. They would dedicate their efforts to their sister, Domenica, and help her and Michele raise their family. They all promised Neto that, even oceans apart, this family unit would retain a strong connection.

Neto, being the emotional, sentimental man that he was, found it very difficult to say good-bye. It was a sad and sobering thought that he might not see any of his family again, and he pushed it out of his mind. Amid tears and good wishes, they all said *"Arvëdse,"* and saw him off on his journey into the unknown.

As he waved and they faded from view, Neto felt lonelier than he had ever been in his life. As he watched his homeland disappear, he felt very much on his own, with just hopeful expectations for companionship. Only courage allowed him to look ahead to the future, to the mines of Colorado, and the day he would walk through the door of the Sartore's Saloon in Silverton, Colorado.

Going by steamship and surviving life on the steerage level was not glamorous in any way. Traveling alone could be dangerous, and Neto was careful to stay to himself. People on the ship were sometimes beaten and robbed. Cramped, dirty quarters and the poverty of these passengers made the journey miserable, so he kept his money "stashed" in different places on his person. He made friends with no one, not trusting any friendly smiles or greetings. This made him feel even more alone, and at times he was frightened by the magnitude of his decision to emigrate.

Landing in New York in 1901 and waiting many days to be processed into the new country was agonizing. Neto began to realize just how difficult things were going to be because he did not speak any English. He was ignored and pushed aside, suffering abuse and insults when he could not understand what to do. He was made to feel shabby, unworthy, and lower than a common animal. He felt pathetically awkward and lost in an endless sea of immigrants.

He finally trusted himself to a group of Italians who were also struggling with the many problems of where to go and what to do. With the help of these *paisan*, he figured out how to change his money and buy a ticket to ride the train across the large continent of the United States to reach Colorado. Some of these Italians were heading to California where there were vineyards, others to the copper mines of Michigan. Many were going west to Utah and Colorado, to the mines around Denver and Pueblo. Each person had a separate dream driving him forward.

They all laughed nervously when it was decided that they should adopt American names. Pronouncing these new names sounded strange to their ears, and they teased each other as each new one rolled off their tongues. Neto, whose full name was Giovanni, would now be known as John.

When John Baudino finally arrived in Durango, Colorado, he found that he would have to wait overnight to catch a train to Silverton. Durango was a pleasant looking town, but he was not sure what he should do now since he had only fifty cents left in his pocket. A knifelike fear pierced his gut. He didn't know how to handle this next challenge, so he walked from the depot down the street until he came to a saloon with an Italian name. He took a deep breath and entered, hoping to find a cheap meal, if nothing else.

It did not take long for John to relax and feel comfortable. He was greeted warmly and served a small meal and a glass of wine. The bar patrons recognized John as being fresh from the Old Country and gathered around him, anxious to talk about things back home.

John learned that there were many Italians in Durango, and this was comforting after the trauma of first landing in America. He also learned that there were few success stories and no one had become rich overnight. Most were struggling to survive in terrible work conditions with customs they did not understand. These fellow Italians expressed how they had been taken advantage of and told of lessons learned the hard way.

"*Terra dei dollari—Terra dei dolori,*" one man said, meaning dollar's country—sorrow's country. "It is a little Italian pun that shows that earning the American dollar is difficult and does not always bring happiness."

"There is another saying for Italians that come to America," another bar patron spoke up, and he emphasized each word dramatically. "In Italy, the streets are not paved, and we heard that, in America, the streets were paved with gold. What we didn't know is that we were the ones expected to pave the streets."

John nodded his head, slowly understanding the wisdom and truth expressed in all these words. Perhaps he had underestimated the enormity of this venture. Would life forever see him in the role of a peasant?

It was embarrassing for him to admit to those around him that he was completely broke. He had his ticket to Silverton in his pocket, but otherwise they were empty, and he had nowhere to spend the night. When he finally spoke of this to the Italians at the bar, they told him not to worry.

One of them took John to meet a person well known for helping newly arrived immigrants. Mr. McWiggins gave him a few dollars and they shook hands, with John promising to repay the money as soon as he could. This transaction was made with the help of a translator. When they left, John was given directions to a boarding house with cheap rates. He slept fitfully, his dreams tortured and jumbled with new fears. But when he awoke he shoved it all aside, restoring his equilibrium to its usual level of confidence. He would push forward!

Anxious to see Silverton, he boarded the puffing, smoke-belching, narrow gauge train that would cross the rugged mountains and take him to the remote mining town. After months of planning and traveling, he would soon arrive in Silverton.

He sat enraptured by the beauty of the landscape as the little train careened and rocked its way around curves and maneuvered cautiously on the edges of cliffs, with a sparkling river far below. He loved the aspen trees swaying in the early summer breeze and marveled at the towering pines.

A rain shower in the high mountains left the air smelling fresh. He opened a window to enjoy the cool breeze, then closed it quickly when the smoke and cinders from the engine poured in. Undaunted by this, he sat back and sighed happily, thinking that his dreams might come true in a place so beautiful.

John arrived in Silverton and asked directions to the Belleview Saloon. It was a short walk, so he started out toward Blair Street. When he saw the black wreath on the door of the Belleview, he felt a shock run through his body. *"Que ch'a jé capità belesì?"* "What had happened here?" The door was locked and it appeared that no one was around.

He decided to inquire across the street, and he entered the Rock Saloon. A hush permeated the room as John asked in Italian, heavy with Piemontese dialect, if anyone could tell him about the Sartores. Two men at a table stood up, and John could see they wore guns. With great haste, the young man behind the bar came to his rescue and guided him toward the door.

"T'se nin de ste part, nè früstér." "You are new to this area, stranger. You asked about the Sartores, and I think they will arrive home from church soon because it is Sunday morning." He then told John about the death of Louis Sartore. John shook his head sadly, confused by this news and the strange reaction in the barroom.

"J'italian a sen divis a Silverton." "Italians are divided in Silverton," the young man explained. "There is trouble between Tyroleans and Piemontesi, and this street is the dividing line." He said this motioning with his hands. "You need to stay over there to be safe." John thanked him and started to walk away. Smiling, the bartender said, "Put in a good word for me with Mrs. Sartore. I would like very much to court her daughter, but she chases me away."

John tried to not to look perplexed and puzzled as he said his thanks again. *"Grassie d' l'ajüt."* Walking to the other side of the street, John now realized another fact. Every man in Silverton was probably in love with Katie Sartore. How naive and stupid he had been to think there was a chance for him. He felt discouraged and bewildered by the circumstances and the reaction he had experienced in this strange town.

Soon, the Sartores returned from church and discovered John waiting by the front door. *"Varda, a jè'l Neto!"* "Look, it is Neto!" Dragging him inside, Angelina greeted him like a long, lost friend, hugging him and asking about things at home in Italy. John presented the package from her parents and Angelina all but wept with joy. She unwrapped the soft woolen cloth and held it lovingly to her chest.

Eventually Katie and Phil stepped forward and welcomed John, trying to remember him from days that seemed so long ago. John's blue eyes shone with admiration as he looked at Katie, who had removed her black mourning hat and veil. He admitted to himself that she was even lovelier than the photos had revealed. She had soft brown hair and large brown eyes. Her skin was white and as smooth as porcelain. But more than her beauty appealed to John. He liked the warmth she conveyed with her smile, and the dignified bearing of her physical presence.

After they were caught up on news from their homeland, Angelina asked John about his plans. He explained his need to find a job working in a mine. He told them of the sadness he felt and the admiration he held for Louis. He expressed that his goal was to someday have a saloon as grand as the Belleview. It was strange discussing these innermost thoughts, but he felt safe, as if he were with family. Being alone during the long trip had been difficult, but he was now among friends, and soon it would be time to put his ambitions to the test.

John asked to rent a room for the night and pulled fifty cents from his pocket. Angelina insisted that he would be their guest for dinner and gave him back change. In the meantime, she suggested that Phil show John around Silverton. Phil, anxious to be away from his mother, quickly changed out of his Sunday clothes, and they were soon on their way out the door.

Silverton, as a grand city, did not live up to John's expectations. It was the weekend: Drunks staggered everywhere, and heavy booted miners covered with grime walked along the road. Blair Street was full of saloons, gambling halls, dance halls, and cribs. Even though the area consisted of only a few blocks between Eleventh and Thirteenth Streets, this part of town was like nothing John had ever seen. It was a flourishing red light district, with bordellos and saloons actively working around the clock. As they passed the many saloons they could hear boisterous, loud talk and sounds of gambling. At each doorway, the air was thick with the smell of stale liquor and cigar smoke.

Phil directed him to the main part of town, called Greene Street, and pointed to the new Miner's Union Building where John would come tomorrow to find work. They continued strolling up Greene Street past a general store, saloon, a drug firm, and other businesses. On the nearby corner stood the Grand Imperial Hotel, sometimes referred to as the Showplace of the Silver Kings. John nodded his head in appreciation that this was a place for the wealthy. Some people had become very rich and successful in Silverton.

John also found it interesting that most of the buildings were new or had been built just a few years prior. Silverton seemed to be in its prime in 1901.

Phil continued to explain that Silverton was completely surrounded by the San Juan Mountains and very high in altitude. The town was often snowed in during the winter months, and it was, at times, a world all its own. Despite the hardships due to being remote, Silverton was a bustling town with newspapers, banks, liveries, churches, and many stores and businesses. It prospered because the mines of the area produced much valuable ore, such as gold and silver.

It disturbed John, however, to realize the lonely plight of the immigrant miners. He could see that most of them worked and then reveled in an endless cycle that took them nowhere.

Phil was still young at age fourteen, with a quiet, easy personality. John, wondering how the family was coping, asked Phil about life without his father. Phil gave a shrug and a quiet laugh and started relating stories.

"Last week some men came to the livery to rent a buckboard. They loaded it up with supplies for a mine they were working clear up in the canyon. I told them I had to go with them to bring the buckboard and horses back, so they said okay. When we had gone about six miles, they pushed me out of the wagon and continued on their way. I ran after them, but they just laughed and kept pushing me out of the way. I was pretty beat up when I finally walked back home."

John shook his head in sympathy, asking, "What did you do about the buckboard? Couldn't the sheriff help you?"

"Macché, a l'era nin basta 'mpurtant." "Naw, it wasn't important enough. The sheriff doesn't leave Silverton unless there is a murder or something serious," Phil replied, shaking his head, trying to make the story light. "I just got Angelo and two other friends and we rode

horses up to the mining area. We found the buckboard and horses tied out in front of a building. All the supplies were unloaded, so we just drove it back home."

As they walked back to the Belleview, Phil talked to John about the saloon business and how he helped his mother run the bar. John saw Phil as a youth with an adult's understanding of the harshness of life. It was evident that the boy was being forced to become a man before his time.

Dinner was a succulent feast of Katie's special gnocchi, or potato dumplings, with a light dressing made from meat drippings and sprinkled with Parmigiano cheese. This was followed with a special dessert of *pesche ripiene*, peaches stuffed with crushed Amaretti cookies.

John enjoyed the meal and the warm feeling of home that it generated. But later he tossed fitfully, trying to sleep in his room in the Belleview. He was amazed at all that had changed in just one day. Katie had revealed to him, while her mother was out of the kitchen, that she cared for the young Tyrolean across the street. She spoke to John in a familiar manner, as if he was her brother. He realized he should be happy that she felt comfortable enough to confide in him, but he had come too late to win her affection—or perhaps she never would have considered him in the role of suitor. John took a deep breath and tried to put his thoughts and dreams back into perspective. *"Que che fù belesì?"* "What am I doing here?" Suffering with this feeling of disappointment, he could not ignore the tug of pain in his heart.

Early the next morning, John joined the other "new hire" workers as they headed up into the mountains. There, they were supplied with carbide lights on their miner's hats and kerosene lamps to carry for more illumination. John learned that morning that the Silverton district was rich in veins, which contained more base metals than even those of the Telluride district on the other side of the mountains. It was explained that the deposits of ore in this area were often simple veins or lodes averaging about three feet in thickness. At this time, the lead, zinc, and copper ore contained about $22 in gold per ton, and also some silver.

When they reached their destination, they were first told to stand back for the explosion deep within the mountain. After the detonation of "giant powder," or dynamite, they waited until the dust settled and the okay was given to enter the tunnel.

The narrow, low passageway was musty, damp, and clammy as they entered the cavern. Water dripped along the walls. As they moved deeper into the tunnel, they soon could not see daylight from the opening. It was a new tunnel, twisting and turning, going in about 500 feet. Suddenly a downdraft of wind blew out the lights, and they were engulfed in darkness.

John gasped and fought against the monstrous fear of total blackness: Shivers ran through his body, the drumming of his heart deafening. Some of the new miners cried out. Everything was black, and it was terrifying, like being buried alive! This was not a job that a young man, working in the sunny grape fields of Italy, had ever imagined. They were instructed to once again light their lanterns, and John struggled to do so with trembling hands. Once they could see again, they were told to clear away the debris.

"Mucking" was the term given to the job of removing ore and rock after the dynamite blast. It was common to find that the nationalities of the men doing this job were mostly Irish and Italian. They would first load all the debris into wheelbarrows. The rocks containing ore would later be separated from the dirt and put into an ore car on rails or moved down the mountain by pack trains of mules or burros. Some mines were situated so high on the mountain that the only way to move the ore was by dumping it into tram buckets that went to the canyons below, where it would be sorted, once it reached the mill. "Muckers" would toil in the darkness, from sunup 'til sunset, for $3 a day in pay. The endless digging, and being in darkness, would become their way of life.

CHAPTER VIII

 Mining Towns

PART 1—CALUMET, MICHIGAN

Angelina found it difficult to face life without her husband, because she had never anticipated life without him. However, as she became more secure in her new role, she began to realize she was now free to make her own decisions. With this new self-reliance, she thought constantly about returning to Italy. She could see, however, that none of her family wanted to leave Silverton. Would she want to be in Italy without them? She remained confident and undaunted by their lack of interest, certain she could eventually sway their feelings.

She pondered this quandary as she wiped down the bar in the saloon. Jennie was now married to an Austrian, and neither of them had any interest in going back to the Old Country. Phil flatly refused to even consider leaving Silverton, and Katie was blinded by love.

At this thought, she looked out the window and stared for a moment at the Rock Saloon across the street. It sickened Angelina that her daughter was infatuated with the Tyrolean bartender there. It didn't matter that he was part owner, he was Austrian and therefore not suitable for Katie to marry. Under her breath she uttered an oath, swearing she would not let this romance get out of hand. Angelina's mind returned to this thought over and over. Finally her face brightened with an answer to the problem. She would take Katie away from Silverton.

Angelina reasoned that she could take Katie with her to Italy, and there they would secure all the inheritance belonging to her late husband. She would take Katie away, and hopefully the Tyrolean would find someone else. Perhaps there would be a suitable marriage prospect for Katie in Italy. There were many things to consider before she tackled the permanent move, but this idea gave her hope.

Angelina stopped and found her thoughts leading her in another direction. Letters from her sister, Catlina gave her reason to worry. From the time of Jennie's wedding, Angelina had understood that all in Calumet, Michigan, was not going well. Catlina had written that they wished the bride and groom well, but could not afford to send a wedding gift.

The letter sounded dismal, and Angelina suddenly wondered if she should investigate the situation. She could easily travel to Calumet. Her two sisters were both settled there, so this would be a perfect opportunity to be reunited with them. Perhaps if things were not going well, they would all agree to return to Italy together.

She left the cleaning unfinished and hurried to inform Katie that she would be going along on a trip to Calumet, Michigan. The trip to Italy would have to wait! Angelina wasted no time putting her new travel plans into action, and in the summer of 1901, she and Katie boarded the train and headed northeast to Michigan.

Katie did not like being forced along on this journey, but Angelina's excitement did bring a certain amount of reprieve. She had only seen anger and heard words of dissatisfaction from her mother since her father's funeral. Angelina was now aglow with the happy thoughts of seeing her sisters once again. During the long days of railroad travel, Angelina shared childhood stories of life in Italy with her two sisters, reliving glorious moments spent growing up together. Thus, the anticipation of the visit reached a fevered pitch by the time they arrived in Michigan.

In Calumet, there was much interest in the Colorado relatives. Margherita and Catlina were both anxious to greet their older sister as they ventured out to meet the train with their families in tow. The three sisters had not been together for many years, and they were each eager to exchange stories. The strained sense of expectancy in the air was irresistible. As the train pulled up to the Mineral Range Depot, they could easily spot Angelina. She was leaning out the window, waving with one hand, holding onto her large hat with the other.

If she hadn't had long skirts and a body of large proportions, Angelina would have leapt from the train in her excitement. With her heart overflowing, she treasured the joyous moment of hugging her sisters once again. From the very first moment, before they even settled in, they chatted away incessantly, comparing life's situations, all talking at once and expressing tales of happiness and woe. Katie followed along, taking turns holding the hands of the Boggio and the Nigra children.

It was only a short walk from the depot to the Nigra house, so the three sisters settled in the comfortable Nigra kitchen and turned their attention to serious matters. One by one they told their stories. Angelina appeared to be better off in some ways, but she had lost her husband. They all agreed that her future was uncertain because of this.

The Boggio family. Left to right: Giovanni, Maudie, Tony, Katy, and Margherita, circa 1904.

Catlina sighed when she related her current situation. She was the mother of six children, and her husband, Antonio, had left them all to return to Italy for an extended visit. They were left destitute without his salary from the job at the copper mine. Because the family didn't have enough money to make ends meet, she was taking in washing. After a day of washing other people's clothing, she had to do the work of the boarding house and prepare food pails for the miners living there.

Margherita and her family lived across town, near the Richetta Boarding house, where they had all lived when they first came to Calumet. She explained that life in this community was not lucrative and the mines were not profitable for the workers. They could only hope to make a meager salary and barely support a family. Her husband, Boggio, walked a mile each way to Swedetown to work twelve-hour shifts that started at four a.m., and he worked a six-day week. When he returned home each day he was so exhausted that he would eat, sleep, then start all over again the next day. Boggio hated the dangerous mine work and feared ending up with consumption. Margherita told of the pain they had witnessed—of miners with wracking coughs as the sharp dust ate at their lungs and throat lining, allowing them to live a few years at best.

She then related the horrors of a terrible mine accident, explaining that the Red Jacket Mine was a vertical shaft reaching almost 4,000 feet deep. The hoist could raise a cage from that depth in less than two minutes. At the top of the shaft was an operator who, after hearing a signal from below, would prepare to slow the car down to a stop. On May 1, 1893, the operator was either asleep or otherwise occupied. The man-car came up too fast and, for some unknown reason, no one slowed it down. It flew through the roof of the shaft and went back down 4,000 feet to the bottom. All miners in the car were killed.

Silence prevailed in the room while the women contemplated the terrible dangers of working in the mines. Margherita then emotionally expressed her desire to return to Italy. She and Boggio were saving money in hopes of going back to Italy with their three children, Tony, Maudie, and Katy.

As Margherita talked about Italy, Angelina put her hand over her heart in an expression of understanding: Her sister's words were the encouragement she needed. Both sisters were comforted with the idea of returning to Italy together and pleased that they were thinking along the same line. However, Catlina interrupted at this moment, shaking her finger in protest, making it clear to them that she would not be a part of their plan and that she would never return to Italy. Her objection to the proposal set a heated discussion into action, and soon they were all talking at once again. Catlina motioned with her hand that she wanted to speak and make clear her reasons, so the arguing ceased for a moment.

She explained that Antonio had worked as a timberman in the elaborate wooden infrastructure that supported the mine. They had struggled to own and operate a modest six-room home as a boarding house. They were too proud to live in a company home, so they catered to shift-working copper miners. For this piece of property, they were allowed to obtain the five-year renewable ground lease offered by the company. The cost was $5, but there was the risk that the company could ask you to leave at any time if they discovered ore and wanted to dig under the house. The modest house consisted of four downstairs rooms, two upstairs, and, of course, a basement that held the barrels of wine and beer they made every year.

Catlina told them that she enjoyed her church life at St. Mary's. She also loved the diversified neighborhood where everyone pitched in and helped with the midwifery, sickness, and other crises. They all exchanged various homemade goods, and she explained proudly that the Cornish even brought her saffron bread in exchange for Antonio's beer. Catlina emphasized the point that she had worked to make this her home, and she would never leave.

There was again silence in the room. This was a setback to Angelina's plan, but it appeared that there was nothing she could do. She threw up her hands in resignation. She would respect the decision her sister had made.

As things settled down, Katie helped with the cooking and routine work associated with keeping boarders, but she spent many special moments bonding with her younger cousins. She enjoyed talking with the two quiet young men, Tony Boggio and Joseph Nigra. There was happy chatter when two Boggio girls, Maudie and Katy, were around. She spent pleasant times with both Frances and Kate Nigra and loved the moments spent with all of them, chasing around the younger Nigra children.

In accordance with her usual habits, Angelina kept herself busy by assigning tasks to the others. But her happiest moments came when she would sit with her sisters and talk about the past.

As their stay lengthened, Angelina and Katie were able to better understand the community of Calumet and compare it to Silverton.

They learned that upper Michigan is the only place in the world where copper comes out of the ground in large pieces of metallic

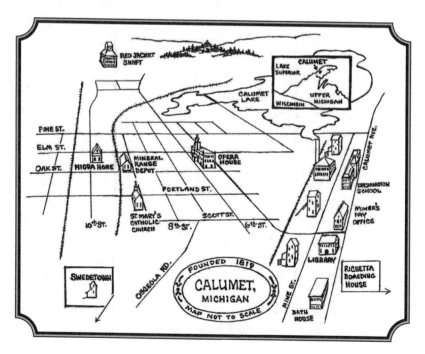

copper. In rare discoveries, some boulders were as large as 6,000 pounds, and the largest on record was 420 tons. However, the Calumet and Hecla lode always yielded a stamp-mill product that needed to be smelted, the same as the ore from Silverton.

The Calumet lode was discovered in 1864, and was the first major mining boom in the United States. The residents were proud of the fact that at Ellis Island, everyone heard mention of Calumet, Michigan, as "The Metropolis of Copperdom" or the "Queen City of the North." Newly arrived immigrants learned immediately that in Calumet, jobs were available. Calumet was an industry in itself, American and yet foreign with its multicultural population.

At this time in 1901, it was a community with a population of over 66,000. Of this number, 28,150 had been born in other countries. In comparison, Silverton numbered only around 3,000 residents, including the many miners working up in the mountains.

Unlike the mining area around Silverton, Calumet was developed as a company town. The Calumet Mining Company provided housing for families at a nominal fee, ran the grocery and dry goods store, and provided medical attention. They had even built hospitals, schools, libraries, and bathhouses by the early part of the 1900's.

The residential community was near the shafts, which finally reached 9,800 feet deep down into the earth. The workers came home each day, after various shifts, and were not separated from their families as they were in Silverton.

It was interesting for Angelina to see that the ethnic diversity in the Calumet community caused tensions, much the same as in Silverton. All the different cultural groups had their own associations and did not mingle very much.

The first miners to arrive were the English, Cornish, and Germans, and then came the Finns and Swedes in the 1870's. The Italians, Poles, Greeks, and French Canadians started arriving in the 1880s. New immigrants were sent to work in the more dangerous operations. As they became more experienced, and if they survived, they could move on to better jobs or work areas.

The English and the Cornish were the mine bosses, because they spoke English. This was the case in most mining areas, including Silverton. These bosses were called "Cousin Jacks" by the workers of various nationalities and were much hated. Their derogatory nickname implied that immigrant laborers could be easily replaced with

English-speaking countrymen, and these received preferential jobs and treatment.

But to the Cornish, mining was their life, and they were proud of their skills. They counted themselves among the elite of American mine workers.

During these days of many discussions, it was decided that Angelina and Catlina could help lighten each other's load. Catlina had six little mouths to feed, and Angelina needed extra hands to help keep the business alive in Silverton. It was decided that it would benefit both of them if Angelina took her sister's two older children, Joseph and Frances, back to Silverton. Joseph was eighteen and would be able to work in the saloon and Frances was thirteen and could help with the boarding house work. This would be a temporary situation for them: They would return to Calumet when their father, Antonio came back from Italy and resumed his job.

Young Kate Nigra and Katie Sartore in 1901.

Little ten-year-old Kate Nigra was the next oldest child, and it was decided that she would stay home and help take care of the younger children. Kate was a clever little girl and helpful to her mother, devising ways of keeping the three younger siblings entertained and under control. If they misbehaved, she would make them sit under the dining room table. She was a favorite of Katie Sartore, and they spent many hours together. Little Kate hovered around the kitchen with her older cousin while they cooked, chatting about life and discussing its various problems. This helped form a bond that would keep them connected throughout the many years to come.

In the autumn of 1901, when it was time for Katie and Angelina to return to Silverton, they took young Joseph and Frances Nigra with them.

Watching them with tearful eyes was young Kate. She would have loved being chosen to leave the disorder in Calumet to go off with her older sister and brother on what appeared to be a fairy-tale journey to Silverton. She knew her mother needed help, but now the burden would fall heavily on her young shoulders. She would eventually be pulled out of school to help with the remaining three children. It wasn't an easy job because one of the children, Dominic, had a club-foot and couldn't keep up with the others. She sighed, watching her older sister and brother leave. She then turned to her task: She gathered up the younger children, herding them under the table and feeding them bread to keep them entertained.

PART 2—SILVERTON, COLORADO

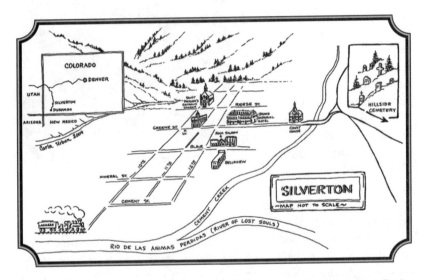

Back home in Silverton, Angelina eagerly planned her return to Italy. She knew it would take some time to work out all the problems for a permanent move, so she decided to first make a short trip to secure the inheritance of the property in Italy, now that Louis was gone. She needed to make certain that Phil would inherit the Sartore house and its property in Pasquaro. Before his death, Louis had also purchased another part of inherited property from his brother, Joseph. Angelina wanted to legally claim all that was due. One day it would all belong to Phil.

Jennie, Katie, and Phil were all sceptical about their mother's plan to visit Italy, because they realized she was viewing this as a prerequisite before a permanent move. They also knew that she would expect them to follow along and leave Silverton. They talked anxiously amongst themselves, wondering how this could be prevented.

The two Nigra children blossomed in the mountain community after living there for several months. Joseph worked in the bar and also helped Phil with the livery, because he loved working with horses. Frances was so happy that she begged to remain in Silverton forever. However, Catlina wrote that her husband had returned from Italy and the financial situation was improving. It was time for the children to return to Calumet.

Angelina was ready for her trip to Italy and decided to travel with the Nigra children to Calumet, and then continue on to New York. She was aglow with happy anticipation when she called for Phil to bring two of the large trunks up from the basement in the Belleview.

For Jennie, her mother's antics involving this trip were becoming impossible and out of control. "What are you doing?" Jennie asked her mother, her voice heavy with irritation.

Angelina had decided to pack Jennie's wedding gifts, including the fine silver service and other valuables, and take them to Italy. Jennie argued with her mother as Angelina loaded these valued possessions into the large trunks.

"These things will be there for you when we all move back to our home in Italy," Angelina said with authority, confirming that what she was doing was right.

Jennie scowled, throwing up her hands in an outburst of anger, but she knew there was nothing that would convince her mother otherwise. None of them had any intention of leaving behind the lives they had in Silverton. Besides, in a few months Jennie's first child was due. Throughout all of this preparation, Angelina was excited to think about her first grandchild and content to wait until after the birth to leave.

Katie was happy to have her mother distracted with the packing and planning, using every opportunity to sneak out to see Peter. These treasured moments had to be spontaneous, whenever the opportunity arose. Angelina had not wavered from her earlier decision, making it very clear to her daughter that she was not to see the Tyrolean under any circumstances, and Jennie had put a stop to any help from Bonavida. Katie and Peter looked for each other at social gatherings or dances, but it was becoming more and more difficult to arrange time together under Angelina's watchful gaze.

One evening when it was quite late and it was certain that Angelina would be working in the bar, Peter came around to the back of the Belleview. He could see a small light coming from one of the rooms, so he took a chance and tapped on the window.

Immediately, Katie's startled face appeared, relaxing into a smile when she saw Peter. Motioning for him to stay where he was, she put her finger to her lips to warn him to be silent. She moved out into the night and quietly closed the door of the family entrance, joining him outside in the moonlight.

Fading into the dark shadows of the alley, they held onto each other. A billion stars blazed up above and moonlight gave off a silver radiance as they strolled hand in hand. With their heads close together, they smiled at each other, speaking softly. For these young lovers kept apart by prejudice and jealousy, the angry world ceased to be, and time stood still for a few brief cherished moments.

The blessed event of the birth of Jennie and Louis Bonavida's baby girl, Angelina, on June 2, 1902, was a happy celebration for the family. No one was more infatuated with her namesake than Angelina. She was now a grandmother, "Nonna," to a beautiful child, who everyone called "Little Lina."

After the christening of her grand-baby, Angelina wasted little time. She prepared the Nigra children for their return home, giving an ultimatum to Katie that she was going along. She made it emphatic that Phil was also required to make the trip because he was the male heir. Once again, they loaded the trunks on the small narrow gauge train and left for a trip to Italy by way of Calumet, Michigan. They planned to return to Silverton in about six months.

Little Lina and her Nonna, Angelina in 1902.

For Katie, the trip to Italy was difficult, because leaving Peter to please her mother was complicated. Peter had talked seriously about marriage and Katie was deeply in love with him. It was a terrible agony, being apart for such a long time. She tried to keep secret the letters she wrote to Peter because Angelina roared with anger over any mention of him. She also had to hide the letters she received from him, but Angelina knew what was going on and continued to discuss finding a suitable match for Katie with Italian friends and relatives.

Angelina was happy in Italy, finding enjoyment in the house she had left behind. This was her home, and she loved it. The pretty bedroom with the roses on the wall was her pride and joy. Phil would some-day own this house, and that was the reason they had come to Italy, to secure this property for his future. She ignored the fact that he was morose and uninterested and seemed determined to make his mother miserable with his glum outlook. He wanted to be back in Silverton. But Angelina chose to attribute this attitude to his age: He was almost sixteen, and she used this as an excuse for his discourteous behavior.

Angelina was extremely relieved when they stood in the solicitor's office and signed the papers officially recognizing young Phil Sartore as the living heir to Louis' land and home. The house and property were now safely within her control, and she would continue plans to make them her permanent residence once again.

The autumn of 1902 found John Baudino in a dreary mine shaft, deep in the San Juan Mountains. He was learning that working in the cold, dark caverns, blasting and digging for veins of silver and gold, was not for him. No matter how strong his ambition, he didn't want to stay in Silverton. Riding the trams that hung from cables stretched across the canyons was frightening even to the stout of heart. Living in a boarding house in the high mountains, a building that hung on the side of a cliff, working many weeks straight, chipping and blast-ing in dark caverns, and then going into Silverton to get drunk was not the life he wanted.

John didn't want to admit to the misery he felt. The frustrations he encountered didn't seem to complete his purpose in life. Yes, he had so far failed in his quest for a better future, but he was still young and strong, and this was only a temporary derailment. It was a good time to leave because the winter season was approaching, and many of the mining operations were slowing down. Avalanches, huge piles of snow, and severely cold weather put things on hold up in the high mountains, and "Mother Nature" remained the supreme ruler.

The pay in the mines was not bad, but it offered little hope of owning any mine interests. Before the 1890s there was a chance, if a promising claim was discovered, that one could become instantly rich. That hope had been taken away by ownership of large companies, and now miners were only day laborers with minimum pay.

Also, some of the big mines were playing out, and The Great Silver Panic of 1893 had caused silver prices to be unstable. Silverton seemed vulnerable to the same vagaries of all boomtowns, so John made a decision: He would quit this job when they closed for the winter and move to Durango. This seemed a viable choice, because Durango appeared to be more of a settled community.

Besides, Katie was not interested in him. She and Angelina were gone, on their way to Italy, and they would be away for months. Angelina had told him this on his last visit into town. He had understood her words all too clearly when she said, *"E vöj turnàr a cà! Custa a l'é nin cà mia!"* "This is not my home. I want to go home!"

There were many times that John felt the same way, but he wasn't ready to forego his dreams and return to work in the fields in Italy. He was, however, surprised when Angelina had spoken confidentially to him during that visit. Her pleas of desperation concerning Katie alarmed him.

"Neto, I need to speak to you," Angelina said, a troubled look covering her face. "My heart is heavy with worry about Katie. She is too foolish and doesn't know what is right for her. I want you to talk to her. Perhaps if you show her that you have an interest, she will listen to you."

John had to think quickly to interpret the meaning behind Angelina's words. Was she insinuating that he was to propose marriage to Katie? What about Katie's feelings for the Tyrolean? He stood there looking at Angelina, but he didn't know what to say.

As if reading his thoughts, Angelina assured him that Katie's infatuation with Dalla was a temporary one. John felt uncomfortable with this topic, so he gently bowed out of the situation by saying that he had nothing to offer in the way of supporting a wife and family, but that he hoped someday to own his own saloon. Angelina quickly offered to lend him the necessary money. This was tempting but he gallantly declined, letting Angelina know he valued her friendship, but that he first wanted to try things on his own.

So now John Baudino was ready to leave Silverton, wanting to be away from this place where everything reminded him of how he had dreamed of a better life. He scoffed at himself for imagining that success and wealth would come easily. It was all a foolish fantasy, and he rebuked himself saying, *"E vöj turnàr a cà! Custa a l'é nin cà mia!"* "You are a stupid fool!"

He was tired of being lonely, and the only thing keeping him going was news that his brother, Tony, was seeking emigration and would join him in Colorado. With this in mind, John planned to try his luck in Durango working in the coal mines. Mining in any form was terrible, but what else could he do? He remembered, fondly the vineyards of Italy, nurturing the plants in the sunshine. Now he toiled in the dark of the mountain tunnels.

John reminded himself, *"A forsa 'd tirar drit e divento na përsuna da rispetàr."* "I am still young and my back is strong. I will keep going and become someone respectable." It was with a heavy heart that he collected his pay and prepared to leave the San Juan Mountains behind.

He had some time after he purchased his ticket to Durango, so he decided to stop by the Belleview. It seemed he was always drawn to this place; when he walked in, he was happy to find Jennie and her husband there tending bar. They explained that Angelina had insisted Phil make the trip to Italy and they talked congenially of news from there. They all discussed the fact that Angelina wished to move back to Italy permanently.

Bonavida had recently returned to Silverton after spending the summer at the Silver Ledge Mine. It was the first time John had met Louis Bonavida, and he liked him immediately. Jennie and Louis radiated excitement and happiness, relating the news of the birth of their baby girl, who was asleep in a bedroom in the back. John gave them his happy congratulations. *"Cumplimènt!"* He then pulled himself away from these pleasantries, because it was time for his train to leave.

They wished John well, extending an invitation for him to visit when possible. *"Ciao! Fa bun viage!"* "Good-bye! Have a pleasant trip!"

PART 3—DURANGO, COLORADO

As John rode the chugging little narrow gauge train back to Durango, his blue eyes glinted almost silver with determination as he stared into the empty space within him. He remembered his first trip into these mountains. Now, swaying back and forth with the rocking of the train, he studied the recent events of his life. He was a different person, changed with the hard knocks of reality. To find success in America was not an easy task, but he had not lost that burning desire. In fact, it never gave him rest! His aspirations seemed out of reach, but he was willing to believe in them and follow where they would lead. He thought to himself, *"A jè 'ncur tante strà duerte 'nt ës munt."* "There is still opportunity in this new uncharted world."

When John once again spent the night in Durango, he felt he had returned home: He was comfortable in his decision to leave Silverton. The next day he asked around about jobs and found work in the City Coal Mine located in Horse Gulch, almost within the Durango city limits. The mine employed many immigrants, mostly Italians, so John felt comfortable despite his lack of English. He did not have time to study the new language because he worked all the time, but he tried to pick up words when possible. He knew he would always be considered a second-class citizen if he didn't learn to speak English.

In the months that followed, John tried to save every penny possible, so he lived in a very cheap boarding house down near the river in south Durango. Whenever he had time off from the mine, he liked to walk around town.

He learned that Durango was established by the railroad in 1881 when they laid tracks into Silverton to bring the ore out of the mountains. Because of railroad backing, Durango was a fast-growing community. The flourishing business district had been established on the lower plateau near the river bottom, and the residential area was developed on the steps above, reaching eastward.

John enjoyed walking up a few blocks to the grand residential area of Third Avenue where there was a boulevard with a tree-lined parkway separating traffic. Houses being built here along this lovely avenue were the magnificent structures belonging to rich, successful people. He felt self-conscious when people stared at him; and he knew he was out of his element in this neighborhood. People recognized him as an immigrant mineworker and wondered what he was doing there. John tried not to be intimidated by this. These outings fueled his new dream, so he walked this path whenever time allowed.

John spent most of his time in the south part of Durango, because this was where most of the immigrants settled. He did not feel out of place in the area near the train depot. This section of town was less desirable to the proper citizens because of all the smoke accumulating there. One thing that could not be ignored in south Durango was the giant, smoking monster that was the smelter. At this time it employed

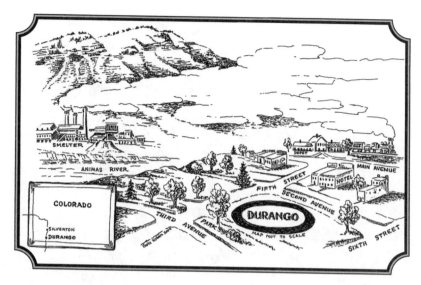

more than ten percent of the payrolls of Durango. The San Juan and New York Mining and Smelting Company had established the smelter in 1882. This was a regional smelter, convenient by location and necessary to produce a metal from the ore delivered from the mines. The Rio Grande railroad tracks were laid to all the mining areas, reaching Silverton, Rico, and Telluride. The smelter was fed by coal, and without coal there would be no smelter; fortunately, the area west of Durango had more than a sufficient supply of bituminous coal, which was excellent for coking.

Most of the homes were heated by coal, and the railroad was also fueled by coal. Between the Rio Grande Railroad Depot and the smelter located in the south part of Durango, pollution covered this part of town like a blanket. But through the haze, John began to see new dreams materializing. *"Nt ël carbùn a jé la furtüna."* "In coal, there lies opportunity."

Durango was willing to put up with the smoke, since these businesses were the mainstay of the economy and coal was necessary. Local coal also powered the dynamos that started generating electricity, so Durango had electrical power as early as 1887. John realized that all of this was part of Durango's success as a community. He could see the importance of the smelter, the railroad, and the coal. *"Eh sì, 'l carbùn a l'é 'mpurtant!"* "Ah, yes, coal is important."

John was at the Durango Rio Grande Depot to welcome Tony on that happy day in 1902. Seeing his brother's face as he disembarked

The San Juan & New York smelter at the base of Smelter Mountain in Durango, Circa 1900.

from the train, brought tears to John's eyes. *"Tone! E t' é rivà final-ment!"* "Tony, you are here at last." They took many moments to study each other, talking with excitement and letting the ten months apart fade away.

They were soon both employed at the City Coal Mine, digging and blasting for long dreary hours, but John was more relaxed with his brother working beside him. He had someone with whom to share his thoughts and ideas. Tony was by nature more fun loving, and he seemed to float above life and its troubles. This created a good balance for John's overly serious side, but he often had to bring his brother back to earth and reality, as Tony was susceptible to harmful ways. Tony would be happy sitting in a bar visiting with other customers, drinking up all his wages. John would not allow this to happen.

Together they supported each other, stabilizing their differ-ences. John talked with seriousness to his brother, disclosing his ideas and all that he had learned and experienced. With excitement in his voice, he tried to explain that in America, at this moment, true opportunity did exist.

"Me ch'a và che 't dise parèj?" "Why do you say that?" Tony ques-tioned.

"Because it's true." John continued. "As long as there is plenty of land to be had in America, people will be able to choose their own destinies. All the land in Europe was claimed centuries ago, and everything there is tied to the past."

"So we should work to become land owners," Tony replied factually.

John answered with passion in hi voice, "Yes. *Parèj e j'an nin da travaiar mé 'd bes-ce për ièt.* So that we don't have to work like slaves for others." They both nodded their heads in agreement with this statement.

"Que ch 'et pense che devan far?" "What do you think we should do?" Tony asked.

Antonio (Tony) Baudino in 1902.

"I think we should own a saloon and boarding house, like that of Louis Sartore in Silverton." This, John thought, was his destiny.

Tony raised his eyebrows but nodded his head in agreement answering, *"Va ben, se 't crese che posan faila!"* "Okay, if you think we can do it!"

The goal to own their own business kept them from the despair that can come with heavy labor in a dark cavern. John became an expert with explosives and learned to detonate a new opening in the mountain when veins of coal were discovered. Because he was a small man with a brave attitude, he was often the one they sent in after the blasting to check for air and other conditions, such as dangerous gases. Both of the Baudino brothers were hard workers and were respected for their ethics, exerting their strength and effort whenever needed. John always took the initiative, taking on any new or dangerous mining project. When difficulties presented themselves, it was Tony who made the going easier with his humor and easy attitude toward life.

John and Tony knew many Italians in Durango, and when a new opportunity was handed to them, they jumped at it. They were offered jobs in a local saloon owned and operated by John Sategna. This was employment that would benefit their plan for the future by way of experience. The San Juan Saloon catered to Italians, so their inability to speak English would not hinder efforts to communicate. John, being cautious, was afraid of this new venture, but Tony shook his head, saying they could always return to work in the mines if this failed.

"At least we will be cleaner and not covered with coal dust at the end of the day," Tony said, and both men smiled at this thought, slapping each other on the back in happy agreement.

So in 1903, the two brothers quit the coal mines and took jobs in what they considered a "more respectable" line of work. After a few months at the saloon, John wrote a letter to Angelina in Silverton, telling her that he felt a step closer to achieving his goal. He also mentioned that there would be an opportunity for him to buy into the business when the proper amount of money was available. Angelina wrote back immediately, inviting the brothers to come see her in Silverton. John took the next day off, leaving Tony to work the bar. It was decided that John would accept a loan from Angelina if one was offered.

John didn't know what to expect as he rode the little train back to Silverton. He was nervous! He felt himself too bold in asking for money from Angelina. She had brought up the subject once before, but he didn't know what the circumstance would be this time. Did Angelina expect something from him in exchange? Why did he allow himself to do these things that were daring and beyond his capabilities? He did not want to be indebted to anyone. Why was he doing this? He flinched at the thought that what he was doing was rude and brazen.

John walked to the Belleview and found Angelina alone as she cleaned the area behind the bar in preparation for the evening crowds.

"Neto, I am happy you have come," Angelina greeted him, but it was clear that she was feeling in poor spirits. She sighed heavily and motioned for him to sit at a table nearby. "Nothing goes right for me," Angelina said as she plopped into the chair, seemingly weighed down by her problems. With a heavy heart she related her worries. She was losing many of the business ventures her husband had worked to secure.

"Louis' business partners are trying to take everything," she told him. "I don't even know about most of the business dealings and I don't know who to trust." She complained that she was being taken advantage of because she was a woman.

After carrying on about her many troubles, she turned her attention to John, positioning herself for a new subject. She seemed interested in everything John was telling her, and his excitement grew as he confided his thoughts to her. He expressed that he now hoped to become part owner of the saloon in Durango where he was now employed.

Angelina listened, and in return John gave her his complete attention, trying to advise her in matters he knew nothing about. She insisted John stay to eat something before he left, so he followed her to the family quarters and into the kitchen.

Katie was there, and John's heart almost stopped when he saw her. It had been more than a year since he had last seen her, and it surprised him that she appeared even lovelier in person than he remembered. It embarrassed him to admit to himself that she remained the object of his fantasies. Would another woman ever be able to live up to the image this special paragon had become to him?

All of these thoughts were difficult enough as Katie greeted him and prepared food for him. The worst part was that Angelina ignored Katie and they seemed at odds. Katie placed a large bowl of chestnut soup, heavy with rice, and slices of French bread and cheese in front of him along with a small glass of wine. Neither Angelina nor Katie spoke, so John ate as quietly as possible. He felt conspicuous, finding it difficult to spoon up the soup and chew the bread without making noise in this atmosphere of tense silence. His attempts at small talk seemed to fall flat because Katie and Angelina refused to even look at each other. There was nothing he could do but eat quickly and break the silence by preparing to leave.

As he did this, Angelina told him to wait a few moments and she quickly left the room. While she was gone, Katie opened up to John and he relaxed a little. "Mama is constantly telling me to marry someone she has chosen," Katie whispered. "She parades every man in Silverton in front of me and refuses to understand my feelings for Peter. Mama just pushes me aside when I try to talk to her. The fights we have over this are terrible."

In response, John simply nodded his head in understanding.

Angelina returned with a box. She opened it and handed John a bundle of money. "Take this, Neto. You deserve a chance to operate your own saloon." Lifting her hand at his protests, she insisted he take the money, saying he could pay her back whenever it was possible. She then walked John to the door, wishing him luck and happiness. He was speechless!

He turned to walk to the train depot, pausing to wave and shout his thanks to Angelina. She returned his wave and turned to go back inside.

On the trip back to Durango, John could not believe what had happened. Nothing was as he had imagined it would be. It hardly seemed like a business transaction had taken place. He felt foolish that he hadn't been able to talk more directly to either Angelina or Katie. He wasn't sure what to think about the entire situation. Somehow he now had to make this venture work so he could pay Angelina back for the kindness and trust she had so generously bestowed upon him. As for Katie, he tried not to think about her at all.

Life took on new meaning for John and Tony now that they were part owners of the San Juan Saloon. However, John had specific ideas about the way the bar should be run and often argued with Sategna. This made things uncomfortable at times, but for the most part they were doing all right. After almost a year of work, they were making preparations to pay most of the money back to Angelina. This gave them both a huge boost of confidence and encouragement.

One day, during the early months of 1904, a customer came in from Silverton and many of the patrons gathered to hear the gossip and news he carried from that neighboring area. The discussion turned to the disputes between Tyroleans and Piemontesi Italians in Silverton. "The Sartore girl is engaged to marry a Tyrolean," the young man was saying, "and the Piemontesi Italians are creating havoc. The Italians in Silverton are divided, and the girl's mother is dead set against the marriage. *A l' periculùs për tüjt.* It is a dangerous situation for everyone involved."

CHAPTER IX

Peter Dalla

Angelina was furious over Katie's plan to marry, but she remained hopeful that it wouldn't happen. Katie was not defiant by nature, so it didn't seem likely that she would go against the wishes of her family. Angelina reasoned that if things became difficult, Katie would back down and break off the engagement. But Angelina was beginning to worry, convinced that her daughter was being swayed by the devil himself. She could not understand the hold the Tyrolean had on Katie, but Angelina swore her vengeance and intended to ward him off, pledging, *"E laso nin che susì a sücedo!"* "I will not let this happen!"

Katie's engagement was not Angelina's only problem: Her financial struggles continued, as well. *Le fumne aj pijan mai sël serio.* Debts owed to Louis were often not paid, and some of his business partners took complete control of shared assets. Louis' brother, Joseph, worked with her trying to help, but she became suspicious even of him. She accused him of trying to deceive her for his own advantage. Angelina became more hardened and difficult, trusting no one.

At this time in 1904, Phil was still young, not yet eighteen. He was belligerent and not much help. Despite all of this, Angelina was determined to keep what business interests remained intact for him to inherit. She would hang onto as much of the Sartore investments until Phil was old enough to take over. In an attempt to make a show of strength, Angelina reclaimed the Belleview Saloon, legally making it her own and renaming it the Belleville Saloon and Boarding House.

She was also aware that Phil had discovered women and frequented the cribs on Blair Street. She worked the bar and could not help but hear the rumors. She reasoned that this was not unusual for a young man, living with the temptations of this boomtown environment. She also recognized that her constant vocal reprimands were having no effect on the situation. In fact, she wondered if his actions were a reflection of his defiance of her wishes. She hoped this phase would pass and he would marry a decent young lady, reasoning that men don't marry prostitutes. *J'oman a 's marian nin cun le pütane.*

Angelina had been disgusted when, in 1902, it was announced that Mary Sartore would marry her father's business partner, Ludwig

Vota. "Mary was promised to my Phil!" Angelina protested, knowing that the circumstances were different now. It seemed that no one in America paid attention to the custom of marital arrangements determined at the birth of a child.

Joseph and his wife ignored Angelina's arguments. To them it was evident that Mary and Ludwig had chosen each other. Everyone, except for Angelina, was happy when the engagement was announced. To Angelina, it was another slap in the face. "It's as if I am of no importance and promises are broken like cheap glass!"

Angelina's head spun with all the problems. Katie was engaged to marry a Tyrolean, Phil was seeing prostitutes, and Jennie was struggling financially because Bonavida was having very little luck with his mining projects. Jennie complained to her mother constantly about her financial woes and the fact that Bonavida spent most of his time at the mine.

Bonavida continued to work and invest money, certain that the mine would eventually prove to be a lucrative endeavor. It had become necessary for him to acquire several business partners in order to buy a water pumping system to remove the water that perpetually seeped in. This pump weighed several tons and cost thousands of dollars, but without it going twenty-four hours a day, water would quickly flood the working level of the mine.

Angelina listened patiently to Jennie's problems, feeling a close relationship with her oldest daughter. She opened her heart to Jennie but felt she was losing control of Phil and Katie. She asked herself, in moments of despair, "How can I, alone, keep this family from ruin?"

When the problems seemed too burdensome, her one consolation was Jennie's baby daughter. Little Lina's face would break into an angelic grin at the sight of her grandmother and her tiny arms would reach out, begging to be lifted and loved. Angelina would hold onto her granddaughter warmly, saying over and over, "Lina is the light of Nonna's life."

In her husband's absence, Jennie continued her work as a seamstress but spent many afternoons at the saloon. There, she and her mother exchanged complaints of their miseries and together cursed the world for their suffering. Mutually, they targeted Katie's marriage to Peter Dalla as a threatening menace. They kept their facial expressions impassive as they discussed Katie and the dignity they would lose if she married the Tyrolean.

The one fact they could not ignore was that they needed Katie. She worked in the kitchen, kept the boarding house running, and the boarders fed. This was a main source of income and the only business showing profit. Now Katie had announced her engagement, a situation that would cause things to change. This fact alone made Angelina furious! She could not afford to let Katie leave.

"Mama, I plan to be away this afternoon, but I'll be home in time to finish supper and serve it to the boarders," Katie said as she walked into the bar, wiping her hands on her apron. Angelina and Jennie stilled their conversation and raised their heads to look at her.

"*Que?* You don't bother to ask if you can go out. You are insolent and a disappointment to this family and to your heritage!" Angelina spit this out in anger, rising from her stool behind the bar and throwing her fist in the

Katie Sartore circa 1904.

air. "Go on! What does it matter that you break your mother's heart! You have made your decision with that Austrian ring on your finger. Get out! *Vatne via!*" Angelina screamed this, her face red with anger, making the few customers at the bar squirm uncomfortably.

"Mama," Katie protested, "I am twenty-three years old. I have tried to accept the fact that you don't like Peter, but..."

"Remember this, you stupid girl," Angelina interrupted. "It is not right to marry against the wishes of your family. Your actions are insulting and vulgar. You persist in going ahead with this wedding, but your family will not stand with you. A family should be united at a wedding. There are responsibilities and traditions in the joining together of two families. You don't care about us, or those obligations, and make plans for yourself alone. This will never do, my ungrateful one. *E t'jè vultà la schejna a tüte i tò!* You have turned against us!"

Katie stood there for a moment, lowering her head at her mother's harsh words. She had nothing more to say after going over and over this subject many times. She had sacrificed and struggled to help keep the Belleville in business. Now she was twenty-three: How much longer did her mother intend for her to remain here? She wanted very much to please her mother, to make her understand, but it was impossible. Besides, she loved Peter and she would not consider marriage to anyone else! She and Peter had previously put marriage plans off, waiting for better times, but it was becoming apparent that things would never improve.

Katie realized that Angelina always found excuses, and this would be the case until she relented and agreed to marry someone of her mother's choosing. Her mother was arrogantly refusing to acknowledge anything respectful about her engagement to the man she loved.

Angelina's objections to the wedding were well known and she expressed them openly within the community. This added fuel to the already burning fire, causing the warfare between the Italians to blaze out of control. The two divided groups met in frequent acts of violence against each other on the streets. Anger was directed at this marriage. Against their will, the young couple was being drawn deeper into the perplexities of the situation. Storm clouds of prejudice were ever present, yet they were determined and directed by love.

Katie looked over at her sister, Jennie, whose eyes would not meet hers. Jennie was now almost eight months pregnant with her second child. Little Lina, now a toddler, was taking a nap in Angelina's bedroom. Jennie had always treated her younger sister with a mixture of affection and condescension, but Katie could not understand the harsh tone of hatred that was evident lately in Jennie's voice. Katie needed someone on her side, but Jennie remained steadfast with Angelina.

After a deliberate pause, Katie sighed and turned to leave. She could feel the burning wrath of her mother and sister as they watched her turn to walk into the kitchen. This display of loathing cut into her like a knife being thrown into her back.

"She is meeting with that Austrian bastard again," Angelina said to no one in particular after Katie had left. *"A cres 'd vureje ben."* "She thinks she loves him," she added with mocking tones. "Love and passion don't necessarily work in marriage, because those things do not allow for practical reasoning. Besides, he is only using her to get into the family and take over our holdings."

"I would gladly marry Katie and let you maintain this crummy saloon," one of the bar patrons replied with a laugh. "She is the most desirable Italian woman in Silverton—who is *not* married, of course," he added, looking at Jennie. She laughed good-naturedly, making humorous remarks about her budding, pregnant figure.

Angelina and Phil at the bar in the Belleville Saloon circa 1904.

"A l'é na fola," "She is a stupid girl," Angelina scowled. "Katie has brought dishonor on the family in her choice of a fiancé. A marriage should be planned by the entire family and have blessings from both families. This Austrian bastard has no family and wants to bleed this one dry."

"It's a free country," another bar patron offered. "She's old enough to do what she wants!"

"We'll see about that!" Angelina muttered under her breath. Just then, Phil came in and she turned her focus on him. She yelled out. *"Da 'ntè ch'e 't rive?"* "Where have you been?"

"E jù da far!" "I have things to do!" His remark to his mother was insolent and tainted with disrespect.

"E t'é sfacià e maleducà!" "You are impudent and insulting!" Angelina shouted, almost turning purple with rage. "What have I done to deserve children that hurt their own mother with hateful words and bad behavior? You are not yet eighteen years old and you spend all of your time with prostitutes!"

Phil ignored his mother's ranting and worked around the bar, preparing for the evening crowd. "It's like a circus coming to the Belleville these days," one miner sitting at the bar said, grinning at Phil. "We pay for drinks and get entertainment free from La Signora."

Most of the other bar patrons agreed and laughed jovially. Phil only shrugged, as if none of it were important.

Angelina knew about Phil and his rumored "affair" with the prostitute everyone referred to as "Black Minnie." She heard most of the stories from Jennie.

Minnie Meyhew Heberling was a short, buxom, heavily painted-up, outrageous, out-spoken and well-known lady of the evening. Her skin was not black: She was called Black Minnie because of her wild bouts of temper. She fought like a wildcat for certain customers and felt especially possessive of Phil. Minnie had a crib across the street from the Belleville, up the stairs above the Rock Saloon.

"Me ch'a ja pudü capitar tüt susì?" "How could this happen?" This had been Angelina's outburst upon hearing the gossip. All she could think of was that another problem had its source at the Rock Saloon.

Minnie sought out Jennie's expertise with a needle and thread, as did many other sporting women in Silverton. Minnie did this mostly out of curiosity, hoping to get to know Phil's family.

"Honey, can you sew something real pretty out of this blue satin?" Minnie asked Jennie at a fitting. "Phil thinks I look pretty in blue."

Jennie's face took on a blank expression, not knowing what to think upon hearing this. It was now obvious that Phil, at age seventeen, was sexually active with prostitutes.

"I'm happy to know his family," Minnie continued in brassy, confident tones, assuming a stance that accentuated the shape of her body. "Phil and I are very close."

The two friends with Minnie snickered at her use of words. "You mean you're close at times," one of them added with a lewd and wicked grin.

Meanwhile, Katie hurried to meet Peter Dalla. Feeling the cold, she pulled the heavy scarf tightly around her head. With all the worries she carried within her, she was scarcely aware that the clouds were grey and heavy and snow was lightly falling. It was March, and this was not unusual weather for Silverton, but no amount of bad weather could keep her from this important rendezvous. She moved quickly, her long skirts swishing through the newly fallen snow. She slowed at times to remove her glove and look lovingly at the engagement ring on her finger. Her face relaxed into a smile, and she quickened her step as she saw

Peter waiting at the Catholic church on Reese Street. He hurried to greet her, stepping forward to take her hand in his.

"I'm sorry I'm late, Peter," she began to apologize. Even though she was trying to put on a brave front, he could see she seemed both agitated and distressed. Knowing of her struggles at home,

St. Patrick's Catholic Church in Silverton, Colorado, at 1005 Reese Street. Photo taken in 2002.

he always did his best to remove the troubled frowns from her lovely face.

"*Stai bene, cara?*" "My darling, are you okay?" With this question, he hoped to sooth her. He lovingly put both hands on her shoulders and smiled directly into her face, his eyes glistening with something that could only be tenderness.

"*Le persone che si vogliono bene devono essere contente. Non mi vuoi bene?*" "Lovers are supposed to be happy. Don't you love me?" He teased her, trying to charm her into smiling. A twinkle lit his eyes as he took off his hat for a moment, allowing snowflakes to dot his dark hair.

"Peter," she sighed, "things are so difficult for me at home." She went into his arms, leaning against him for strength, while they stood in the quiet of the late afternoon snowfall. There was a taste of smoke in the air, and their coats wore the faint smell of wet wool. As she stood with him, she experienced again the thrill of attraction, and how effortlessly he'd always been able to make her forget her fears and uncertainties. She felt warm and safe against the cold March storm as he whispered words of love into her ear, treasuring each one as it rolled off his tongue. It made her laugh when he stopped to catch falling snowflakes in his mouth.

Peter once more took hold of her hands and looked lovingly into her face, his eyes warming, while his expression became intense. Viewing her in the veil of the falling snow, he asked for reassurance.

Katie looked at him, and, searching his face, she found a mixture of doubt and pride, humility and strength.

"Katie, do you want to take more time to think it over? I will wait forever, my love. If it were up to me alone, I would have us married today, at the courthouse or anywhere. However, I know it's important to you that we marry in the church. I want to do what makes you happy, but we know we can't wait until your mother gives in to the situation. We have waited almost three years for her to change her mind and give us her blessings. She will get used to it after we are married and have children. You know she won't be able to resist the little ones."

She slid into his arms once more and Peter held her. She hugged him in return, smiling with the thought of her future with Peter and their family.

"She will learn to accept another Tyrolean son-in-law, but you have to be certain it's what you want. I hate to see you so unhappy, my sweetheart."

"No, Peter, I love you and I don't want to wait! We will meet with the priest now as planned, and set the date for the wedding. I don't want to go through life without you. We'll do the best we can with my family situation as it is. What else can we do?"

Katie took a deep breath and struggled to relax in the sanctuary of Peter's closeness. She raised her head to look directly at him, and her voice quivered with excitement as she spoke. "How does May 15 sound to you? It's only two months away. This will allow the anniversary of my father's death to pass, and Jennie will have her baby in April. My mother will be busy and involved in these events."

He smiled, eagerly nodding his head in agreement, causing snow to fall from the brim of his hat, and they both laughed. Their spirits were lifted with the excitement that came with the decision, and soon their happy laughter filled the air. She threw her arms around his neck and he lovingly put his hands on her waist and lifted her gently into the air amongst the flurries of snowflakes. As her feet once again crunched into the few gathered inches of white snow, they kissed. Together, in this snowy scene, they shared the exhilaration of love and pledged devotion to each other.

"Soon you will be Mrs. Pietro Dallapiccola."

As the world turned white all around them, she dusted the wet snow from her face and eyelashes. She buried her head against Peter's shoulder and closed her eyes, allowing the fullness of love to overflow in her heart. They then walked together, entering the little church to make arrangements for the wedding ceremony that would unite them as man and wife.

CHAPTER X

Foul Play

Things seemed to spin out of control as Katie and Peter made plans for their wedding. The protests at home were worse than anything imaginable for Katie. Angelina was like a volcano, erupting, crying, screaming, and hurling curses and spiteful words toward her daughter at every given opportunity. The depth of her fury seemed to have no bounds.

Jennie continued to side with Angelina, wanting it plainly understood that she and her husband would not attend the wedding. Bonavida kept his thoughts to himself, careful not to take sides in this family argument.

Katie remembered when there had been a bond between her and her sister, a foundation built on shared secrets and memories. If Jennie would speak up in her defense, Angelina might be swayed to accept another Tyrolean into the family. But the fact that Jennie had turned against her broke Katie's heart. She shook with anger and disappointment that such a special time was marred with rage and hate. Katie felt that the source of this problem was the afternoon gossip sessions staged between her mother and sister.

Perhaps Jennie felt it unfair that Katie be allowed to choose her own marriage partner since she had not been given that opportunity. However, it simply appeared that Jennie didn't like the loving attention Katie received from Peter. Even though the impact of Katie's engagement brought a negative reaction from the Italian community, it was more notice than Jennie could tolerate. It appeared that Jennie harbored more than just a touch of jealousy. She even put a stop to any help the couple might be receiving from Bonavida. The family's objections toward Peter were unfounded, and the vengeance was uncurbed: there was no restraining the vicious attacks from both Angelina and Jennie on the subject of this wedding.

In this bleak atmosphere, Katie sat alone, sewing her own wedding dress. She was denied the usual traditions of family preparations. Fighting back feelings of resentment, she recalled the excitement of Jennie's engagement and beautiful wedding. This brought forth a deep sigh, released with shuddering breaths. It was painful to her that her wedding would be marked with unhappiness and sorrow and her family would not be present.

The wedding would also be humble, because she and Peter could not afford to be extravagant. She cried openly, remembering her father's generosity and his concerns that everything be perfect for Jennie's wedding. It was reasonable to think that he would have been more than willing to do the same for her wedding. In her heart, she even felt that her father would have been accepting of Peter. She needed her father now, needed the strength his presence had given the family. It didn't seem fair that he had left her to handle this problem alone.

Wiping her face with her hands, she tried to shake off this mournful mood. *"Ah, se papà a füs sì! a saris tüt divèrs!"* "It would all be different if papa were here."

These conflicting emotions and sentiments must not be allowed to tear her apart and ruin this special time in her life. Her mother and sister were acting in a deplorable manner, but the wedding would happen—would go on as planned. With each stitch of the needle, she grew more resolute in this purpose. She would make the best of things and dare to choose her fate rather than have it chosen for her.

Not even the insults and objections of all the Italians in Silverton would be able to stop her from marrying Peter, although it seemed crazy that her wedding would divide the town. In a moment of remarkable clarity, she realized with disgust that the feud between the Piemontesi and Tyroleans was being fueled by the hatred of her own family!

Katie's cousin, Mary Vota, remained close and steadfast through all this turmoil. Mary agreed to stand with Katie at her wedding even though Angelina threatened to disown everyone involved. Because of this, Mary, was no longer welcome to come to the Belleville.

On April 15, 1904, a wonderful diversion entered the family in the form of another Bonavida baby girl. Beautiful little Anna was a welcome distraction for the family, and even Angelina seemed to forget the complications of her life with Jennie's two little angels around. Angelina, as a grandmother, was a different person. It pleased everyone to see how she doted on little Lina and baby Anna. Her demeanor seemed transformed into a subdued and gentle nature when the little ones, *"le cite,"* were in her company. Seeing this softer side of her mother gave Katie hope that somehow Angelina would come around and finally accept Peter.

The harsh winter of 1904 was finally showing signs of melting into spring as May arrived and the snow receded. A hint of green edged the slender white-barked aspen trees and warmer days arrived in the high country. The air was still brisk, but the breezes held a refreshing hint of warmth. With the thawing of ice and snow things began returning to life, and activities picked up around the little town of Silverton.

At night, however, on Blair Street, the bars rumbled with ugly talk. Conversations centered on the wedding scheduled in two weeks. The loathsome concept of a Piemontese woman marrying a Tyrolean man caused tempers to flare at a time when the feud between the two groups of Italians was reaching a fevered pitch.

Angelina drew hope from these outbursts, which were often violent. It appeared to her that if there were incidents to discourage the Austrian bastard, he would call everything off. Katie would be heartbroken at first, but she would recover and find someone else.

Angelina knew she didn't have much time, so determination drove her with fanatical commitment. She sought solace in her sessions with Jennie, and at these times she would vent her venomous feelings. As comrades on a shared mission, they allowed this hatred to override all other feelings and, working together, they let anger and hostility consume common sense.

Because Jennie agreed with her, Angelina did not hold back the obsessive conduct that welled up inside her. She decided she must do something to stop this union as her thoughts dictated. The wedding would not be allowed to take place!

Through all this confusion another matter surfaced for Angelina. The entire community was aware that her son, Phil, appeared to be courting a prostitute. This news drove Angelina to distraction.

Phil did not attempt to hide his liaisons. Minnie coaxed him to spend more and more time with her, and they were often seen together, even in the brightness of daylight. Phil would take Minnie for buggy rides, picnics, shopping, or anywhere she wanted to go. In the harsh light of the sunny outdoors, Minnie's rouged cheeks appeared to glow even brighter against the paleness of her powdered face. She happily flaunted her new position in society and frequently referred to herself as Phil Sartore's fiancée.

Minnie made it known that Jennie Bonavida was her seamstress. She hired her to design special creations, and these were original in every way. Even though the style of the day called for long, modest dresses, Minnie had Jennie make all her skirts knee length. The colors of these outfits were usually gaudy and bright, but it was of great importance to Minnie that they be made of expensive materials, in clouds of silk, satin, velvet, and lace. Minnie had not been born with a silver spoon in her mouth, but she wanted, more than anything, to triumph over the obstacles that caused her to dwell on the lowest rung of life's ladder.

Minnie had a fetish for shoes and owned an assortment of fancy, colorful, very high heels. She was short in stature, not quite reaching five feet, so the shoes greatly enhanced her height. She enjoyed walking arm and arm with Phil who was tall, a bit over six feet, young, handsome, and well established in the community.

Gaily attired in these outlandish outfits with large matching hats, Minnie looked outrageous. But her persona was outgoing, warm, and friendly, and this made her good company for the quiet, sullen Phil. He jumped to carry out her every wish.

Things hadn't been easy for Minnie. As a young child she was tossed around between two parents who often went in different directions. When her mother remarried, she and her sister were abused, neglected, and left on their own. While they were still children, they had to support themselves in order to eat. Minnie scrubbed clothes in a laundry, toiling for a pittance of a salary. That tedious episode in her life ended when someone pointed her in the direction of prostitution.

Minnie Meyhew Heberling in Silverton, circa 1910.

Minnie professed to be the same age as Phil, who at that time was seventeen. They had known each other since she first came to Silverton, at about age fifteen. Minnie often boasted that she was Phil's first and only lover and she intended to keep it that way. She affixed a secure hold on him, never letting him too far from her clutches. She cared for Phil, but she also recognized that he was her ticket to respectability.

Angelina knew that even if she were successful in thwarting Katie's plans to marry the Tyrolean, she still had an enormous problem to solve with Phil and his "fallen angel." Jennie refused to help her in this case, because she liked Minnie and expressed this openly to her mother.

Angelina's thoughts reeled and her shoulders slumped forward in response to the weight of these problems. Life around her had been in a downward spiral since the death of her husband. Something must be done to rectify these appalling circumstances, or everything would soon hit rock bottom! With a new feeling of determination, she made up her mind to prove that she could handle things once and for all.

Phil loved baseball and enjoyed watching the Silverton team, especially when they played their rivals from Durango. He had a system that made it possible for him to watch parts of these important games even while he was tending bar. He would saddle up one of his horses and leave it out front of the Belleville. Setting up everyone at the bar with drinks at the same time, he would run out, hop on the horse, ride down, and catch an inning or two. By the time he returned to the saloon, everyone would be ready for another drink.

He had already made a couple of trips to the ball field at the edge of town this overcast spring day. He was returning to the saloon to set up another round of drinks when he heard loud noises and some sort of ruckus coming from the Rock Saloon.

Phil heard a woman screaming and recognized the voice as Minnie's. The calls of distress came from the upstairs rooms of the Rock Saloon where Minnie had her crib. A sort of commotion was going on, and Phil stopped in his tracks, listening. Suddenly he felt alarmed and ran in the direction of the confusion to see what was happening. Why would Minnie be screaming?

Phil retained a sort of neutrality during the feud among the Italians. The Tyrolean patrons of the Rock Saloon paid Phil no heed, knowing that he and Minnie had a "type" of relationship. However, now Minnie was shouting and throwing things in some sort of struggle.

Apparently a group of young Piemontesi had converged on Minnie, threatening her and demanding she stop seeing Phil. Minnie was no milquetoast and fought back when they tried to rough her up.

By the time Phil worked his way around the two taller buildings that penned in the Rock Saloon, he was caught up in the brawl. Tyroleans from inside the bar had heard the uproar and they stormed outside from the rear door, ready for a fight. Some of them almost collided with Phil as he ran down the back alley and headed for the stairway inside the back door of the Rock Saloon.

ROCK SALOON

Phil started up the back stairs to Minnie's room, but in a matter of minutes a battle ensued and he was caught up in the free-for-all. He was jerked off his feet and shoved against a wall. Fighting to rid himself of an aggressor, he almost went down as then a fist slammed into his face. Soon there were men rolling down the stairs, wrestling with each other. Phil stumbled to make his way to the second floor, tripping over bodies as men fell and regained their feet. Reaching Minnie's room, he heard glass from the window shatter as someone dived out the window. Finding her alone, he pushed his way into her small room, shoved Minnie back inside and shut the door. She was still screaming hysterically.

Most of the fighting was now outside the building, and suddenly a shot was fired, bringing all the chaos to a stop. Phil looked out of the broken window to see Peter Dalla with a gun in his hand, motioning for the fight to disperse. Piemontesi Italians ran in the direction of the Belleville, to the safety of the other side of the street. However, one man stopped to punch Peter in the face, making ugly threats before taking leave of the area. Peter was knocked down with the force of the blow and struggled to remain conscious. His jaw throbbed with pain.

Looking stunned as he staggered to his feet, Peter dusted himself off and tried to make sense of the situation. He was getting used to the physical abuse and threats, but he didn't understand why this fight had happened. Spying Phil at Minnie's second-story window, he motioned for him to come down, and Phil obliged.

"Young Sartore," Peter said as he stepped closer to talk to Phil. "We don't want trouble with you. Soon you will be my brother-in-law." Peter smiled and, placing one hand on the younger man's shoulder, he turned to talk seriously with Phil. "You need to take Minnie away from this area. Take her to a nice room somewhere where she doesn't have to work like this anymore. Those men meant to hurt her, although I don't know why."

Phil slouched and awkwardly shifted his eyes to the ground. He had spent the last few years doing things in contempt of his mother's efforts to dictate and control his life. He had enjoyed a strong sense of gratification watching the anger burn on her face as he defied her attempts to force him to stop seeing Minnie. But Phil understood the dangerous situation this now presented to Minnie, and he felt the need to listen to Peter's words.

"Minnie's a nice girl who has never been given a chance," Peter continued, "and we know you two care about each other. Get her out of here so the two of you can be together." Phil nodded his head in understanding, and when Peter offered his hand, Phil shook it in agreement. Peter patted Phil amiably on the back and turned to enter the bar area of the Rock Saloon. Phil went back up the stairs to Minnie's room, where he went inside and closed the door.

Minnie was still crying and, when she saw Phil, she ran to him, clinging in desperation. She was fearful of what would happen now. Would she and Phil be forced apart? What would she do if she lost hold on the one strong hope in her life? If she lost Phil, she would sink into a quagmire of filth and be forever lost in degradation as a prostitute.

She felt panic rising within her body as Phil pulled away from her and sat down on the bed. He had to move things aside, because the room was in shambles. Minnie watched him, but his face was unreadable.

She was clever enough to know that this was not the time to crowd Phil into a corner. He was only seventeen and not ready for a permanent commitment. She would be careful not to make a fool of herself and beg him to help her—that might scare him into running off for good. She would struggle to gain her composure and act in a cool and dignified manner, forcing herself to concentrate on fact, not fantasy. Phil was not ready to marry a prostitute, even to spite his mother.

She gathered some of her personal things that were now strewn around the room and sat down on the bed next to Phil. She placed her hand mirror, hairbrush, and some cosmetics in her lap.

"I'm a mess after all that trouble," Minnie began, brushing her hair while she looked into the mirror. "I hate for you to see me looking like this."

He watched her steadily, his expression closed, as she fixed her hair and added powder and paint to her face. Her fuchsia and black dress was torn, and one sleeve hung in shreds at her arm. He studied her, recognizing this as a turning point in his life. He could easily walk away from this situation, but he had nothing better waiting for him in the other direction. He was oddly content in his relationship with Minnie, but he wasn't sure what to do. He had seen her eyes filled with fright when she had been accosted, and it scared him to think what might have happened.

"Phil," Minnie said, interrupting his thoughts, "don't you wish we could be like ordinary people? Know what I mean? You could come and call on me like I was a proper lady. I'll be lucky if I live to be twenty at this rate, doing this job. I wish you could stay here and we could tell all the customers to go away. I feel safe with you here."

He lifted his head and looked up through the broken window where the sky still held a flush of daylight. His mother would be angry that he had left the bar, and it would soon be time for him to work the night shift.

"Of course, your mother would probably not approve of me, even if I were a real lady," Minnie continued. She glanced in his direction and said, "Do you think she sent those men over here?"

There was something about that last question that strained Phil to the limit. He stood up and pulled her to her feet. "Pack up your things," he said. "We're moving you out of here!"

Inside the Rock Saloon, Peter was listening to the rumblings of more trouble as complaints against the Piemontesi continued to grow. How would these, his countrymen, react to his wedding? Perhaps the problems would mend if somehow his marriage could unite the two groups. He wondered what kind of future he and Katie would have with such hatred around them. It gave him hope to consider the fact that Bonavida was Tyrolean and he had married Katie's sister. How was this marriage different?

Late that night at the Belleville Saloon, Angelina was made aware that another job had been botched. "Phil has moved Minnie away from the Rock Saloon, down the street to a private room in the house of Pasquardo," a bar patron was telling her. "There is talk that Minnie won't work anymore and Phil will support her."

Angelina angrily shook her head and her fist pounded the bar as she listened. She planned to confront Phil, but he quietly worked his side of the bar, staying away from her, avoiding her looks of scorn. Phil knew she wouldn't make a huge scene in front of the customers.

Angelina couldn't have imagined that things would get worse, but now they had. She felt a need to put a stop to this invasion of Austrians and the problems they generated. She needed to talk with Jennie.

It was May 14, the day before the wedding, and Katie had decided to be happy at all costs. Her ivory wedding dress hung on her wardrobe door in readiness for the big day. She was marrying the man she loved, and she felt that this marriage would make everything right.

She was paying the price for defying her family, and none of them spoke to her at all these days. Phil was neutral, as always, but of no support to her at a time when she felt very alone. Her mother complained only of the need to find someone to replace her in the kitchen.

"I can continue to work here after the wedding, Mama," Katie offered.

A hard glare was all the reply that came from Angelina.

Katie was locked out of the security of the tight family unit, and she cried herself to sleep on a night when all should have been joyous in anticipation of such a special celebration.

Late that night, at 11:30 p.m., Barney Fiori quietly entered the rear door of the Rock Saloon. He shouted threats, then waved and pointed his long-barrel Colt .44 revolver as he shouted an order for them to put their hands up. Firing two shots at Peter Dalla, he then fled from the scene. Dalla fell as one bullet passed through his left leg, shattering the bone. A doctor was immediately summoned and Peter was taken upstairs to his room.

Katie was sleeping lightly but she heard the uproar coming from across the street. She was used to hearing noise from Blair Street, so even the sounds from gunshots didn't seem unusual. She lay there with her eyes open, listening. Suddenly she jumped out of bed, running to the window. Something was going on at the Rock Saloon, and she felt a pang of fear. *"E s'aj füs capità quejcòs a Peter?"* "What if something has happened to Peter?"

She pulled on a robe over her nightgown and ran to the side door that opened out to the back area of the Belleville. From here she could see out in the direction of the Rock Saloon. There were people gathered in the street and she could hear shouts of anger.

What could she do? She couldn't just walk over to see what was happening. She stood still, straining to see and hear anything that would tell her what was going on. She spied Phil, moving away from the crowd, walking back toward the Belleville. She called out to him. *"Flip, que ch'a jé? Que ch'a jé capità?"* "Phil, what is it? What is happening?"

Phil came over to her and told her that Peter had been shot, but that the news from the doctor was good. As Phil looked into her shocked, dazed face, he muttered gently that Peter was going to be all right. He took her hand and patted it, saying nothing more. He then mumbled that he had to get back inside to the bar and walked away.

Katie stood there in the doorway. The late night air was making her shiver but she couldn't go back inside. She wanted to go to Peter. She stood there, watching the crowd across the street slowly disperse.

Angelina opened the door leading from the bar and saw Katie standing there. Neither spoke, but their eyes met briefly before each one looked away. Angelina walked past her daughter and, going directly into to her own bedroom, she closed the door behind her.

By the time Katie gathered her thoughts and returned to her bedroom, the clock read 2:30 a.m. She sat there, not knowing what to do. She would have to wait until morning to check on Peter. Her eyes, now accustomed to the semi-darkness of her room, moved to the ivory wedding dress hanging on the door of her wardrobe. Somehow she knew she would not wear the dress as planned. Her feelings shifted from those of fear to those of sorrow. Not allowing herself to spill the tears that pooled in her eyes, she dropped to her knees and prayed fervently that Peter would survive this horrible incident.

Katie was still awake at the first light of dawn and watched as the sky began to fade from deep blue to lavender. She dressed and tried to remain calm, despite the unrelenting panic rising in her body. She took deep breaths and continued looking outside, across the street to the Rock Saloon. She knew she would have to wait until late morning before someone would arrive and open it up for business. Her mind struggled to sort out what could have happened to cause this catastrophe. Inhaling deeply as she heard her mother moving around in the kitchen, she fiercely fought the desire to cry. She wished silently that she had someone to help guide her through this terrible crisis.

Around ten o'clock in the morning, Katie saw activity across the street and she could wait no longer. Not allowing anything to detain her, she drove herself forward, thinking of nothing but reaching the Rock Saloon. Before she realized it, she went out the door and walked quickly, so wrapped up in her thoughts that she didn't realize where her feet were taking her. All she knew was that she had to find out about Peter! She ignored her mother's protests as Angelina shouted after her. She kept moving across the street toward the Rock Saloon.

When she pushed open the door and entered the unfamiliar saloon, there were no surprised looks from the few men gathered there, only somber faces with sympathy. *"Dov'è Peter?"* She spoke in Italian, her Piemontese accent clear for all to hear, but there were no harsh feelings demonstrated.

Because they all knew that this was to be the morning of her wedding, arms wrapped around her as if to console and protect her. They ushered her inside, seating her in a chair. She listened as they related the story of what had occurred the night before. Peter was resting, but they assured her that from all reports the chances were favorable for his complete recovery. The doctor didn't think the wound would leave him permanently crippled. They told her that Barney Fiori had been arrested.

Katie was shocked when she heard this. Her brown eyes blazed with dark fire and her head swirled with the accusation of what this meant. *Barney Fiori a jà sparà a Peter!* Barney Fiori had shot Peter!

She listened to the entire story several times and could hardly make sense of the conflicting thoughts jumbled in her mind. In flashes, she recalled her mother pushing her toward Barney Fiori and saw images of Angelina spouting words of hatred about Peter. Finally, tears began to fill her eyes. She wanted only to see that Peter was alive. She accepted the fact that she could not disturb him at this moment, but her mind worked ahead to the problem of how she would be able to see him and help him recover. She would need to take care of him. She needed to move him to the other side of the street, because her mother and others would not approve of her going to the Rock Saloon repeatedly.

Katie graciously shook hands with the Tyroleans, thanking them for their help and concern. Giving them a confident smile, she inwardly vowed to be strong, fighting through all the chaos and confusion the shock that morning had brought. She wasn't certain that she could endure her mother's behavior for another moment, but she would faithfully return to her side of the world and try to think of a way to bring sanity to this nightmare.

As she walked across the street she thought to herself, "My life feels as if it belongs to somebody else. How could this be happening?"

She approached the Belleville from the side entrance and, as she stopped before the opened door, she spied the small building next to the saloon. It was standing unused in the back of the yard near the alley. This storage shed had been fixed up and rented out at times, but it was empty at the moment. She reasoned that she could bring Peter here, to the little building in the backyard. Here she could take care of him and help him recover.

She set her jaw stubbornly and decided against confronting her mother to ask if she could use the building for Peter. She knew her mother would emphatically say, "No!"

It suddenly disturbed Katie that her mother constantly reminded everyone that someday the Belleville would belong to Phil. Why? It was simply because he was her son. The daughters would not be allowed any part of the saloon as inheritance.

Jennie had explained to her that it was Angelina's fear that Peter would claim part of the saloon after the marriage. The laws dictated that properties of the wife belong to the husband. Katie knew she had no claim to the Belleville, so she did not understand the problem. That worry was nonsense, anyway, because she and Peter had no interest in the Belleville. Peter was satisfied with part ownership of the Rock Saloon and proud that he had worked to accomplish that on his own.

She momentarily let a thought enter her mind that Angelina might have offered something to Barney Fiori. She brushed it away. It disturbed her, but she found it almost impossible to believe that her mother would take part in anything that despicable!

Barney Fiori had often made threats against Peter, convinced that Katie would be engaged to him if it weren't for Peter. Katie knew this wasn't true: She had no interest in any relationship with Barney Fiori and had given him no encouragement. But now she was worried about her mother's association with Fiori. Even if Angelina had only expressed her feelings to him, words can be harmful and spark violence. Katie knew how strongly her mother spoke out against Peter.

"No!" She didn't need permission to use that small building. It belonged to the Sartore family, thus it belonged to her as well. She now burned with such determination and anger that her hands balled into fists. She would use that building, knowing full well that Angelina would not approve.

She gathered up a ring of keys from the kitchen and went back outside. Pushing open the door of the little shack, she looked inside.

It would need cleaning, but it would do nicely for the purpose at hand. She would prepare this small room and have Peter moved over here. Starting on this cleaning project immediately, she worked as if she were on fire. She swept the floor vigorously, stirring up a cloud of dust, fuming and venting her anger with each stroke of the broom.

It took almost a month before it was deemed safe to move Peter, because the wound was more serious than originally thought.

"We still have to get married!" he joked as his friends carried him across to the Belleville on a stretcher. "I missed the big day."

Katie's heart warmed at his jovial attitude and she took hold of his hand, loving him all the more. It was a relief for her to know that he would soon be nearby where she could be with him. His cheerfulness, despite the pain and discomfort he was suffering, was a blessing to her. Weak with worry since the night of the shooting, she had spent the lonely days that followed in an unsteady state of mind. Now, when he gave her a bright smile, it made her flutter inside with happiness.

"Peter, I think we should call the priest and he can marry us now. I don't want to wait, and my mother will just have to accept things," Katie pleaded, touching his forehead to smooth back the dark hair.

"*Cara,*" Peter responded in a heavy voice as he struggled with the pain the move had caused, "you need a proper wedding, in a church with your beautiful white dress. You need a husband who can walk. What if I never walk again? I may be a cripple, only able to limp along."

"Nothing else matters, Peter. *Non mi importa niente altro!* You are my love, whatever the future brings."

The summer brought with it many happy days, as Katie and Peter were together more than had ever been allowed. She fed him and took care of his every need, helping him to walk, slowly at first, around the tiny area of the room. Peter responded to the loving care and soon looked as healthy and handsome as ever. As late summer warmed the streets of Silverton, he walked slowly across the street to resume work at the Rock Saloon.

Katie ignored her mother's snide comments and stayed away from her as much as possible. She knew that it was her own mother and sister spreading scandalous gossip that she was "living in sin" with Peter. There were just a few people actually involved in the Italian feud, but everyone in Silverton seemed involved in spreading the gossip.

Katie now resolved to be firm against all odds. She openly defied her mother but faithfully continued her job of cooking for the boarders at the Belleville. Lost in the love for each other, she and Peter struggled to ignore the problems and the persisting threats.

Early in September they once again set the date for their wedding, choosing September 24. "It will be the week after my birthday," Katie said cheerfully. "I will then be an old lady of twenty-four."

On September 15, one week before the wedding, and two days before Katie's birthday, residents were awakened at 3:30 a.m. by a terrific explosion. During the darkest hours of the night, several sticks of Giant Powder had been suspended on the outer wall of the small building near the Belleville where Peter slept. Peter Dalla met his death when he was blown up in an explosion of dynamite.

CHAPTER XI

Death at Dawn

Katie sat straight up in bed, uncertain of what had awakened her in the early hours before dawn. She felt a sense of alarm, wondering if someone was moving around the buildings. Just then the ground shook with a thunderous explosion near the saloon. She grabbed her clothes and pulled them on as she ran from her room, dread in her heart at what she might find. All of Silverton heard the sound of exploding dynamite and many hurried to the site.

When Katie reached the scene she gasped. Covering her mouth to stifle her cries, she viewed the devastation of the small building Peter had occupied since the shooting in May. *"O Nusgnùr, que ch'a jé capità?"* "Oh, no! What has happened?"

She stared at the view in front of her, eyes blazing with disbelief. She struggled to see in the darkness, calling out for Peter over and over. Her voice was tense and high pitched, and her state of mind frantic. She moved amongst the still-settling wreckage, looking for signs that Peter was all right. The north side of the building was almost completely blown out, and suddenly she could see Peter's life-less body, thrown across the oppo-site side of the small room. She gave a small cry of hope as she ran toward him, but arms reached out to pull her back. As her friends pulled her away, she stooped to retrieve some-thing from the pile of  rubble thrown aside by the blast. Her hands were trembling as she lifted a photo she had given Peter, a picture of herself. She had often found him holding it to his chest during the days he spent recovering from the gunshot wound.

Katie felt frozen to the spot, and her eyes could not look away. The tragedy before her was brutally oppressive. What she saw was the death of all her dreams. Last night he had kissed her, and her hands automatically went to her lips to retain any of the feeling that might remain there. Uncontrollable sobs shook her as she buried her face in her hands and blurted out, "Oh, God! How could this happen?"

More people gathered and there were quiet murmurings as they whispered among themselves. They shook their heads in understanding of Katie's distress. Everyone knew that this love story had ended in the worst possible way. There would be no wedding for Katie Sartore and Peter Dalla.

It was not remarkable that the dynamite had blown up the small building and not touched the larger structure of the Belleville, even though it was just a few feet away. However, another small adjoining building was destroyed. The dynamite was obviously set by someone with a miner's skill of moving rocks against huge mountains. Many miners were capable of this feat.

Peter's body was not mangled and the only wound was a skull fracture. He had bled slightly from the mouth and ears but showed almost no evidence of the horrible fate that had befallen him.

Finally, Katie was gently persuaded to leave the scene as friends guided her inside to her room at the Belleville. Angelina was there, looking out the window at the crumbling remains of the little building and, as they passed by, she cried out, *"Mia povra cita!"* "My poor baby!" Angelina then reached out to hold her daughter, but Katie shook her off in a moment of conflicting emotions.

Katie felt something stir inside, as a tangle of terror, rage, and hatred came alive. She wanted to let loose her fury and strike out against her mother. The realization of what had happened, and why, caused all the hidden currents of bitterness to rise to the surface. Words to her mother could not be expressed, and her hand went to her mouth as if to smother them. At that moment a sound rose from her chest like a distant wail as pain ripped out of her. Her friends guided her to her bedroom, away from Angelina, who stood looking wide-eyed and shocked at the entire spectacle.

The whole day was lost to madness as Katie blacked out, awaking at times to a haze of voices in her room. Friends stayed at her side, afraid for her to be alone, as the magnitude of this terrible act was realized. For Katie, time passed in delirium. She opened her eyes intermittently hoping to break free from the nightmare. Her sleep was filled with images of people with harsh, menacing voices, and always amongst them was the contorted, enraged expression of her mother.

In one dream she saw a puppeteer wearing a mask. At the end of the strings was a puppet trying to run away, but the puppeteer only laughed and kept the helpless doll dancing in place. Dark shadows flickered against the background as the masked demon seemed to glare closer and closer, laughing grotesquely. When the mask was discarded Katie saw the distorted, angry face of her mother. She sat up in bed screaming, terrified and unable to think clearly. She was soothed back into her feverish daze by comforting words from those in her room.

The sunlight at the windows changed, first glaring, slowly working its way through a series of colors, and then disappearing entirely.

As the evening shadows of this dreadful day spread across her room, Katie listened to the whispers as those around her discussed the feud between the two factions of Italians. These faint sounds interposed themselves between sound sleep and full consciousness as the small group mentioned possible motives for Peter's murder.

"It isn't every Italian who is involved in this feud," she heard them saying quietly. "It's just those two rowdy groups with troublemakers on both sides."

"Perhaps it was Barney Fiori again," she heard someone speculate. "He seemed determined to do away with Dalla. Everyone knows of his threats. We all remember the shooting in May, and he was just recently released from jail. He was in love with Katie and she shunned him."

"What about Angelina?" someone whispered. "She was against the wedding and swore it would never take place."

"Shhhhh!" came the reply. "We don't want Katie to hear us talk of this." For a few moments the room was silent, but the shock of the event could not stop the need to talk.

"I have heard it said," one older lady offered, "that it isn't unusual for murders to happen in saloons. If a man is somehow different, he isn't accepted. Most saloons are patronized according to nationalities, and others are not welcome!"

They chatted quietly in a round-the-clock vigil, worried as to what would happen if they left Katie alone.

Days of pain passed and Katie refused to acknowledge any part of activity around her. Her life had been thrown off balance, and she was left with a heartache as bleak and stark as the deepest part of winter. At night she often quaked and screamed with terror, and in the light of day her face became a grey, expressionless mask. She remained shrouded in her misery as friends, her cousin, Mary, and her sister, Jennie, tried to force her to eat and keep up her strength.

"Now, now, little sister, you need to eat and live," Jennie prodded. "It is important to keep going through difficult times. You are stronger than this! You must keep on living!" Jennie struggled with strict tones to revive the despondent, lifeless figure lying on the bed.

Katie suddenly sat up at the sound of music in the distance. She recognized it as the Eagles Cornet Band leading the procession to the cemetery. "What is that? *E devo 'ndar da Peter?* Are they burying my Peter? I must go to him. He needs me there." The sobs and tears flowed from her as she ran about in disarray and confusion. Jennie tried to calm her, but Katie was crazed and thrashed about as she attempted to dress and tidy herself, even in her bewildered state of mind.

Jennie hurried out and returned a few moments later with her husband. Bonavida motioned for Jennie and the others to leave, and settling Katie with his quiet manner, he reached for her hand and told her to sit down. Katie wore a look of wild-eyed terror: She hadn't eaten or slept; she was disheveled and pale. Katie looked to him for answers. Her face clouded with a troubled frown and her brow was furrowed, but no sound escaped her lips.

"I know, sweet Katie, that you loved Peter very much, and he loved you, too." Bonavida spoke softly. "Peter was a fellow country-man, a Tyrolean, like myself, and we must talk about the truth. All these twists of stories and lies need to be straightened out."

"We have to find the ones who killed Peter!" Katie blurted out, and her hand went to her mouth to suppress her sobs. "I have to go to the funeral."

Bonavida spoke softly. "Katie, you cannot go to the funeral. There is still much hatred and, at this moment, it is best you do not go. It will just stir up feelings on both sides for you to be seen there."

"But that is impossible!" Katie sputtered, "I have to go, for my Peter. He needs me! *Peter a jà damanca 'd mi!* All we have is each other!" Her face twisted with pain, as she broke down in tears once more. It was hard for her to admit to herself, let alone to Bonavida, that she was alone and doubted her family's affection. They had closed her out and now she truly wondered if they cared for her at all.

"Katie, what I have to tell you must never leave this room. For the sake of your family, you must never repeat what I will now tell you."

Bonavida cleared his throat nervously, looking at the pitiful expression on Katie's face.

"Katie, your mother and your sister are involved, but I don't think either of them intended for it to become murder. They love you, very much, and thought that what they were doing was justified. You must forgive them. We all must. It's time to move on and not to focus on revenge and retribution. Peter is gone, but he would want you to carry on with your life and not to become bitter with hatred. Peter would want you to continue to be the beautiful person he loved."

Katie's look was blank and expressionless as endless tears streamed down her face, but she didn't brush them away. Bonavida wondered if she would ever blink or take a breath. The weight of his words bore down on her, and she felt the isolation and emptiness all the way to the bone. The puzzle had been completed with words she didn't want to hear and facts she didn't want to know.

She finally responded, "I don't want to continue to live, Louis." He took hold of her hand and they sat together as if frozen in time, allowing the silence to persist and the words to settle into place.

Bonavida rose and, patting her hand, he made a motion that he would leave. "I will go now to the funeral and give your words of love to Peter. Please stay here, Katie, and think about what I've told you. Your family loves you and didn't intend for this to happen. I will give Peter your message of love."

After he left, Katie remained sitting, staring into space. It was as if an hourglass had run out of sand and time was now an endless void. Sadness wrapped around her like a heavy cloak, weighing her down. Everything seemed to hurt; and from the hollowness in her chest to the heaviness in her heart, there was one vast empty ache. It was an emptiness as real as if something had been physically wrenched from her body. She was nothing but a shell. How could life continue? Murmuring quietly to herself, she said, "When I do leave this world, Peter, it will be loving you. You will always live in my heart." She wept quietly as grief crushed down on her like a dark enveloping cloud, shutting everything out.

Angelina and Phil kept the bar running as talk and tempers flared with the events of the last several days. There were threats on both sides, and the bar patrons talked of nothing else.

"You are guilty as sin, *cara signora*," one of her countrymen was saying for all to hear as he sat at the bar. "Nonsense!" Angelina shouted back at him. *"Ch'a 'm piasèjs no, ma e 'l'ù nin masà mi."* "I didn't like him, but I didn't kill him."

"You didn't fuse the sticks of dynamite," the man continued, "but you killed him just the same! *A l'é culpa tua!* You are guilty!"

The taunting accusations made Angelina feel uneasy, so under this pressure, she left the barroom with the excuse of checking on Katie. Angelina knew she needed to clear the air with her daughter, but she wasn't certain what she would say that would allow them to make a fresh start.

She would start by saying, "A mother's love is absolute," and then continue with, "It's a parent's right to protect her children." Katie would understand this. Angelina prepared no words of repentance. She wanted to tell her daughter, "Someday, when you have married someone else, you will understand why I was against your marriage to the Tyrolean."

Angelina entered the darkened room, waiting for her eyes to adjust so she could locate the bed where Katie lay motionless. The silent, ominous shadows seemed ready to devour both of them.

Angelina sat in a chair next to the bed and reached out to touch her daughter's hair, smoothing it and stroking her head. She scanned the room, her eyes resting on the ivory wedding dress hanging on the door of the wardrobe. It was a ghostly reminder of her daughter's shattered dreams.

Katie was half-awake but didn't respond or acknowledge her mother's presence. Even now, after all she knew, part of her wanted to reach out and be comforted by her mother. At the same time, she fought against the disgust and hatred that rose like bile in her throat when she thought of how her own mother had denied her the happiness of marriage to the man she loved. How could things ever be right again? What had life become for all of them?

The following was printed in the *Silverton Standard* newspaper on September 17, 1904, the date of Katie Sartore's 24th birthday.

Residents of this city and particularly those residing on East 13th near Blair and Mineral Streets were awakened at 3:30 Thursday morning by a terrific explosion, and as they hastily arose from their couches, grave fears were entertained of some dreadful disaster.

In a very few moments the streets were thoroughly crowded with anxious persons seeking the scene of the wreckage and possible bloodshed. All were headed for a point between Blair and Mineral and here found the little frame cottage occupied by Peter Dalla with the north side almost blown out, the interior furnishings badly wrecked and the lifeless body of Dalla deposited in the opposite side of the room from where the explosion occurred.

A thorough examination of the premises revealed the fact that several sticks of Giant Powder had been suspended on the outer wall of the building and near the head of Dalla's bed. All being satisfactorily placed and the intended victim fast asleep, the combustibles were ignited in some unknown manner with the result above given. So great was the force of the explosion that a building adjoining the occupied by Dalla was also badly wrecked—doors blown off, framework splintered, windows shattered, and furnishing demolished. Fortunately no one was in the cottage at the time or other victims would have been registered. There is no absolute clue to the murderer of Mr. Dalla, since no one but the perpetrator of this dastardly deed seems to have been witness to the explosion, and yet there is little doubt in the minds of officers and friends of the victim who recall details of an attempt on Dalla's life at 11 o'clock on Saturday night, May 14 last, by Barney Fori [sic], and this same man, it is reported, has made numerous threats since.

Standard readers will doubtless remember the assault upon Dalla by Fori in the former's saloon on Blair Street. Fori entered the place through a rear door and, with a Colts Revolver pointed at persons present, commanded all hands go up. Two shots were fired at Dalla, one taking effect in his left leg just above the knee.

The ill will existing between Dalla and Fori is said to have arisen from the infatuation of each for the same girl. Dalla was successful in his suit for the hand of this fair young maiden and twice has a date been set for the ceremony uniting their lives, but as many times has their purpose been thwarted. This time the affair is forever cancelled by death of the successful suitor.

Fori was found at Animas Forks by officer Walter Campbell. He was in bed partly dressed. He was arrested and is now behind bars in the county jail.

Eight witnesses were present to testify, one of the most impor-tant being Florence Baker, an employee of one of the Blair Street dance halls, who had seen two men in the alley near Dalla's room between the hours of one and three o'clock Thursday morning. She was taken to the county jail but could not identify Fori as being one of the parties seen in the alley. The shift boss at the mine where Fori works could not be had at this hearing but it is thought he will prove a valuable witness.

There was no let up in the Italian feud as the anger continued to grow, and this time, John Fiori, Barney's brother was involved. On September 24, 1904, *The Silverton Standard* printed the following story.

Tuesday night an Austrian decided to make a target of John Fiori, an Italian. The same evening Pete Ray, night watchman at the Gold King Office, was shot at twice, one ball passing through his coat sleeve and the other close to his head. There are too few arrests made for the carrying of concealed weapons these days and a gen-eral roundup would be beneficial to the public in general and inci-dentally to the town treasury.

No further evidence, unless possessed by the secret detective society, has been obtained as to the party or parties implicated in the killing of Peter Dalla by dyna-mite last week. Barney Fiori, the suspect, is in jail and awaits a preliminary hearing. A feud of long standing between the Italian and Austrian elements of Silverton may have some bearing on the matter but to date no pos-itive proof has been obtained.

Barney Fiori was never convicted of the crime and the murder was never solved.

As the sunny warm days of September 1904 turned into the deep cold of winter, Angelina decided to give up her work in the bar. It was getting increasingly difficult for her to put up with the banter and keep things under control. Phil, now eighteen, was not old enough to handle the bar by himself, nor did she deem him responsible. He was living openly with his girlfriend, Minnie, and this was painful to Angelina's heart and ego. Jennie had developed a friendship with Minnie, so Angelina was left to fight this battle alone. She was tired of fighting. Besides, it caused her heart to ache when she looked at Katie. Her daughter was now a shadow of her former self, silent and full of sadness.

Angelina worked out a lease with John Giono. She would continue to run the saloon and upstairs boarding house until July 1, 1905. After that, the rent was to be $70 per month for the Belleville, and the lease would run until 1915. She and Katie would maintain the family residence in the single story quarters to the rear of the Belleville.

"E n'ù fina 'dzur dij cavèj. E na pöss pì!" "I have had enough!"

CHAPTER XII

The Courtship

When citizens in Durango heard the news of the murder in Silverton, it fueled gossip and speculation. "It is a crazy feud! Her mother didn't want the wedding." To most, it was just another problem caused by too many foreigners who brought their ancient customs and grudges with them to cause trouble in America. Newly arrived immigrants were considered to be no better than unwanted rabble.

But the news of the premeditated malice had a different meaning for the Italian community, and the topic spread with a quiet, hushed-up effect. They knew they were looked upon as outsiders, but no one seemed to understand the hardships and difficulties involved in the blending together of cultures and traditions. The complexities were many. It would take the passing of several generations before the mixing of nationalities and conflicting beliefs would all come together peacefully. To the immigrant Italian community, it was as if the Peter Dalla murder had simply evolved from these differences, and they spoke of it in whispers. Only amongst their own did they talk about it, a parent's right to control their children, and the prejudices of Italians against Italians. *'D chi ca l'é la culpa?*

John Baudino was aware of all the talk, and he stiffened with a strange feeling of mixed emotions. His heart felt a deep sadness for Katie, and he knew that she must suffer great heartache. *A starà mal.* He was plagued with suspicion as he wondered about Angelina's involvement in the murder, knowing how she felt about Katie's engagement. He had witnessed firsthand the estranged relationship between mother and daughter.

He thought about going to Silverton to offer his condolences, but he didn't want to anger Angelina. Because she had loaned him money to start his saloon business, she would expect his loyalty. It would be a long while before things would settle down, so he knew better than to approach the Sartores at this time. But he followed the news about the trial and the search for the murderers of Peter Dalla. It hurt him to know that Katie would be facing all of this alone.

John tried to put these worries aside, because he was busy with his own problems. He and Tony were working long hours in the saloon in

Durango, and the situation was getting out of hand. They had agreed to a fifty-percent partnership when they bought into the saloon, but conditions were becoming unbearable; John was impatient to run the business the way he wanted. Tony knew that once John convinced himself of something, there was no arguing with him, so as far as this business deal was concerned, change was coming.

Tony was nervous about John's desire to split with their business partner. They were making good money and their savings increased weekly. Part of their earnings went to Italy where their older brother, Carlo, invested it in strong Italian currency. They also frequented the First National Bank in Durango, making deposits and becoming familiar figures to all the bank employees. John was becoming known in the community for being honest, fair, and willing to lend a helping hand or a few dollars. He had a simple philosophy and often expressed it as "A good name is worth more than money." Tony felt John was obsessed with his reputation, but he valued the respect that it inspired.

John made a business of loaning money, but he wasn't a loan shark and didn't foreclose on his loans. Knowing that the bank would not lend money to newly arrived immigrants, he helped many businesses get a start in Durango by making funds available. He tried to use careful judgment when fellow Italians approached him to borrow money and he was right most of the time. He lost in some cases, however, and wasn't popular when he pestered for payments. He continued to work to keep his name clean and honest, and the interest from the loans added up in their bank account.

John made it a point to get to know the townspeople, non-Italians included. Tony stood back in this, not learning to speak English, but he was honest, hard working, and pleasant, so he added credibility to the Baudino name. The Baudino brothers slowly earned a place in the Durango community as they struggled for acceptance and respect. John became the better known of the two because of his capability in handling business deals. Tony was the good-natured older brother; John was the younger, motivated, serious one.

Eventually the brothers were able to bring an end to the saloon partnership, with Sategna agreeing to buy them out. It would be done with the condition that he pay them over a period of one year, and that they would continue to work and earn their 50% until that time. The saloon was now an established meeting place for the Italian community, so, with persistence and perseverance, the Baudinos would be able to retain the money they had invested. It would give them enough financial security to start their own saloon.

So, heavily weighted with the enormity of this new decision, John and Tony put a cash down payment on a piece of property on Durango's Main Avenue, only a few doors away from the Sategna saloon. The dream to create a business of their very own was about to become a reality, when, in 1906, they applied for a building permit. A sense of exhilaration surged through the air as they made plans to build their saloon and boarding house in Durango, just as Louis Sartore had done in Silverton. John decided it was time to write Angelina with the news.

John and Tony Baudino in 1905.

Tony's head was in the clouds, feeling the new world of possibilities, while John was the worried one, burdened with all the difficulties involved with turning this dream into a reality. Neither he nor his brother had received their United States citizenship papers yet, and they could not get the building permit approved because of this. The problem was solved when a good friend, Pietro Filippi, later called "Pete Phillips," agreed to sign the papers with them.

During the time of proposed construction on the building, John frequented the bank, making certain all details and loans were secured in the proper manner. He was feeling the strain of this business transaction when he ran into a friend he knew from his early days of mining in Silverton. After pleasantries were exchanged, they began to discuss news from Silverton, and the topic became the subsequential fate of the Sartore family.

"Angelina leased out the saloon and Phil is running the livery," the man explained. "Jennie and Louis Bonavida are still trying to get gold out of that mine near Chattanooga."

"E la Katie?" "What about Katie?" John inquired, with a flash of worry in his eyes.

"She is a problem for the family," the man said shaking his head. "It is sad that a beautiful girl has such sorrow. She won't have anything to do with any man after the murder of the Tyrolean she was engaged to marry. Her mother is crazy with worry. Angelina asks about you, John. *E 't duvrisse 'ndar a truvaje.* You should go see them."

John was disturbed to hear this, because the fate of the Sartores was always in the back of his mind. When they shook hands to part company, John thanked his friend for the information. He assured him a trip to Silverton would be planned as soon as all his building worries could be straightened out. *"Grassie 'd le növe."*

John passed this news on to his brother and expressed the desire to go to Silverton. Tony understood. He was fully aware that John patterned himself after Louis Sartore, but he didn't share his brother's enchantment with the Sartores; on the contrary, he considered them troublesome. Perhaps it was because he was a little jealous of the way John idolized them. He also realized that his brother was more than mildly interested in Katie, so it didn't surprise him when John decided to make the trip to Silverton later that same week. Tony chose not to go along, knowing full well that John's heart was involved and that he needed to work this problem out for himself. He would let John go alone and hope that he would not do something stupid. He emphasized to his brother that this was not a good time to let the heart rule the head. *A l'é nin 'l mument 'd lasàse piàr dai sentiment.*

So, going against his nature and better judgment, John put aside their many business problems, boarded the little narrow gauge train, and headed for Silverton.

During the trip over these now familiar mountains, John once again let his fantasies run free. He imagined himself married to Katie Sartore, living in a big house on Durango's Third Avenue with the tree-lined boulevard. He made up his mind to try for her hand once more. What did he have to lose? He realized that he didn't sound like a practical person, even to himself. He was beginning to sound like a dreamer with no understanding of the real world.

As the narrow gauge train jostled him on his way, passing over the bridges and around the cliffs, John looked out at the mountain scenes of early June. Snow could be seen on the high peaks, but the air was fresh with the feeling of late spring. Forgetting past experience, he opened the window to more fully enjoy the cooling rain shower that made the air smell clean with the piney scent of the forest. Immediately, the soot flowing from the chugging engine quickly enveloped him, blowing cinders in his eyes. This helped bring him back to reality and he quickly closed the window.

What did he plan to say to Angelina—or to Katie, for that matter? He had no experience in the ways of winning a woman's heart. He didn't know what women liked to hear. He had been away from his sisters a long time now, and he wasn't used to being around any women. He wasn't sure how he should approach the situation, now that he was on his way. If he were home in Pasquaro, his sisters, Domenica and Camilla, would find someone for him to marry. Pasquaro had about one-hundred inhabitants, and they all knew each other. Marriages were easily arranged and were governed by strict, traditional rules. This wouldn't have been a problem if he were still living in Italy.

But why would any woman choose him over the many men wanting marriage? He only knew a life of hard work and hadn't had time to learn gentle graces or etiquette. He now realized the enormity of the task he had created by taking this trip. He cursed himself for once again being so stupid, saying, *"E su mac senpre 'l solit fulatùn."* "I am a fool once again."

As the train entered Silverton his heart was heavy. "Now what will I do? I'm here, so I will carry on and visit the Sartore family. *Fuma parèj!* That's all!" As he climbed down from the train car, he lectured himself inwardly, acknowledging that courage was the only magic that would get him through these next few moments. Pausing, he took a deep breath, trying to restore his equilibrium to a decent level of confidence. He straightened his shoulders and strode the now familiar path to the Sartore saloon.

When John arrived on Blair Street, he noticed with some curiosity that the Belleview was now called Belleville House. Walking into the saloon, he recognized familiar faces as they called out for him to join them for a drink. Not wanting to face Angelina or Katie smelling of liquor, he told them, as a friendly gesture, "Perhaps later." John worked in a bar, but he only had a glass of wine now and then and rarely drank beer or whiskey.

He asked how to locate Angelina and was directed to the back area behind the saloon, where the family still lived. Angelina and Katie were in the kitchen and John had a flashback to a previous visit here, when he talked with Katie and learned of her love for Peter Dalla. It had been almost five years ago, and many things had changed since then.

Angelina spilled over with hugs and happiness at the sight of him. *"Oh, che bel! Neto a l'é gnü a truvane!"* "Oh, how wonderful, Neto is here to see us!"

John was soon seated and food piled on his plate. He inhaled the mingling fragrances in front of him. The aroma was wonderful! He noticed that Katie was silent, moving slowly around to warm and serve the food. She said nothing and her face expressed nothing. She hardly acknowledged him.

Angelina was the opposite, talking a mile a minute, telling him of all the recent problems, explaining the necessity for renaming the saloon. "I had to combine resources and pay off some of Louis' partners. We worked through all the legalities and now the saloon belongs to me. I had to fight to keep it because I want Phil to inherit it." This was stated emphatically, the emotion in her words obvious. She then ranted on with biting aggravation in her voice, about Phil and his problems. "The worst part is that Phil is now living with a whore, so what choice did I have but to lease out the saloon?"

John nodded his head in agreement, enjoying the delicious home-cooked meal that started with a clay pot of *bagna cauda*—bread and vegetables to dip into the warm olive oil and anchovies mixture. Large onions stuffed with Italian bread and roast beef followed and was served hot from the oven. The food and familiar ambiance gave him a comfortable sensation, as if he were at home in Italy.

Angelina soon wanted to know all about his life and the new saloon about which he had written. Because she had originally given him money for their first business venture, John knew he owed much to Angelina. He paid her due homage by saying, "Without your help, none of this would be possible." Angelina smiled at this statement, looking very pleased.

Happy to hold her interest, John continued to explain the details of his project. He and Tony hoped it would be finished by this time next year. "It will be a good, strong, beautiful building made of brick on Main Avenue in Durango, right across from the train depot."

Angelina was pleased with all he was telling her, because she liked Neto and admired his intensity of purpose. John and Tony had paid back the loan, including interest, as she knew they would. Appearing to be deep in thought over his words, she responded with approval when he finished. "You are to be much respected for your ambitious plans, Neto. I am certain you will be successful. Bravo! I always knew your attitude and abilities would accomplish much."

Angelina glanced over at Katie, her mind once again set on playing matchmaker. When she rose to leave she said, "You sit here with Katie while I go and get Jennie. She will want to see you and show off her beautiful babies. Katie, take chairs outside and sit with Neto. It's a wonderful, sunny day."

Katie looked perplexed, as if she didn't want to be bothered with his company, but she picked up a chair to go outside and he followed her, doing the same. Sitting there, to the side of the saloon in the backyard area, the high-altitude air of Silverton seemed especially clear and bright. At an elevation of more than 9,000 feet, even summer days could be cool, but the bright sun on his back felt warm and reassuring. Katie looked disinterested and remote, but John decided to start talking anyway. Fear hammered in his chest as he spoke.

"What are your plans now, Katie? Will you continue to live here with your mother?" He wondered about his words as they tumbled awkwardly out of his mouth. Katie raised her eyebrows and tilted her head, seemingly agitated, dodging his glance. The feeling in the air between them was strained as he waited for her response.

"I am thinking of cooking at the Chattanooga Cookhouse. They always need cooks there."

John gave her a stern look. He was shocked that she would even consider such a situation. "No, Katie, that is a terrible job! Cooking over those hot stoves for so many miners every day will make an old woman of you in a short time. *A l'é nin na buna idea!*" "It is not a good idea!"

Katie stared at him as if to say, "What business is it of yours?" But no words came out of her mouth. She finally did comment, *"Que che pöss far d'aut?"* "What else can I do?"

John began to feel hot and uncomfortable, and it had nothing to do with the sunshine. His palms were sweating! He realized that this was the perfect time, probably his only opportunity, to tell her his entire plan—even the part about marriage.

"Katie, you could come to Durango and work there. You have all the experience necessary, and we need the help, especially in the boarding house."

"You're offering me a job?" she questioned him, squirming with annoyance at this disturbing topic. John could see uncertainty in her eyes.

"Not exactly a job." He stammered and thought for a moment that he couldn't continue. "We could be partners," John made a quick intake of breath. "I was thinking that you could be my wife." He said this in a matter-of-fact tone that had her staring at him in disbelief. Now her face wore a slightly startled look.

"John, I am not wanting to be anyone's wife," she said as she looked away and fingered the engagement ring she still wore.

"*E capisso.*" "I understand," he said with anxiety building in his voice. "I *do* understand, and I don't care if you carry love for him to your grave. I think it is sad to waste your life when you have much to offer! I can give you a partnership, a good secure life, away from this town that only reminds you of sadness."

He had said it all and stated his case! He sat quietly waiting, but there was no response. John glanced over and noticed that Katie sat staring into space. He studied her, noticing her bony wrists and the body lost within the baggy folds of clothes. She had lost a lot of weight and she looked frail and vulnerable. Perhaps it was just the sadness about her that made it seem that you could almost see right through her. She never smiled, and her eyes looked...empty. It made John hurt to see her this way.

Katie couldn't respond. How could she explain to anyone that her life was just an existence? She lived only in the past, remembering every moment spent with Peter. Every memory was kept inside, pulsing in her mind whether awake or asleep.

Just then the tension of this moment was broken by the squeals of two little girls running toward them from around the corner. Even Katie broke out in a semi-smile for the adorable children who climbed in her lap and smothered her with kisses.

Lina and Annie, the little Bonavida girls, soon made John feel like part of the family. They warmed to him with charming loving gestures that only children can bestow. He was immediately smitten with Jennie's children, so he reached into his pocket and retrieved candy. Noises of delight once again pierced the air, and John knew he was successful in winning their hearts. As they filled their mouths with the treats, Jennie came and opened her arms to embrace him. She was very pregnant again and laughed as her enlarged belly came between them. She started talking, asking questions, happy he had come to see them.

"Mama tells me you are building a new saloon in Durango. When will it be finished? What's it like? This is exciting news, Neto. *Dine tüt!* Tell us all about it!"

The afternoon passed quickly, and John needed to catch the train returning to Durango. He explained that he and Tony were working at another bar until their saloon was ready to open. As he once again hugged them all in readiness to leave, Katie said, *"E penserù a que che't m'è dit."* "I will think about what you said."

He was so stunned that he almost missed hearing Angelina's invitation, asking him to return for the Fourth of July events. She was saying, "Silverton has a parade, baseball games, concerts, and the firemen have a hook and ladder race." He graciously said he would try to return and thanked them for everything.

He smiled, listening to the happy rhythm of his heart as it pounded in his head. Boarding the train to return to Durango, he took a seat and sat there, bemused, confused, and delighted. She would think about it! That was enough to keep him going for a long, long time. Her parting words were on his mind all the way home. So, as the little train chugged its way back to Durango, John—Giovanni Grato Baudino—let happiness burn its way into his heart.

Disappointment clouded John's hopes to celebrate Independence Day in Silverton. Both he and Tony needed to work at the bar because it would be extra busy for the holiday. They needed all the money possible for the building construction of the saloon, so this was no time to relax and have fun. He would go to Silverton another day, but he felt downcast thinking of the festivities he was missing.

It was only a few days later that he heard the news of another devastating blow dealt to the Sartore family. On July 9, 1906, Angelo Sartore had been shot and fatally wounded while allegedly stealing horses from the logging camp of the Honaker brothers, near the small mining community of Chattanooga, a short distance north of Silverton. John knew Angelo Sartore was a relative of the Sartore family and as close to Phil as a brother. John decided to take time off. He would attend the funeral in Silverton and give condolences to the already disconsolate family.

Both John and Tony boarded the narrow gauge train dressed in their best suits. They would attend the funeral of a fellow countryman, comforting the Sartores the best they could. John gave thought to this situation, talking to his brother as the train blew cinders and smoke into their lungs. He wondered if things would ever settle down for the Sartores. Tony shared his feelings on the subject, saying that the Sartores seemed to make their own trouble.

Indeed, this was yet another complicated and perplexing incident for the Sartores, and they were all surprised and grieved by Angelo's death and the circumstances. Phil was anguished by what had happened and wore a bleak, shocked expression. They held services for Angelo in the Catholic church, and for the burial Angelina had his coffin placed in the Sartore family plot at Hillside Cemetery. A large concourse of Angelo's fellow Italians followed in procession to his grave.

James Honaker was arrested and charged with the killing, but he was released. It was suspected that Angelo had an accomplice, but he died taking the name of the collaborator to his grave. It appeared that this was another crime and murder that would never be solved. There was no evidence as to who had actually fired the shot, and no evidence to prove that Angelo had been stealing the horses.

The Baudino brothers didn't plan to stay long at the funeral, wanting only to spend enough time to pay their respects. However, Angelina didn't let them leave until she had served them food, and she repeatedly expressed her appreciation that they had come. Everyone was concerned about the effect this would have on Jennie, because she was due to deliver her baby soon.

Katie cried constantly, saying that Angelo could not be guilty of such a thing. John did not approach her with words: He knew that it was best to support her sorrow by being silent and respecting her sadness. He promised to come back another day, and he and Tony left to return to Durango.

It was autumn before that day arrived. The colors of the aspen trees in the high mountains were turning gold and the air cool, a reminder that winter would come soon. John enjoyed this season and the journey on the train. He decided to let himself relax. Things were taking shape in Durango. Even though Katie had not yet made a decision, perhaps she would want to work at the boarding house but not commit to marriage. He would be agreeable to whatever she decided.

The pervasive atmosphere was peaceful as John arrived in Silverton. Jennie had given birth in late August and had named her baby son Emilio. John spent time greeting the family and giving candy to Lina and Annie. After these pleasantries and formalities were accomplished, Katie suggested they go for a walk.

It was a warm September day and, at first, they each felt uncomfortable in the other's company. As they walked around the outskirts of the town, Katie suddenly started to talk. She explained how difficult each September was for her. In a few days it would be her birthday, and as she wiped tears away, she told him how it would always remind her of Peter's death. John listened patiently, trying to stay composed. He offered his handkerchief and let her release those painful memories of that September only two years ago. She continued to talk, confiding her innermost thoughts and secrets. As she explained the details of her family's involvement in the murder, it pushed his sensitive feelings to the brink. Listening as she expressed her despair and sadness, he couldn't contain the tears and he cried along with her.

When the flood of emotions had almost drained both of them, they stood looking into Cement Creek, watching as it passively made its way through town. In the warmth of that lovely autumn day, Katie began to feel a sense of relief. She could relax with John, and he seemed able to look beyond the complexities she carried in her heart. They had both grown up in the same part of Italy and knew much about each other. It wasn't surprising that they could come to an understanding and form a special bond, a trusting relationship.

Katie looked at John with his tear-streaked face and saw a gentle, caring man. It occurred to her that maybe it was time to concentrate on what could be accomplished, rather than allow herself to continually mourn. She could start a new life. This thought materialized, even though it meant that she would be giving in to her mother's wishes. She wanted to punish her mother forever, but was it worth the price of adding to her already wounded heart?

She turned her attention back to John, asking about his project and how the saloon was taking shape. He told her of the construction, letting the excitement of the project warm his features. She studied him as he spoke. His eyes lit up, projecting his enthusiasm for all that was developing in Durango.

"Perhaps I would be able to come to Durango and see your new building," she offered, saying she could stay with friends there.

He was pleased to hear her talk in a pleasant manner, free from emotional disturbances. But he was thrown off balance by her change in mood and almost failed to realize what this interest in his saloon might mean. John felt his face flush as he grasped both her hands in happy excitement. "You want to see the new building? You would come to Durango? What about the wedding? *Et vötö dir che 't vöj spusate cun mi?* Does this mean you will marry me?"

She lowered her eyes and responded, "If you want, I will marry you."

She then continued, letting her decision push her forward. "The wedding could be next autumn, on September 24. That is the day I was to be married before. I already have a dress," she said, looking away to hide the tears forming once again in her eyes.

"That will be fine," he said in understanding. "Things will be better now. *Aura a 'ndrà tüt ben.* Somehow I will make thing right for you."

Katie took his hand, guiding him in the direction of Reese Street, to the little Catholic church where she wanted the wedding to take place.

John's head was spinning as he rode the little train back to Durango that evening. So many things had happened in one day. The course of his life had changed—or had this been his course all along? Katie Sartore had agreed to be his wife. Isn't that what he wanted? Could he make her happy? Would she ever forget that she loved another man?

Somehow he had faith that Katie would make a good wife, and he would work like the devil to give her a secure and respectable life. He wanted to make up for the injustices she had suffered. His thoughts were solemn on this trip home, because the future was a serious matter. "I have a big job ahead of me," he muttered to himself. He listened to the incessant sound of iron on steel as the train rocked and swayed him on his way back to Durango.

CHAPTER XIII

Mascot Saloon

On Wednesday afternoon of September 24, 1907, Katie Sartore married John Baudino in a small ceremony at St. Patrick's Catholic Church in Silverton. There was no extravagance spent on this wedding: The celebration and the photos were basic and simple. All of the extended family were present, including the Joseph Sartore family, John's brother Tony, the Bonavida family, and Mary and Ludwig Vota. Two photos were taken: One was of the bride and groom, and the other included Jennie's two daughters, Lina and Anna.

Katie and John Baudino with Anna and Lina Bonavida on Sept. 24, 1907.

They ordered a few extra wedding photos to send to John's relatives in Italy, but it was nothing like the vast amount of photos of the wedding party taken at Jennie's wedding. There was also no elaborate dinner or grand ball, as there had been for Jennie's. They simply married, had a quiet reception, and boarded the train for Durango.

As the couple waved good-bye, Angelina stood dabbing her eyes with a handkerchief, misty-eyed and happy. She approved of the union wholeheartedly, giving the couple her blessing. "Things will be right for Katie now," Angelina thought to herself. "A good match can often be more enduring than love. *A l'é me ch'a ventava ch'a füs.* This is the way it should have been in the first place."

As the narrow gauge pulled slowly away from the Silverton depot, the guests threw flowers and rice, wishing the newlyweds health and happiness. During the festivities, Katie had been unaware and oblivious to her feelings. It was like a dream…a blurred, bewildering dream. She suddenly awakened, moving out of a foggy haze, realizing she had been numb throughout the ceremony. She was married. It was done! For a moment she felt bewildered.

John sensed her distress and reached to catch her elbow so she wouldn't fall. She quickly steadied herself and gave her husband a feeble smile. It wasn't his fault that her thoughts of a wedding were marked with confusion. She had promised herself she would not punish him with any feelings of disappointment. To cover her mood, she hastily threw her bride's bouquet out the train window. This brought wails of happy laughter from everyone present, because Jennie's two little girls raced to catch the flowers. With that, Katie waved, managing an air of cheerfulness. Glancing beyond the crowd of well-wishers toward the town of Silverton, she whispered, "Good-bye."

John ushered his new bride into a seat near the window and then settled in the seat next to her. She tried telling herself that a part of her life was now over and before her was a clean slate on which to start fresh. She outwardly displayed a calm manner, but this was simply hiding the disturbance she felt on the inside. Her hands remained knotted together in her lap, and she wondered if she was doing the right thing in accepting this new direction in her life.

It was true that she felt some optimism about the future, and she wanted to put the sadness behind her. Letting go of those painful yesterdays would remain a challenge, but she would try to live her new life with dignity. She promised to do what was expected to honor the good man who was now her husband. John Baudino was responsible for giving her this opportunity.

Thinking of the new saloon in Durango gave purpose to her life, and she could feel some spirit returning. She was infused with the energy that flowed through John. By convincing her that she was needed and important, he was breathing new life into her. Thanks to him and the warmth and attention he showered on her, Katie's emotions were beginning to untangle. She had confidence that she could help with the business, but she gave no thought to success or vindication for all she had suffered. She simply wanted to get on with life and find a reason to keep living.

Her sister and mother would still be part of her life. She had no desire to close them out, but there was regret. What they had done in the name of love was too difficult to understand or completely forgive.

Thinking back on her life, she could only remember the loving relationship she had shared with her father. There was now a permanent shield between herself and her mother and sister. However, she already missed Jennie's children and her brother, Phil. It was promised that they would all come spend time in Durango after she settled in. She felt shame, as she inwardly admitted that it was a nice feeling to be separated from her family.

She also had to fight the guilt that caused her torment—feeling responsible for Peter's death. "He was murdered because I refused to do what my family wanted. *A l'é culpa mia se Peter a l'é mort.* He would still be alive if not for me."

The narrow gauge train that climbed along the mountain tracks was moderately full of passengers that day in late September. Most of them ignored the splendor of the golden autumn scene on display. The travelers mostly talked or dozed, anxious to get to their destination. As Katie gazed absently out the window, she could not help but overhear the chatter coming from the two women sitting in the seat directly behind her.

One woman was talking emphatically. "Things are different today, and we must be aware of that. If you're not happy in your marriage, and it's obvious that he treats you terribly, you have every right to divorce him. A woman shouldn't have to cower in a corner knowing that her husband will beat her up after spending all his earnings on drinks at a saloon. There are new laws now and they will protect you."

"But what about the children?" a submissive voice pleaded quietly. "He's a mean devil and would take the children away from me just for spite. Worst of all, my own parents would disapprove of a divorce." It was easy to hear the pain in her voice as she added grimly, "The marriage was arranged by my parents. They scrimped and saved to put something aside each year for my dowry. With that money, we purchased the house and property. With a divorce, I would lose everything to him."

"No, no!" came the comment from the other. "It's better now, especially here in Colorado. There are laws of equality for men and women. Aren't you aware that women vote in this state? Perhaps your property would be divided, but you would have the right to keep your children and part of the property. Women now have more control over their destiny and no longer need to depend solely on a man or their parents to make all the decisions."

"But how would I, as a divorced woman, live?" The sound of desperation quivered in her breathless voice as she succumbed to sobs.

Katie tried not to listen as this personal conversation continued, but it triggered memories of her mother's lectures on a young woman's duties. It was natural for parents to control the destinies of their children, and after marriage it was the right of a husband to continue this control. These social rules of etiquette had ruled families for generations. Katie knew that even though Angelina had suffered social injustices herself, she would not have considered allowing her children to make their own decisions. Honor thy father and thy mother, for they know what is right! *Übidìsje a tò pare e a tua mare!* These are the words that she had been taught, and she still heard them ringing in her ears.

What would Angelina's views be on equality between men and women? She would think it all nonsense! She was in charge of her household and family and didn't care what went on outside of that.

It was of no use that Katie had tried for freedom of choice when she decided to marry someone her family didn't find appropriate. America reverberated with voices of independence, but she came from an Old Country Italian family that lived by traditional rules. She knew of the suffrage acts taking shape in the United States and the advances women had made for equality and justice, but this had no effect on her life. She had not been allowed the freedom of choosing her own husband.

Women's Suffrage was especially well supported in America's western states. It was said that pioneer life fostered independence and equality, and lawmakers and judges were more responsive to the demand for reform when their attention was directed to unjust treatment of women. Also, it was a thousand times more difficult to repeal an unjust law in an old state than it was to adopt a just law in a new state. By 1907, four states on the western frontier had equal rights for women and men—Wyoming, Colorado, Utah, and Idaho.

In these newly settled areas, laws unfavorable to women were not as firmly entrenched or had not been included in the legal codes. Women thus worked to gain rights concerning control of property, guardianship, divorce laws, and increased opportunities for education and employment. Before the suffrage acts, married women could not sign contracts, they had no control of title to their own earnings, they had no property rights, nor could they claim guardianship of their own children in cases of separation or divorce.

Yes, there were improvements in state laws, but Katie knew that no law would have saved her from the wrath of her family. She had lost the battle in the most terrible of ways. Now she would accept this fact and live the life her mother had chosen for her. Would it be the same someday, if her daughters wanted something other than their mother's wishes? She couldn't imagine she would be indifferent to their feelings. (But, old traditions run deep!)

Thoughtfully she wondered about her new life, married to a man she respected but did not love. Would she want a divorce like the woman in the seat behind her? "Divorce" was not a word even considered in the vocabulary of her immigrant Italian society.

Her gaze moved to her new husband and she studied him as he spoke to his brother. It seemed as if she had known him for a lifetime, but she didn't *really* know him.

In appearance, John was slightly built, with shoulders broadened by years of hard work. He had a shock of light brown hair, finely boned features set off by a smaller Roman nose, and he wore a moustache. He was an unimposing man, shy in some ways but bold in others. He was shorter than she was and not educated, speaking only broken English. His blue-grey eyes took on the look of steel when they sparkled with purpose, and there was an intensity to him that was compelling. He seemed to possess a dynamic balance of opposites that shifted from moment to moment. He had determination and courage, and yet he was completely unpretentious, with a serious outlook on life. Despite this, he had a gentle, pleasant nature. Some of this puzzled her. She admitted to herself that she was not attracted to him in a passionate or physical way, but in his presence she somehow felt safe and comfortable. There was something about him, something steady and reliable.

A slight smile crossed her lips as she recalled Jennie's children running eagerly to greet John, vying for his candy and attention. John would be a good father, she reasoned, but in her mind's eye she had to push away the vision of Peter. *Mè por Peter!* Peter should have been the father of her children, and with that thought, she slowly closed her eyes.

"Have you heard about the Anti-Saloon League and the Women's Christian Temperance Union?" Katie once again tuned in to the voices behind her. "I think they will someday close down all the saloons as these organizations become more powerful. That will solve all the problems of men getting drunk all the time. Women and God-fearing men should vote for that law."

Katie's eyes flew open as if in alarm. "This would not be a good time for all the saloons to close down," she thought anxiously to herself. She was depending on the new saloon to bring a sense of security to her life.

The golden shimmer of aspen groves brightly marked the autumn landscape as they passed through the canyons, with the little train rocking, causing passengers to sway from side to side as it moved them slowly around the dangerous cliffs. With a deep sigh, Katie left thoughts of Silverton behind. She sat next to her husband, with Tony seated across the aisle. They each sat rigidly, thinking their own thoughts.

In an impulsive moment, she felt the desire to slip her hand companionably over her husband's arm, but something stopped her and her body lurched forward instead. John looked at her, questioning her abrupt movement, but she gave him only a stiff half-smile and turned away to look out the window.

John was also aware of the conversation coming from the seat behind them. They were just idle women talking, and he couldn't imagine that laws against liquor would ever be established. The drinking of alcohol had been around for a long time, and he reasoned that more people would vote *for* alcohol than *against* it.

He could hardly wait to get home to Durango. He had work to do, but most of all he wanted to show Katie around the new building. It would now be her home, and he hoped she would be pleased. He couldn't wait to show her the surprise gift he had chosen for them to share: a brass double bed. It was an extravagance, but he wanted only the best for his new wife. It was his wish that their married life start out in proper style. There was the expectation that perhaps the brass bed would bless their wedded life with love and children, but he also wondered if Katie would be happy with him as a man. This worry was always in the back of his mind.

Whatever the future brought to their relationship, John knew he would value her abilities and experience in running a business. He knew she had worked hard in running the boarding house at the Belleville: her skills would be a great asset. Speaking perfect English, she was charming, gracious, and beautiful. Yes, John was pleased that she had agreed to be his wife. Whether or not love would ever enter this picture, he had no idea, but he felt that he had just won a great prize. She was the only woman he had ever wanted.

Soon they would be alone, just the two of them. He had made reservations to spend a couple of days at the Trimble Hot Springs Resort in the Animas Valley, located outside of Durango on the train route to Silverton. A fresh new environment would be a good way for them to become familiar as man and wife. They would take a walk around the beautiful grounds of the resort and have dinner in the special dining room.

His only hope was they would not feel uncomfortable in each other's company. He really didn't know what to expect, as they had never really been alone together, and neither had spoken any words of love. Looking out the window, he recognized the Animas Valley. They were approaching Trimble, and he felt a bolt of fear going through his body. He thought himself a fool to be afraid of his wedding night. He would more easily enter an unsteady mine shaft!

As the train pulled up to Trimble, John and Katie nervously picked up small valises, and prepared to disembark onto the platform. Awkwardly they said their good-byes to Tony, who would continue on to Durango. He would be in charge of the three trunks containing all of Katie's belongings. Angelina had given her the Giordano trunks from the original trip from Italy.

Drawing of Trimble Hot Springs Resort as it looked in 1907.

Always the one to worry, John was busy giving last minute instructions to his brother for all the details concerning the business. Tony waved him off, telling him it would be all right. Nothing would fall apart in the two days John would be away. *'A 'ndrà tüt ben! Preocupte nin!'* "Things will be fine! Don't worry!" As Katie and John stepped off the train at Trimble, they turned to wave, watching the train pull away as it continued on its way to Durango.

Tony pulled his hat forward and took a deep breath, settling back for the short remaining distance of the trip. He realized that everything would be different now and he would have to guard his feelings carefully. John now had a wife, and he had been replaced in the eyes of his brother. John had always sought his advice and kept him in his confidence. Now Katie came between them, making it difficult for Tony to feel like an equal partner. He had heard the expression of feeling like a fifth wheel; he was actually only the third wheel. Perhaps what the wagon needed was another wheel.

John had touched on the subject that it was time his brother found a wife, but Tony shook his head with a feeling of disgust at this notion. He deemed it impossible to find someone to marry in Durango. Any unmarried Italian girl was in demand and surrounded with suitors the moment she arrived in town. It was an impossible situation, because immigrants were not considered socially suitable for mixing with proper citizens. *As pol nin viver parèj!* Tony grimaced thinking of the terms and slang words he heard used to describe him and his countrymen. It was difficult to be looked upon as less than others. He often watched as John pushed himself forward, putting himself in situations, hoping to gain respect from distinguished businessmen and the community. John took the benefits with the blows and was able to establish a good name. But Tony knew that no matter how successful John became, he would never be considered someone of prominence. The lines were drawn!

Even their new business, the Mascot Saloon, was placed on the "immigrant" side of town. Durango's Main Avenue ended at the railroad depot and the new saloon was on the block, right across the street from the depot. Yes, it was a good location for business, but perhaps there was little choice allowed them as "foreigners."

The street ended because of the Animas River, and the smelter loomed, belching smoke, on the other side of the river. It wasn't the desirable side of town. South of Sixth Street was the dividing line, and

The railroad depot in Durango, Colorado in 1907.

this area was always covered in dark clouds as the smelter and train filled the air with black smoke from burning coal.

No, Tony could not find a wife in Durango, but there was a possibility that he could make a trip to Italy and find a wife. His sisters were there, and he knew Dominica and Camilla would delight in finding a wife for him! He and John had talked about making visits to their family in Italy. The new business venture and the wedding had interfered with those plans, but as soon as things stabilized, it would be a consideration. This gave him much to think about. As the train pulled up to the Durango depot, Tony went to the baggage car to locate Katie's trunks. He claimed them and set them aside, then walked the short distance to the Mascot Saloon.

He stood there in front of the new building, thinking it resplendent in the dim light of dusk. For a long, drawn-out moment he stared at the new saloon, letting his eyes rest on the words written on the windows— "Baudino Bros." He felt intensely proud that he and his brother had worked like the devil to make this possible. It would soon be open for business.

The last rays of sunlight cast their golden hue on the thick walls that rose up two stories, and Tony was suddenly filled with emotion. In huge white letters across the top of the two-story building, a sign read, SALONE ITALIANO. Tony felt tingles of pride as he let his eyes take in the words sparkling in the last light of day. He was proud of his heritage, and Katie and John had agreed with the placing of those large letters on the front of the building. He smiled and walked to the saloon down the block to find friends to help him carry the large, heavy trunks. He felt comfortable in this area of town. He didn't need to speak English or be something more than

Mascot Saloon in Durango, Colorado. Drawn as it looked in 1907.

what he was. Yes, he was an immigrant, but now this was his home! *Custa a l'é ca mia!*

After the trunks were placed in the family living quarters above the Mascot Saloon, Tony walked with his friends to the saloon down the block to join them for a drink and catch up on the local news. The topic of interest was the same as those conversations in bars around the entire country—talk created by the imposing influence of two powerful pressure groups, the Anti-Saloon League and the Women's Christian Temperance Union. These groups had become strong enough to back presidential candidates and were especially effective in states such as Colorado, where women had the vote. A new political party was being formed to aid this movement against the use of alcohol. It was called the Prohibition Party, and they were preparing a candidate to run for president in the 1908 election.

Katie easily took charge of the boarding house and the kitchen. Even Tony had to admit that having her there was a great benefit as the building was always warm and rich with the delightful aroma of delicious food being prepared. The boarding house offered one meal a day with a rented room.

Katie was frugal and wasted nothing, creating magical dishes with anything, even leftovers. *Süpa 'd pan,* or bread soup, became John's favorite meal. This was an Old Country Piemontese recipe made with day-old bread, beef broth, cabbage, and cheese. It is a simple, common dish made succulent with skills that were handed down from generation to generation.

The location near the train station proved to be advantageous as the brothers thought it would. They were kept busy with customers both in the boarding house and the saloon. It quickly became a popular place with the Italians of the area, but the Baudinos had competition, since there were other places in the area offering the same facilities. They worked hard to set up a friendly atmosphere with low prices

Koshak Saloon and Boarding House, circa 1907. Courtesy of the La Plata County Historical Society.

The Koshak family ran a similar boarding house just a block away, and the Sategna Saloon was only a few doors down from the Mascot at 534 Main. Because it was also Italian owned and operated, the San Juan Saloon vied for the same customers as the Mascot. Each bar had its own group of Italian patrons and shared gossip about the clientele at the other saloon. Sometimes a customer would go to the rival saloon just to listen and report back the news.

This was just a diversion from the jobs of manual labor and otherwise dreary lives they led. Because they were fresh from Italy, they found comfort in talking about relatives and situations in the Old Country as well as the problems in the New World. In this area south of Sixth Street, they bonded together. Eventually they would learn to speak English and adopt the new ways. They knew it was important to become part of the community and replace the term "immigrant" with that of "citizen."

Katie easily made the adjustment to married life because the boarding house kept her busy. Throwing herself into work was a healthy distraction: it gave her little time to grieve the life she might have had. She found the strength to accept her new circumstances, but at times she still mourned her loss. In that safe place in her memory, she was with Peter, and their love was unchanged by time. She found these moments both painful and strangely gratifying. Some people go to their graves never experiencing what she had shared with Peter. She would not allow time to erase this love.

Almost from the time she arrived in America, she had cleaned rooms and fed boarders. Now she was doing it again—but this time she felt in charge, and her experience made her an expert in this field of business.

Katie and John had a congenial relationship, based on a common feeling of respect and trust. Theirs was not a romantic or passionate love, but they frequently put their heads together to work out problems, consulting on matters of business. Was Katie happy? This would be a difficult question for her to answer. By simply throwing herself into the work that needed to be done, she never had to face her response.

She fingered the brass on their bed one day, letting her mind wander, as she paused from straightening the sheets. It was here that their marriage was consummated. During their stay at Trimble, John had only held her close as they shared a bed, wanting to give her time, to adjust to him sleeping beside her. The beautiful brass bed had been a wonderful surprise and she had expressed this openly. She would never have denied him the marriage rights, but she was relieved that he had been understanding and not forceful. Their relationship did not revolve around the bed, but she smiled as she moved away, touching the brass once more, happy to admit that it was not unpleasant to share her husband's bed.

When she took on a serene, complacent glow, it worried those around her, because this was not explainable. But when she became dizzy and nauseous and found it difficult to complete her work, there was concern for her health. It took a visit from Maestra to point out that Katie was not sick. She was pregnant!

Katie was surprised! She had given little thought to the changes this would bring about, but the idea of a life growing inside of her seemed to spark a strange, new feeling. This child would depend on her for everything, and there would be no time for sadness. Tomorrow suddenly held a new meaning.

John's eyes lit up with the news of Katie's pregnancy. He would have liked it to be a loving, romantic message, but he knew it was just another piece to the puzzle that might bring happiness to his wife and their marriage. Being practical, he also realized this added difficulties to her work in the boarding house: Now she would need help. Finding good maid service was an almost impossible situation. Not just anyone would work for immigrants, so they needed to find an Italian girl! How they were going to arrange this was a dilemma!

When extra help was needed, Jennie often came from Silverton, bringing sunshine into the lives of everyone with her two delightful daughters, Lina and Anna. On most of these occasions, because there was work to be done, she would leave her young son, Emilio, in Silverton with Angelina.

At the times when Jennie couldn't come, Katie could rely on help from Maestra. "The teacher" had lost two husbands to miner's consumption, and her only child died at one month of age in 1900. Now in 1908, the cheerfully warm, outgoing woman was alone. Happy to help when she could, Maestra would board the train in Silverton and come to Durango at a moment's notice.

Tony worked in the bar during the day and often into the night, preparing the barroom, serving customers, and keeping the liquor stocked. It was difficult for him, since he still spoke very little English.

At busy times they hired extra help, turning to a young man they all liked. Dominic Bonaventura was a barber by trade, but was always eager to work, and would tend bar whenever he was needed. They also hired Frank Beltramo to tend bar, clean in the saloon, and do odd jobs. Frank was quiet, trustworthy, and had been a friend of the Baudino brothers since they first arrived in Durango.

John worked the daylight hours, delivering liquor to the local mines in the Durango area. It took many hours with a horse and wagon to transport liquor to mining communities such as Perins Peak and around to the coal mines of Lightner Creek Canyon. He would return home from a full day of deliveries and help his brother in the saloon late into the night. John also did all the bookwork and errands and collected bar orders.

Perhaps to some this wasn't considered "living the American dream:" They worked all the time and still had very little in the way of material wealth. But the business belonged to them and it provided a living. The choices were theirs to make, and they were content.

On July 16, 1908, less then ten months after the wedding, Katie gave birth to their first child, naming the infant baby girl Francesca, after John's mother. The entire family was jubilant, and to Katie it was as if her prayers had finally been answered. John was so emotionally moved as he held his child that tears rolled down his face. For all of them, it was as if their lives had been blessed with the arrival of this healthy newborn baby girl.

It was customary to keep the mother in bed for almost two weeks after giving birth, and just when everything seemed to be falling into a comfortable routine, Katie came down with a fever. Now things tumbled into turmoil; Angelina came from Silverton to help and a search was made to find a doctor. Because it was Sunday, the only available physician John could find was in nearby Aztec, New Mexico. The doctor agreed to come but stressed that it would take a couple of hours for him to get ready and make the trip by train. Waiting became agonizing, and, in this, John was not a patient man. He paced nervously beside his wife's bed, fretting and offering to God his own life, if his wife could be saved. He knew it wasn't unusual for a woman to die during childbirth or soon after. It seemed only a short time had passed since the celebration of his daughter's birth; he couldn't believe the happy moment had turned into this nightmare. He was not a religious man, but all he could do at this time was pray. He was in a fitful state when the doctor finally arrived.

Everyone sat nervously waiting for results from the doctor. It wasn't enough that Katie was very sick, but baby Frances, as they called the newborn, was difficult and quirky, crying constantly. On top of all of this, and unknown to all of them, a problem was developing downstairs in the saloon.

Everything was tossed into chaos because of Katie's illness, so Dominic Bonaventura was tending bar the afternoon the doctor arrived. When a man he didn't know came in wanting to buy a bottle of whiskey, Dominic sold him the liquor and thought nothing of it. The man went outside and sold the same bottle to an Indian waiting there. It was considered a crime to sell liquor to an Indian, and when the Indian became drunk and caused a problem, the finger was pointed at the Mascot Saloon. There would be lots of trouble now, as Dominic was hauled off to jail!

 1908-1909

John was angered by the circumstances, but he paid the bail and Dominic was released from jail. Desperately worried that his wife would not survive, John had let his guard down at the saloon. It wasn't Dominic's fault that the Indian had acquired liquor through another person outside of the saloon. Any one of them tending bar would have done the same thing. The guilt was not placed on the bartender, but the saloon itself. The Baudinos now risked losing their license and they soon would have to contend with a trial that could shut down the saloon. The worst part was that this situation could jeopardize their current immigration status. Neither John nor Tony was legally a naturalized citizen.

At least Katie was feeling better, and the doctor said she could get out of bed soon. John was thankful for this. The diagnosis of her illness was a common one for this era; after giving birth, many women developed infections, and this was probably because they were kept in bed for too long. Everyone had suffered during Katie's sickness, because, along with the confusion of the "Indian" affair, there weren't enough hands to do all the work in the boarding house. Customers had to be turned away, and the brothers were becoming desperate to find reliable help. Cooking and cleaning, washing and ironing were considered jobs for women. It didn't occur to them to hire men to do these chores, even though it was backbreaking work and crucial to their business.

Despite all the problems and worries, the christening day for baby Frances was a joyous celebration, with the Sartore and Bonavida families riding the train from Silverton to join in welcoming a new family member.

Excitement grew from the news that the Bonavidas would soon make a trip to the Old Country. "We're going to Italy to check on the Sartore property and see the family," Jennie told them. "We can go now while the children are young, because they can travel without paying full fare. However, Lina will stay at home with Grandma, because she has to go to school."

During a quiet moment when Angelina was out of the room, Jennie admitted that the trip was mostly for the sake of her mother, who wanted them to return to Italy to live permanently. Everyone knew that it was Angelina's dream for all of her family to return to Italy.

Many things about the trip were discussed, and John made a request that they make contact with the Baudino family while in Italy. The Bonavidas would stay in the Sartore house in Pasquaro, and John's sister, Domenica Naretto, lived only a short distance away, as did Margherita and her family. The Boggios had been living in Italy since they left Calumet in 1904.

It was also decided that while Jennie was in Italy, she would try to find a young Italian girl willing to come to America and help with work at the boarding house. The passage for the girl would be paid and she would be well looked after. It was hopeful that this would solve the problem of finding reliable help.

Angelina's eyes filled with tears, visualizing Jennie in Italy with Margherita and her family. She never gave up the hope that one day she would be in Italy with her sister. It concerned her to hear there was a possibility that the Boggios might soon emigrate to Colorado. Angelina couldn't help but wonder if fate would have her someday living in Italy, all alone.

Besides all this, Angelina had many troubles to think about and most were centered on the Belleville. John Giono had been leasing the saloon since 1905, but he and his wife, Caterina, had recently bought the property and buildings across the street at the end of the block. They tore down the existing three buildings and built a large boarding house and saloon, calling it The Piemonte. It was new, quite grand, and catered to Italian miners. The Belleville would soon be left to Angelina to handle once again. This time she decided it was time to turn it over to her son.

Phil was older now, but the predicament with Minnie was still the same. To Angelina's indignation, he lived openly with his prostitute girlfriend. Angelina knew that Minnie didn't cater to customers anymore, but, to her way of thinking, it was only because Phil paid all the bills. Angelina would never allow that "tainted" woman in her house or acknowledge that Minnie and Phil were partners of any kind. She often said, *"E preferiso murir pitost che lasar intrar cula pütana 'n ca mia!"* "I will die before I let that whore in my house!"

Angelina moved into a lovely house in the block behind the Belleville, next door to the Bonavida residence. This was a convenient location, as she doted on Jennie's children. As a grandmother, Angelina was different from Angelina the mother. With a heavy hand, she worked to shape and control the lives of her own children, but she was warm and gentle with her grandchildren, showering them with love and attention. She often reprimanded Jennie for her strict discipline, and the children would run to find their grandma when their mama was yelling at them. Perhaps this was yet another way of retaining power over her adult children. Thus, another tradition was handed down through time.

Angelina was especially close to young Lina Bonavida. Lina was not at all pleased when she learned that her parents were leaving her behind when they went to Italy. They said she had to go to school, but to a young girl, that wasn't a good reason. She cried to her grandmother that it must be that she wasn't beautiful. Angelina soothed her the best she could, saying, *"Che fularà! E t'é la pì bela 'd tüte."* "Nonsense! You are the most beautiful of them all." Lina cried all the more, saying if she couldn't be beautiful, she didn't want to live! Angelina would hold her closely, trying to take away the pain of this innocent child who could not understand.

Lina Bonavida at age 8 in 1910.

Angelina knew that it was only money that kept Lina at home. They didn't have to pay the fare for the two younger children, but those past six years of age required a full ticket. Money was tight now, and Angelina could hardly remember the good times. She ran the boarding house while Phil worked the bar, but there was now serious competition with the new Piemonte Saloon and Boarding House just across the street.

Angelina looked forward to her trips to Durango to visit Katie and her son-in-law, Neto. She was very much aware that Katie's life was going well. John took care of everything, and they seemed to prosper. She could clearly see that Katie's life was better than that of her sister, Jennie. Bonavida's mine venture was having little success, allowing him only enough to support his family. Of course, Angelina had always seen that Katie would do well with John Baudino, a respectable Piemontese. She would tell her friends, "I know what is best. *Se mach a m'avejsan dèt da mènt.* If only they would listen to me."

In late December of 1908, the Bonavida family left Silverton to spend a year in Italy. Shortly after their departure, sad news came from Catlina in Calumet. Joseph, her oldest son, had been killed while working as a timber boss, deep in the copper mines. The young man's back was broken when falling timbers pinned him down, and he lingered seven pain-filled hours before he died. His father, Antonio, had been working in the same mine two levels below him when the accident occurred. He helped take his son to the hospital. Joseph was only twenty-five years old.

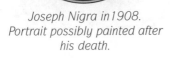

The announcement came late to Silverton, but the exact date of this tragic accident was September 15, 1908. This was the unforgettable date that brought sad memories when it came around each year—it was the same day as Peter's murder in 1904. Katie cried at this news, fondly remembering the days Joseph had spent with them in Silverton in 1901. Now she would have two souls to pray for each year on that dreadful day in September.

Joseph Nigra in 1908. Portrait possibly painted after his death.

Shortly after the holidays, on January 5, 1909, John was called to trial in Denver regarding the "Indian" incident. He traveled the almost-400 miles by train, hiring a lawyer, but he then learned that this would be only the first interview. He returned to Durango a few days later after being detained in snowstorms along the way. It upset him that the situation was taking him away from work. The business was still new, and there was much to do in becoming established.

The actual trial was set for February 26. Struggling to make everything right, John decided to take Katie and the baby along. This would provide proof that the day of the crime was muddled with Katie's sickness, the baby's birth, and confused activities. The alleged date of the crime was determined to be July 26, the Sunday when Katie was sick in bed after giving birth to Frances. They brought the doctor from Aztec who had attended Katie to act as a witness. Baby Frances was now six months old and still cranky and fussy, but they took her along in hopes this would be the final trip. Thankfully, Maestra came from Silverton to help with the boarding house work at the Mascot.

The February weather was bitterly cold and threatened to cancel the outgoing railroad traffic. But despite it all, the train to Alamosa left as scheduled. It was advised that the weather from Alamosa to Denver was blizzard conditions and very dangerous, but John felt it critical that they make it for the trial. Katie tried not to complain, understanding the importance of this trip, but all she could do was pray they wouldn't get stuck in the snow with the baby along.

After a slow, agonizing trip in a snowstorm, struggling with a crying baby, they arrived to spend the night in Alamosa. The weather remained inclement, but despite this the train reached Denver the next day. They arrived behind schedule because of the slow pace through the snow. John pushed and hurried the doctor and his tired, forlorn little family along at a brisk pace. He was concerned that they would not make it in time and the trial would be dismissed.

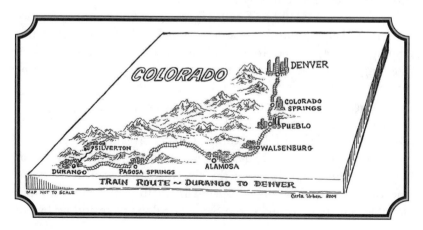

Arriving at the courthouse, they found no information pertaining to the trial in which they were involved. They hurried down hallways and up staircases, trying to find someone to help them locate the place of the trial. After much time spent searching for answers, they finally entered a courtroom. It was empty except for one man who offered to help. "Oh, that trial was postponed," he told them. "The weather has been so terrible in Colorado that we figured it unlikely that the trains would run. The trial was postponed until May."

John started to complain that the family had endured many hardships getting here, but he realized the man was looking at him and not really listening. Because he spoke in the broken English of a simple immigrant his words were not taken seriously. What did the courts care about what happened to him! They hadn't even bothered to inform him of the cancellation!

John was miserable. He had incurred many expenses in hiring lawyers, dragging the doctor away from his practice, and all the endless travel. It had been for nothing. They would have to return to Denver again in May. Now Katie was exhausted and the baby was sick and more fussy than usual. John cursed inwardly, then silently ushered the tired little group to a hotel where they would spend the night.

The next day they began the trip back to Durango, bewildered and frustrated. It was an enormous worry as to how this postponement would influence the outcome of the court trial. When they finally reached Durango on Sunday night, they were struck with yet another blow. Greeting them was a very exasperated Maestra. The story was complex, and as she tried to explain she began speaking fast and incoherently. They finally gathered that the new maid had arrived from Italy but refused to stay at the Mascot.

Katie was beside herself with distress. She knew the importance of finding help to run the boarding house, and now it seemed this attempt to bring a maid from Italy had failed. She was worn out from the long trip and wondered if things would ever settle down and be normal.

"Nusgnùr benedét, che vita! A 'mna va mai ben üna!"

Maestra tried to explain. "Tony and I were there when the girl arrived but she left with her brother, that cobbler in town."

Oh, what a story was going around in Italian circles now! It was a delicious bit of gossip about the girl who didn't want to work for the Baudinos, and it was whispered it was because they were not suitable. The bar patrons at the Sategna Saloon were adding lots of fuel and innuendos to the story. This kept things stirred up in all the Italian saloons.

It was days later that Katie finally learned the whole story. The poor girl was innocent and had no choice in the matter. Giovanna Frasca agreed to come to live in Durango because her brother lived there. It had seemed a perfect situation when Jennie hired her.

As the story unravelled, it was easy to see how a misunderstanding had occurred. Tony Frasca met his sister at the train depot as planned, but Giovanna immediately caught the eye of a young Italian man, Oreste Ferdinando. Oreste started courting her, proposing marriage immediately. Poor Giovanna was very puzzled with this new situation in a strange country where things were happening too quickly.

As was the custom of the time in Italian families, Giovanna's fate was not hers to decide. Her brother felt it would be best for her to marry and she had little to say in the matter. So, the young couple married and acquired a farm on Florida Mesa, south of Durango. Oreste worked hard to pay back the entire fare expensed by the Baudinos.

Unfortunately, Giovanna was never happy on the farm and she came into Durango whenever possible. At these times, she would visit with Katie and they became good friends. The confusion at the beginning of their relationship was forgotten.

Meanwhile, back in Silverton, Angelina worried about the Indian incident. She knew John was cautious and extremely law abiding, and she felt it was jealously that had caused this problem. Someone wanted to ruin him. What would happen if John was convicted of the crime? Would he go to jail? Would he be forced to return to Italy? She didn't want to think about the consequences, but perhaps it would be to her advantage if John and Katie had to return to Italy. But she didn't want to even think about John being in any trouble.

Angelina enjoyed the security John Baudino offered the family. He was strong, thoughtful, and provided well. She felt a pang of longing for the days when her husband had emanated that feeling of strength and had taken care of them. She had no one on whom to rely. Phil would forever do what he pleased and was worthless to her. *"L Flip a na val gnune."*

Angelina lived for the letters Jennie wrote from Italy, and she would immediately write back. She felt a bond with her eldest daughter that she didn't share with her two other children. In this relationship, there was support for her feelings. Jennie didn't mince words, however, and was open with criticism, so their association was close but often volatile. Through it all, Angelina enjoyed taking Jennie into her confidence. So, with the snows of February locking them inside, Angelina decided to write to Jennie and share the news of Silverton.

Yes, Jennie understood, so Angelina would write of the gossip, of the snow that kept the train from coming, and of the polenta they were forced to eat constantly while waiting for supplies. While doing this, Angelina transported herself mentally back to Italy, where there were people she knew. Some of these she held very dear, and there were others whom she despised and would like nothing more than to spit in their faces.

Despite the harshness of Angelina's character, she had a gentle, caring side that kept people coming to her. Some took advantage of her softer side and didn't always pay for rooms or other debts. Angelina cared for Jennie's sister-in-law when she was sick, but then Angelina was pleased to curse all the Tyrolese who could have come to help and didn't. She would forever struggle for the respect she thought she deserved, and she would also continually struggle to make a living. Life, Angelina felt, had been unkind to her. First she had to come to this barbaric country, then her husband died in a foolish accident and left her to fend for herself and raise the children. The ungrateful children didn't heed her advice or appreciate her efforts. *"E sun mac sì për sufrir."* "All I do is suffer."

The troubles stemming from the Indian problem seemed destined to hang over everything like a dark cloud. John finally traveled to Denver in May of 1909 to stand trial. With his American citizenship in jeopardy, the entire family was concerned, and his future depended on the outcome and decision of the Court. Finally, he returned to Durango with victorious news that he had been pardoned, and the Mascot Saloon was found "not guilty" of the accused crime of selling liquor to an Indian.

Everyone breathed a sigh of relief with this matter put to rest. Life could be more relaxed now, but John cursed the amount of time, effort, and money that had been spent on this accusation. He was determined to put their lives back together and make up for the time that was lost. He swore to himself as he thought of how someone had intentionally provoked this incident to smear his good name. His reputation was his greatest asset. Perhaps someone had thought the Baudinos, being simple immigrants, were easy targets. He had to be extra careful at all times so this would not happen again. *"A l'é mac tüta gelusja."* "It's common jealousy," he said to himself, "that causes people to work against each other. It's hard enough to make a living without all these unwarranted troubles!"

Life at the Mascot fell once again into a routine. The tasks were endless, and keeping things in operation caused confusion, but life was busy and comfortable. Katie worked through difficulties without much help, even though finding good maids was still the biggest dilemma. She won over Tony's respect as she worked with obstacles he couldn't take care of due to his lack of English. Katie had baby Frances as a very young toddler to care for, but she still handled the chores of the boarding house and watched over the entire business. Now she appeared to be more radiant than ever. She was pregnant once again, and no one was more pleased than her husband.

John, in his determination to be successful, worked, as he would say, *me'n mul*—like a mule. He did whatever necessary: in the saloon, at the bar, doing all the bookwork, planting a garden in the yard next to the horse stable, making wine and sausage, delivering liquor to the local mines—all the while lending money to friends he trusted.

Tony was helpful but didn't have the desire to work all the time. His easygoing ways didn't make him a determined businessman, but his personality worked well in attracting customers. John realized this and allowed Tony to work at his own speed, valuing his brother's advice and the closeness they shared.

John felt that Tony was lonely and needed a wife. Plans would be made soon to send him to Italy to rectify the situation. Good, hardworking women were crucial in running the boarding house, so if Tony couldn't decide on a wife, he could at least bring back a young female relative. John would explain this to Tony so he would understand the importance of the problem.

It was Katie who decided that it was time to take a moment out from the work and upsets that had befallen them recently. When Angelina and Phil came with young Lina from Silverton for a visit, she arranged to have them all photographed together along with

Maestra. This would be the picture they would send to all the relatives in Italy and to Calumet.

As they posed for the photographer, Katie said lightly, *"Fumje vér ch'é sen tüte 'n salüte, 'd bun emur e pin 'd vita."* "Let us all look healthy, happy and prosperous."

In February of 1910, John received a letter from the Department of Commerce and Labor. The Naturalization Service returned the old certificate, dated April 5, 1904, which had been revoked. The letter stated: "The proper officers of the Government have decided not to institute proceedings to cancel your certificate of naturalization, and you may consider the incident closed." This called for rejoicing! It pleased them all that the judicial system of the new adopted country had been fair and just.

Back row, from left to right: John Baudino, Phil Sartore, and Tony Baudino, Front row, left to right: Maestra, Lina Bonavida, Katie Baudino, and Angelina is holding baby Frances. 1909.

Department of Commerce and Labor

NATURALIZATION SERVICE

OFFICE OF CHIEF EXAMINER

ROOMS 415-416 QUINCY BUILDING

Denver, Colo.

4-17.

FILE NUMBER

Mr John Baudino,

February 3, 1910.

Durango, Colorado.

Dear Sir,

Referring to the matter of the legality of your certificate of naturalization, which question arose when this office was under the supervision
of the Department of Justice, I beg to advise you that I have been instructed by the officer now in charge of naturalization matters - the Chief of the
Division of Naturalization, Washington, D.C. - to return your certificate of
naturalization to you for such use as you may desire to make of it. The proper officers of the Government have decided not to institute proceedings to
cancel your certificate of naturalization, and you may consider the incident
closed.

The certificate of naturalization surrendered by you for cancellation
is described below as an enclosure, and it is respectfully requested that
you acknowledge receipt of this letter, using for that purpose the enclosed
penalty envelope requiring no postage.

Yours truly,

Theo F. Schmoecker

Chief Naturalization Examiner.

Enclosure: Certificate of naturalization (minor) issued to John Baudino
by the County Court for La Plata County, Colorado, April 5, 1904.

CHAPTER XV

Italy

On April 28, 1910, Katie gave birth to her second child, a baby boy, and they named him Luigi, or Louis, after her father. A few days after this blessed event, the Bonavida family returned from Italy. There was much to celebrate when Jennie and Louis stopped in Durango for a short visit before boarding the train that would take them home to Silverton.

The Bonavidas had been in Italy for over a year and it was a treat for everyone to see how much the two little ones, Anna and Emilio, had grown. Anna had just turned six and Emil was almost four. The children tried to play with two-year-old Frances, but she hid from them in her shyness.

Katie remained bedridden after giving birth to Louis, because the doctor had ordered the customary twelve days of bed rest. John hesitated to let her get up early; he didn't want a repetition of the fever and sickness that had caused him to fret when baby Frances was born. He was more than pleased to have a baby boy, but most of all he wanted his wife healthy, with no chance of losing her due to the dangers involved with childbirth.

Katie argued, "I feel wonderful, and I want to hear about my sister's trip. *E vöj nin perdme gnente.* I don't want to miss all the excitement." Because she had been in bed for almost eleven days, John relented, and Katie bounded out of bed. She felt a little weak, but she dressed hurriedly, asking John to help tie up her corset. He swore under his breath when she wanted the ribbed garment with its set of stays tightened more and more. He argued that she didn't need to wear a corset to greet her sister's family, but she insisted. She always wore a corset, even under her working dresses.

Katie smiled radiantly as she greeted her sister and Bonavida. She was especially happy when little Anna and Emil ran to her with arms open wide, offering many hugs for their Aunt Katie. There were sounds of joy when she introduced everyone to the newest member of the family, the tiny bundle, baby Louis. Two-year-old Frances hid behind her mother's long skirts, wanting attention but too timid and confused to come forward.

When it was time for the Bonavidas to bring out the gifts they had brought from Italy, the room began to vibrate with anticipation. Sentiment stirred in all of them as the presents from the Baudino family in Italy were passed around. Domenica's husband, Michele Naretto, was a saddle maker, and he had created a fancy harness with bells for Tony's horse. The leather was soft and the bells were made of gleaming brass—a delight for all to see. The children's faces lit up with excitement as Tony shook the bells, making them ring with lovely musical sounds.

"Che bele ch'a sen!" "These are wonderful! When I parade down the streets of Durango with my horse and buggy, heads will turn!" Tony declared with a happy smile.

There were gifts of suits made of the finest Italian wool and beautiful pieces of wool cloth. Special salami and a variety of Italian treats were included, which were set out and passed around. Expressions of gratitude resounded from the happy group as they admired these precious gifts from loved ones across the ocean.

It might have seemed as if the struggles of life were fleeting at moments such as this. Being together as a family and sharing ties with relatives many miles away was an exceptional treasure, and it stirred a yearning in all of them. It also prompted thoughts and plans for more trips to Italy.

"Prima cosa, Tone a dev 'ndar a truvase na fumna!" "First, Tony must go and find a wife!" John proclaimed this emphatically, and everyone cheered in this moment of joviality. Voices began to badger Tony, and his face flushed as he tried to shrug off the gibes and jokes. In understanding, John quickly changed the subject, bringing the topic back to a more serious matter. "After Tony's trip, it will be time for me to take my family to meet all the Baudino relatives in Italy." And, lifting a glass of wine, he offered a toast to many more safe and happy trips to Italy. *"Salute!"*

Early the next day, everyone crossed the street from the Mascot Saloon to Durango's depot to wave good-bye to the Bonavida family. As they boarded the little narrow gauge train to return to Silverton, Angelina and a disgruntled Lina were waiting for them. Young Lina only wanted to cling to her grandmother after being left behind by her parents and siblings. She felt rejected and unloved by her parents. Now it was very unsettling to young Lina that Nonna Angelina talked often of returning to Italy.

Lina was resentful of any news concerning Italy. She remained fearful that she would once again be left behind, this time by her beloved grandmother. Angelina talked often about her sister, Margherita Boggio, who now lived in the Old Country once again. Angelina could hardly wait to talk to Jennie and hear news about Margherita. She explained happily to Lina that Margherita's husband and daughter, Maudie, would be coming soon to live in Durango. It seemed that Boggio was dissatisfied once again and he had decided to return to America to try to find another type of work in Durango among his many relatives. Margherita was suffering with health problems, so, for the moment, she and her youngest daughter, Katy, would remain in Italy. Angelina thought it a good idea that Margherita and Katy move into her house in Pasquaro because it would otherwise stand empty.

When Boggio and his daughter, Maudie, arrived in America, they stopped briefly in Durango to reacquaint themselves with the family before going on to Silverton to spend time with Angelina. Maudie was a young woman now, and she and Katie were thrilled to see each other again. Katie urged Maudie to return to Durango as soon as possible, convincing her to work at the boarding house.

When Maudie started working at the Mascot, Katie's life changed. Maudie was hard working and competent, yet full of fun and merriment. She was a delight to have around and was soon adored by everyone. Katie and Maudie would laugh together as they worked, lightening the drudgery. Maudie had a simple song that she loved to sing while she worked, and Katie would join in until they were roaring with laughter.

The words of the song meant nothing to them and had no significance. They simply liked the melody and the tune was similar to an old Italian song, sounding much like the American song, "No Place Like Home."

> *I'm a poor little beggar girl, my mother she is dead.*
> *My father is a drunkard and he won't give me no bread.*
> *I sit by my window to hear the angels play,*
> *And God bless my mother for she is far away."*

In reality, this song mirrored the feelings of the Women's Christian Temperance Union and clearly sent a message that alcohol was damaging to the family unit. There were many such songs circulating that were concerned with the dangers of "likker." Even with Prohibition looming before them, the two women did not see a connection, because to their way of thinking alcohol posed no danger. For them, this was a simple little song to sing as they worked.

Maudie was adorable in looks and personality, and it wasn't long before she caught the eye of many young Italian men in town. She quickly became engaged to a young man, named Louis Marchetti. She suddenly decided to end that relationship in favor of an engagement to John Bonaventura, the brother of Dominic, the bartender at the Mascot Saloon.

"I don't know what to do, because I care for John (Bonaventura) very much," Maudie was saying to Katie one day as they changed beds for the boarders, "but I'm a little confused and need some advice."

Katie was charmed that Maudie would ask for her opinion. It was obvious that her cousin was suffering with a dilemma that many women would cherish: Maudie had too many suitors from whom to choose.

"I watch you with your husband, and I want a relationship in my marriage like you have with your John," Maudie said to Katie in serious tones. Katie raised her eyebrows but said nothing.

Maudie then continued, stating that she recognized John as dependable and stable. But finally she blurted out, "Why is it that the heart seldom follows where the mind leads? I love John, but we are like close friends." Then she confided, "I can't help it, Katie. I'm drawn to his brother, Dominic, and he seems to care for me as well. Do you think I'm acting foolishly by letting my heart rule my head? John would give me a secure future, while Dominic is thirteen years older than I am, and—as we all know—he has a passion for gambling. I would be throwing all caution to the wind if I married Dominic. But he's handsome and mature, and when he's around, I feel my skin tingle and butterflies flutter in my stomach."

Katie took Maudie's arm and motioned for her to sit on the yet - unmade bed. Sitting next to her, Katie raised her hand in silent reply and then softly spoke with her advice on the subject of love.

"I love my husband, Maudie. I have learned to love him because he is a good and caring man. But I once had a special love, and if I could, I would go where my heart is."

"What happened to him?" Maudie asked, her eyes wide, wondering what Katie would say.

Not wanting to open any more doors of accusation against her family, Katie looked down saying, "He was killed in a mining accident."

Maudie reached to take Katie's hands and they sat there in silence for several moments. Finally Katie shed the façade, feeling the need to tell the story that was locked away in her heart. As tears flooded her face, she told Maudie about Peter Dalla. She radiated a glow of love as she described him, explaining how his jovial manner had tugged at her heart.

As the story untangled around them, the truth surfaced, and Katie admitted with biting anger that her sister, Jennie, had filled their mother's mind with false accusations, that ultimately led to dynamite being placed on the building where Peter slept. The combination of grief and rage made her voice tremble and some words were hardly more than a whisper as Katie expressed how shattered she was, suffering with the loss of Peter.

"But I finally accepted my life," Katie said with conviction. "Maybe it's the weakness of my memory that allows me to feel less pain, or maybe it's because John has given me the faith to move on."

Maudie again took Katie's hands in hers and they cried together, leaving them both feeling empty and drained. Maudie looked up at last, her eyes swimming with tears. She held tightly to Katie's hands and admitted that she loved Dominic Bonaventura.

The mood of the room changed to that of jubilation as the two women hugged and chatted about Maudie's need to make a decision. "It isn't easy to deny and ignore what you're feeling," Katie said, adding, "I know what it's like to have your heartstrings pulled. You'll make the right choice."

Maudie opened up and babbled absently about the roguishly handsome bartender while Katie smiled, basking in the glow of love from Maudie's radiant face. As the two women continued with their chores, Maudie became more and more convinced that love should be the deciding factor, but she would try to be practical and think rationally before making up her mind.

For a time, Maudie's romantic dilemma was the talk of the patrons at the Mascot Saloon. Everyone wondered which suitor would be her choice for a husband, and they all had an opinion on the subject.

The Baudinos were concerned for Maudie's future, of course, but it was a greater worry that after marriage, she would discontinue her work at the boarding house. With rooms to house twenty people, the

*Inside the Mascot Saloon at 552 Main in Durango in 1912.
The bartender is Dominic Bonaventura.*

boarding house brought in a steady income. They were almost always full, and now they planned an addition: More rooms would be added to the rear of the Mascot. It was a great asset having Maudie there because Katie more than had her hands full. Along with the cooking and cleaning, there were little Frances and baby Louis to care for.

Tony spilled over with excitement one day as he was anxious to share his news. He had learned about a proposed new railroad system that would bring jobs and prosperity to Durango. It was a sluggish economy in 1912 and the smelter was closed. It had been processing ore from the mines for twenty-five years and now things were slowing down. A new railway would help return prosperity to Durango. It would be a wider gauge system, running from Durango southwest into Arizona, with the rails placed on top of existing narrow gauge tracks. The coal mines would have to work steadily to fuel these new trains, and Tony believed that the railroad would bring great benefits to Durango. But the project was ultimately rejected by the railroad companies because it was too costly.

From left to right, upstairs: Louis, Frances, Maudie, Katie, and Angelina. Downstairs, left to right: unknown, Frank Beltramo, Tony Baudino, John Necchi, John Baudino, and Frank Zellitti, circa 1912.

The other disappointment was that their brother, Carlo Baudino, had decided to remain in Italy. They had hoped he would join them in America, but Carlo had secured a good job as manager of a lime quarry *(cava calcarea)* in Rivara, a four or five mile walk from Rivarolo. Carlo understood his brothers' disappointment with his decision, but he promised to look after their Italian bank accounts, because they continued to send money to Italy.

It was with John's insistence that Tony finally set off to Italy in early 1913. The main priority of his trip was to find a woman to help in the boarding house. John's words were, "Without women to do the work, we will have nothing. Tony was instructed to either bring back a wife or one of the young relatives to help in the boarding house.

The trip was also a mission to attempt to collect payments from relatives of those to whom they had loaned money. This was an era when a person's good name and a handshake was all that was needed to close a loan or any deal. The strength of a man was in his word, and his standing in the community depended on this. Even far away in Italy, they would want to protect the family name if a loan hadn't been paid.

When Tony finally arrived in Italy and was greeted by his brother, Carlo, he was surprised to hear that "Neto" had already alerted the family about Tony's quest in finding a suitable wife. Carlo laughed, telling him, in good-natured jest, that their own sisters, Camilla and Domenica, were busy lining up many worthwhile candidates from which Tony could choose.

Tony failed to see any humor in this situation. He wanted a companion with whom to share his life, and he considered this to be a serious matter. How would he be able to choose correctly and not offend his sisters or the women they were consulting?

As he entered Domenica's home, where everyone was waiting to greet him, he was besieged with questions about what he wanted in a woman. Both Domenica and Camilla were certain they had the perfect woman for him. Tony sat down with a groan, explaining he was tired from the long trip and needed to rest for a few days. He didn't feel good about this and was worried about being matched up with women of his sisters' choosing.

It was Camilla who somehow won the toss to choose whom Tony would meet first, and he was sent off down the road to nearby neighbors. The parents of the young woman were thrilled to meet him, welcoming him into their home and introducing him to their very shy daughter. After several days of "courting" visits, Tony realized that they would never have a close relationship. The parents were anxious to have their daughter married to "a rich and successful American," but the girl really only wanted to remain in Italy. She and Tony had no chemistry, and it was painful for him to be in her presence. Camilla kept repeating, *"E 't vesrè che pö a 'ndrà mei, Tone."* "This will improve in time, Tony." But he could see no future with this first contestant.

Now Domenica was thrilled to have her chance, telling Tony that this next prospect would be perfect for him. Realizing that her brother was over forty years old, she hadn't chosen a young girl of twenty, but a robust and merry widow who was anxious to have a suitor. This woman almost frightened Tony, and he was shocked at her aggressive ways and forward attitude. After one visit he was determined to cross her off his list.

Tony was discouraged, and the letter in his hand from his brother didn't make him feel any better. John wanted to know if he had found a woman. How thoughtless of everyone to think they could arrange his life like this! He felt like a pawn in a chess game. He decided right then and there that he would remain single if he chose to do so. He would not marry someone just to please his family!

Before he returned to give an account of his findings to his sisters, he decided to stop at the home of their cousin, Francesco Grivetto. Francesco had left a message for Tony with questions about his own plans to emigrate to America. Pausing at the front door of the Grivetto house, Tony looked around at this familiar place. As he knocked and waited, he found it pleasant to remember happy times from his childhood spent in these surroundings. When the door opened, Tony stood staring at an attractive young woman he didn't recognize.

"Oh, Tony! It's you!" her voice sang with recognition. "I heard you were here. Oh, how wonderful to see you. *Intra, intra.* Come in!"

Tony had to search his memory to put this lovely person into context. She had been only a little girl when he left Italy, and now she was grown up and beautiful. *"E sun Maria."* she said, reminding him of how he used to taunt her when they were both much younger. Remembering her as a scrawny little kid, Tony began to tease her once again. They were soon both doubled over with laughter relating stories of days growing up together.

Maria convinced Tony that he should stay for dinner so he could visit with her brother, Francesco. Tony didn't argue. He was tired of the pressure put on him by his family to find a wife. He would find excuses to tell them later, but for now he wanted to relax in the charming environment created by his cousin, Maria.

At dinner, Francesco and Tony discussed his desire to emigrate and the possibility of traveling to America together in a few months' time. Maria listened attentively, expressing her sorrow that she couldn't go with them. She lamented with envy that men could go anywhere, but a single woman wasn't allowed that choice. Tony had thoughts of telling Maria that she could go along and work as a maid at the boarding house, but something in the back of his mind decided not to give her that option. At that moment, he realized he had feelings for Maria. She was everything he wanted in a woman, but he needed some time to sort through these thoughts and emotions.

Domenica was disappointed that her brother wasn't going to give the widow another chance, but she had a list of others from which he could choose. Tony decided to confide in his sister and ask her what she thought about marriage to a first cousin. *"A j'é gnente 'd mal,"* "It isn't wrong," Domenica shrugged. "It happens all the time."

Tony then asked her to keep this a secret, because he wanted time to court Maria and see what would develop. Domenica gave her brother a kiss on the cheek, wanting more than anything to see him happily married. It added much to his decision to have his sister warmly approve of Maria Grivetto as his choice for a bride.

Tony and Maria were married in Italy in 1913 with the extended Italian relations gathered together for the celebration. Maria was every bit as happy as her new husband as she packed her trunks for the trip to America. She and Tony shared a feeling of closeness, and she smiled thinking of her future with this man that she had always loved.

Tony Baudino and his wife, Maria Grivetto, in 1913.

They sailed to America, leaving her brother Francesco behind in New York City, where he wanted to seek his own fortune. Next, it was on to Colorado to greet their new life and the relatives waiting there.

John Baudino was pleased that Tony had married their cousin, and even happier that Maria would be able to lend a helping hand at the boarding house. Now he would be able to plan his own trip to Italy.

John was anxious to take his family to the Old Country before Frances turned six and required a full-fare ticket. But he felt uneasy with this decision, knowing that this was not the ideal time for them to leave. The work at the boarding house was not yet familiar to Maria, because she had been in America only a few months. Neither Maria nor Tony spoke English, and yet they would have to run the business. Much of the burden would fall on Maudie, because she spoke both English and Italian.

Maudie assured John that she would not run off and marry, leaving the business without her supervision. He felt comforted by this, knowing that she was competent and dependable. But he realized that Maudie was only one person and couldn't be expected to do everything.

In February of 1914, heavily burdened with worries about the business, John and Katie set out on the trip with their two young children. They boarded the train that would take them across the United States, where they would embark on a voyage by steamship to Europe.

The trip to Italy turned out to be a wonderful reprieve for both John and Katie. Their courtship and marriage had been full of serious decisions and hard work. Now they relaxed and watched with delight as their children entertained everyone on board the ship. It was a constant request by other passengers that the little tykes sing American songs, such as "Yankee Doodle" and "My Darling Clementine." These were proud moments for Katie and John.

Both the parents and children were overjoyed when "Jello" was introduced and served on the ship. This was a new treat for all of them! John and Katie enjoyed quiet moments in the peaceful journey across the ocean. They could talk about the future and share thoughts and dreams. Through all of this, they continued to develop a feeling of togetherness, but there remained a void that kept them from being more affectionately intertwined.

Upon arrival in Italy, they were met by John's brother, Carlo, and taken to the Sartore house in Pasquaro where they would stay. Margherita and Katy Boggio were now living in the house and, after happy greetings with the Boggios, they spent some time settling into the new surroundings. Carlo later came for them to make the short walk to greet the rest of the family in Rivarolo Canavese.

"Gni sì, masnè." "Come here, children," Carlo spoke gently to Frances and Louis in the Italian dialect that was familiar to the American youngsters. Taking their hands, Carlo walked with them, pointing out many things on the way. Soon he motioned ahead to a house where an excited group of children was standing by the fence, anxiously waiting. John and Katie joined Carlo in laughter as the littlest one, Teresina, saw them coming first and shouted, *"A sen rivà! A*

sen sì!" "Look! They are here!" This alerted the others, who came running to meet their American cousins.

Carlo thought this to be a magical moment, when he introduced the American children of his brother to the Italian children of his sister. Frances and Louis were shy at first as they met the young Narettos, the offspring of John's sister, Domenica. Francesca, Alessina, and Teresina politely said their greetings to the adults and then ran off to play with their American cousins, who were no longer strangers.

John was anxious to see his sister's two older boys. Giuseppe and Giovanni had been young children when John first left Italy, but now they were teenagers. It warmed his heart to see that they remembered him from the days when he carried them around on his back. Both young men expressed the desire to emigrate to America and talked excitedly, asking many questions. But for now it was their turn to chase and tease the younger children. The boys delighted in swinging their young American cousins around and giving them rides on their backs. It was a pleasant and happy time for all the family to see the children playing together.

It also pleased everyone to be with Margherita and Katy again. It was a special time for Katie to become close to her younger cousin, and they spent many hours together, either exchanging recipes as they cooked or playing with Frances and Louis.

From left to right: Teresina Naretto, Frances Baudino, Alessina Naretto, Louis Baudino, and Francesca Naretto, in 1914.

There were some differences in Italian customs and ways of life, so the American children were mesmerized by the "forno." This was a large public cooking oven in Pasquaro. It had a front opening and a wide stone surface with a domed vault as its covering. Its fire was fed by bundles of twigs and was used by people from the area to bake bread and for other special baking purposes.

Katy Boggio with Frances and Louis in 1914.

They also enjoyed walking the pathways between Rivarolo and Pasquaro and watching people stop to pray at a *pilone*. This was a statue or a sacred picture placed along the road in a charming, restful surrounding, inviting a pause in the journey to offer prayers.

Rivarolo boasted two castles, and this conjured up wonderful fantasies for the American children. Noticing the spires silhouetted on the horizon, they begged to visit the castles and to inspect them closely.

The first *castellazzo* was mostly in ruins, but it had been the residence of the counts of Valperga, who ruled and oppressed the village for many a century. All that was left of the beautiful castle was a tall round tower. Built in medieval times, it at one time had a *bastiun*, or a fortified town or city, attached to it.

The second one, Castello Malgra, was the larger of the two castles and was built in the fourteenth century. It was the ancient mansion of the Counts of St. Martino. Its massive walls and large, round tower were once used as a military fortress. These castles were a nostalgic elegy of past times and reminders of Italy's centuries under the feudal system.

There were more exciting adventures ahead for the children as they were introduced to many of Italy's special traditions. At the end of

September, all the members of the family were called upon for the grape harvest. It was of great joy to the children that they were included in this event. Their care was entrusted to the women, so Camilla and Domenica, along with other female members of the family, patiently showed Frances and Louis how to carefully pick the grapes. Thus, while the work was being done, the children were gaily entertained by these "thin, black-dressed figures" that were the Italian women. When all the grapes were picked and loaded into a big tub, the children were allowed to ride in the horse-drawn cart alongside the tub of grapes. These were never-to-be forgotten memories.

Castello Malgra in Rivarolo Canavese, Italy, circa 1969.

News from Durango was never good and marred the essence of the visit, especially for John. Hearing that Maria was pregnant was good news, but knowing the boarding house work would be difficult for her caused concern. Maria also sent news that Angelina was sick and had come to the Mascot to recover. It appeared that she had suffered a small stroke. John knew that whenever Angelina needed a doctor's care, she came to Durango, and the bill would remain there for him to pay. He accepted this responsibility as if she were his own mother. He would take care of all of them, if necessary. They were family.

A greater worry befell him when it was learned that Maudie was also sick and had to be hospitalized. John wondered if the business would fall apart without her there to watch over things.

As weeks went by, serious problems continued, causing John to persist in his worrying about the business and conditions at home.

Tony wrote that Maria was suffering with her pregnancy, that he couldn't handle things alone, and customers had to be turned away. Tony hired Dominic to work full-time at the bar so he could keep up with the other tasks of the business.

Finally, they received the good news that Maudie was back at work, feeling better, and that the boarding house was doing well. It was also mentioned that Maudie and Dominic had announced their engagement.

This was indeed happy news! However, the excitement surrounding the impending wedding was overshadowed by a feeling of loss. It meant that Maudie and Dominic would eventually leave their positions at the Mascot.

Maudie Boggio and Dominic Bonaventura, circa 1915.

The news from Durango continued to worry John, and he could hardly enjoy his stay in Italy. He was too far away from the business he had struggled to build. It seemed that serious problems were surfacing and he was concerned about financial matters.

He read newspapers from back home, where the talk about the possibility of closing saloons in the United States had grown to be the main subject. Headlines marked it as a serious political issue in the United States. Both the Anti-Saloon League and the Women's Christian Temperance Union were gaining strength and were working to make it illegal to sell alcoholic beverages. The term being applied to this was "Prohibition."

John was disheartened by this news and about the state of the family and business in general. He paced, complaining that life wasn't fair! Katie scolded him, trying to shake him out of his depression. She pointed out that he was preoccupied with gloomy thoughts and worries and was ignoring his Italian relatives. His obsession with matters at home was ruining the visit for everyone.

"A 'm despiàs," "I'm sorry," he sighed after one such confrontation with his wife, "but what if we have to close up the business and go into debt? *Que che faran?* What will we do?"

She tried to counter his negative thoughts, saying, "We'll do whatever we have to do and start over. You can't be so hard on everyone, just because you're worried. *E 't vesrè ch'a l'é nin parèj brut me ch'a smia.* Things probably aren't as bad as they seem. We'll handle it when we get home."

He shook his head and tried to snap out of his gloom, but he couldn't shake the feeling that all he had worked for might be lost. It wasn't in his nature to be complacent about a future where he might end up losing everything. His thoughts were centered on the problems in Durango, and this caused him to feel very anxious.

Through all this, Katie was warm and gracious to her in-laws, winning the love and respect of John's family. They would all cherish the closeness gained from this visit and, from that time forward, Katie became the corresponding link between John's family in Italy and the family in America.

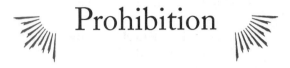

CHAPTER XVI

Prohibition

The news from Durango continued to get worse, and John's frustration increased after reading each letter. He knew that none of the difficulties would be insurmountable, if only he was there to deal with them.

It was good news that Maria had given birth to a baby girl; however, the child was born weak and sickly, and Maria was losing strength, unable to leave her bed. Things were tumbling into chaos at the Mascot, and boarders once again had to be turned away. Everyone sighed with relief when Jennie agreed to come from Silverton to assist Maudie in taking over Maria's work at the boarding house.

Jennie's two daughters, Anna and Lina, now age ten and twelve, accompanied their mother, and this brought lively energy to the downcast residents at the Mascot. With bouncing curls and sunny dispositions, these two young girls helped create a cheerful mood. Young Lina helped her mother in the kitchen and Anna took on the job of watching over Maria's new baby girl. Sweet, young Anna gave the cranky, fussy infant much attention, allowing the despondent Maria a restful break.

Just when things seemed to be improving, the baby's health worsened. Maria and Tony were in a chaotic state of misery when the baby stopped breathing and died. The death was a terrible shock to young Anna and she ran off wondering if she was somehow to blame. Maudie followed her and, finding Anna huddled in a corner crying, she hugged the sobbing young girl. Maudie explained that it was Anna's loving care that had helped keep the baby going. "Now God has called baby Francesca home, and we must resign ourselves to this." Together, they held on to each other and shed tears for the tiny infant who lived on earth for a very short time. Once again a shroud of sadness hung over those living at the Mascot, and the sorrow in Durango traveled by letter to Italy.

As if things weren't already bad enough on the personal side of life for the Baudinos, there were also the business worries centered on Prohibition and the likelihood of the saloon closing. It seemed impossible that things could get any worse, but next would come a blow that would shake the world. The news of the assassination of Archduke

Francis Ferdinand, heir to the throne of Austria-Hungary, and his wife at Sarajevo, Bosnia, sparked many European countries, including Italy, to anger. It was 1914, and the World War I had been set into motion in Europe.

Now John and his family needed to leave Italy earlier than planned, but would they be allowed to go on a ship other than the one on which they were scheduled? It was inevitable that Italy would soon enter the war, so they needed to leave before it took on momentum. They prepared to depart immediately.

There was fear and turmoil when John was detained in Naples and told that he was liable to military service in the Italian army. John argued that he was now an American citizen, but they continued to detain him.

John and Katie found that it wasn't possible to change the traveling dates of their tickets, because people were clamoring to leave Italy, and all the ships were packed full of extra passengers. John realized that they must return to the United States as soon as possible or the family would be trapped in Italy in the middle of war, and he would be inducted into the Italian military. He made a quick decision, attaching all of them to another Italian family. Together, they boarded a ship that was less than desirable, with very cramped quarters.

The trip home to America was a nightmare, and four-year-old Louis didn't understand any of it. He complained constantly of having to share everything with the horrible people. His mother kept telling him that, yes, their companions were crude and obnoxious and the ship was dirty and crowded, but in these difficult circumstances they had to endure. They all wanted to get home safely, and this was the only way.

Meanwhile, back in Durango, the war in Europe was being discussed in every saloon circle, but it failed to overshadow the argument over Prohibition. Tony cursed the position he was in during his brother's absence.

The Prohibition movement in the United States began in the early 1800s. Some of the points in favor of Prohibition were strongly supported by women: They had gained equal voting status and were especially powerful in the western states. Prohibitionists pointed out that there were four main reasons that Congress should pass this law against the distribution of alcohol: medical, economic, political, and social.

It was cited that alcohol damaged health, as many American men suffered from cirrhosis of the liver. Husbands died young, leaving families without fathers, which led to financial problems.

Economically, many laborers got drunk often and couldn't perform the job properly. The absence from work each week was high due to alcoholism.

Politically, it was pointed out that buying beer meant that money was lost to Germany, because most of the brewers and distillers were located there, or owned by German companies.

The social influence was agreed to be the most important. Husbands were spending their families' savings stupidly on alcohol. This led to family arguments, to divorce, and to the overall decline of the family.

There were also those who pointed out the other side, extoling the value of the saloon, and saying the saloon keeper was the only one who kept an open house. It was his business to entertain: The saloon was the common meeting ground of neighbors and made social life possible. What could replace this adequate form of social expression if saloons were not allowed to function?

It was deemed a miracle to John and Katie that they finally arrived home a few days before Christmas in 1914. John had escaped the war in Europe, but now he had to face his brother. He had built up a feeling of rage so great that it would equal any type of warfare. He was extremely angry that Tony had not been able to handle the business problems and had spent their entire savings hiring extra help to keep it in operation.

Tony didn't appreciate having to listen to John express his wrath and disappointment. He felt justified for all he had done in order to handle the difficulties that had beset him. The one problem that John couldn't overlook was the fact that his brother had been doing a lot of drinking in his absence. Tony defended his actions, trying to explain the pain inflicted when their baby girl was taken from them.

"It's all easy for you to say," Tony spat out angrily. "You haven't lost someone through death. My heart is always heavy now, and it's the same for my wife. You weren't here to see the precious baby that was taken from us. *E 't capise nin.* You don't understand."

John didn't want to hear excuses—he only wanted to discuss the damage that was done to the business.

Katie sought to soothe the disagreement between the brothers as she concentrated on giving the children an American-style Christmas. She tried to involve everyone in the preparations necessary to create the holiday, to decorate and celebrate with customs that were still new to them.

Katie asked Tony to go a few blocks down the street where they were selling evergreen trees for Christmas. Tony lifted his hands in disgust. "Send John. He would only find fault with any tree I choose. *Secund chiel mi e su bun a far gnente.* To him I am worthless in all my efforts."

It was left up to Katie to approach her husband and reprimand him for his angry mood and animosity toward everyone.

"Now you are going to ruin the Christmas holiday for all of us," Katie lectured. "For the sake of the children, please put your disputes with your brother aside and help me with preparations. *Fuma pas 'n famija.* Let us have peace within the family."

After his wife's admonishment, John took a deep breath and walked down the street to find a suitable tree for the family to decorate. Later, when the children were asleep, Tony and Maria helped John and Katie string popcorn and hang candy canes and paper ornaments on the tree. They were guided in inspiration by a magazine displaying beautiful decorations on a traditional American Christmas tree. Faces lit up when the work was finished, and the tension was finally broken when they all stood back to admire the beautifully adorned evergreen. Before they retired for the evening, they joined congenially over a glass of wine, sharing a toast for peace and happiness. *"Salute!"*

These efforts were rewarded the next morning when Louis and Frances awoke to the surprise of a fantasy Christmas, with stockings filled and gifts under the tree. There were squeals of excitement from the children and the four adults smiled with the warmth of compatibility. They sat with the children, admiring the toys and gifts in the enjoyment of this newly adopted tradition.

When the holidays were over, it was time for Frances to start school. She had missed the beginning of the first grade because she turned six while in Italy. Now, in January, Katie began preparing her for her first day of school, and when the young girl expressed the desire to stay at home, her mother chided her. "All the little children your age go to school. *Varda la Anna e la Lina.* Just look at Anna and Lina. They go to school and are the smartest ones." This was not a good ploy, because Frances hated being compared to her cousins.

Frances didn't want to listen to more of what her mother was saying about school, and she was horrified when a package arrived from Silverton. "Look here, Frances, your Aunt Jennie made you a new dress to wear on your first day of school." Katie's face beamed as she pulled the garment from the box, but the young girl instantly felt the dress was "hideous!"

Frances stood sullen, not speaking, while her mother insisted she put on the new outfit for inspection. The dress was a dull yellow in color, and Frances thought it made her skin look sickly. In her mind, she envisioned that Aunt Jennie had done this on purpose. Favoring her own girls, she wanted to make Frances look inferior.

The dress was covered in ruffles, and not at all in the style or length that Frances had seen young girls wearing when she accompanied her mama on shopping trips. The fashion of the day for young girls was pleated skirts worn to the knee. Straight lines were in style, not ruffles. Frances longed to wear fashionable clothing and hated the way her family always looked out of place from others in public. She was embarrassed when they spoke to each other in a foreign language and ashamed that they were Italian. How could she explain this to her mother?

With only a couple of days to go until the first day of school, Frances struggled to find the words to explain to her mama that she needed different clothing. She sought out Maudie, whom she adored, thinking perhaps she would understand and help clarify things to her mother.

Maudie flashed a happy smile when she saw young Frances and reached down to touch her head in a loving gesture. She stopped suddenly and, gazing carefully at the top of the little girl's head, ran her fingers around her curls for careful inspection.

"Oh, no! My sweet little girl has head lice! We need to find your mama!"

Katie reacted immediately when Maudie pointed out the problem. With not even a moment to think or discuss this with her young daughter, Katie solved the condition the only way she knew would work. She shaved Frances' head!

Frances gasped when she realized what had happened. Now they wouldn't make her go to school, would they? She couldn't go looking like this!

She heard the adults discussing the fact that the head lice probably came from the journey on that horrible steamship. But they tossed the problem aside, saying she was just a little girl and wouldn't be bothered by this. Their only concern was that she was late in starting school, and they felt there was no way they could keep her back any longer. The other children were now half a year ahead of Frances in their studies.

Frances ran off to be alone and sobbed, tears running down her cheeks. She cried about the ugly dress and reached up with her hands to feel her shaved head. This was appalling, and she knew she would suffer terrible humiliation at school because of the dreadful way she looked. She cried as if her heart would break, feeling sorry for herself because she had backward immigrant parents who didn't understand.

The first day of school was a nightmare. The children pointed and laughed the moment Katie dragged Frances into the classroom. It was bad enough that all the other children had already made friends and were accustomed to the school environment, but to start out with a shaved head, wearing a very ugly dress, was a damaging, shameful blow.

Frances wanted to disappear into the woodwork when her mother left her to face the circumstances alone. The teacher smiled warmly, then matter-of-factly handed Frances her books and showed her the desk she would occupy. All the while, Frances could see the taunting eyes of the other students and feel their snide, teasing looks. She hated school! This was her introduction to life at Park Elementary in January of 1915.

On a daily basis, Frances threw tantrums and refused to go to school. Constantly scolded for these actions by her parents, they struggled with this alarming state of affairs. How could she learn if she didn't attend school? To make matters even worse she was rating poorly in her schoolwork. Katie was upset that her daughter was having such a difficult time, and in an attempt to repair the problem, she crocheted little caps for Frances to wear. Both parents were convinced she would achieve better marks once she settled in and felt accepted by the other students.

Frances was certain that day would never come. She went off by herself at recess or hid around the corner of the school to avoid the devastating jeers and teasing of the other children.

"Her shyness makes her more of a target," the teacher tried to explain to Katie. "If she would just join in with the others, they would finally accept her."

Katie tried reasoning with her daughter, attempting to resolve the problem. Katie was distressed and began to worry that Frances might not be bright enough to fare well in school.

The caring teacher finally detected that Frances had poor vision, so John took his daughter by the hand to have her fitted for glasses. Everyone was hopeful that this would bring the crisis to an end.

Frances came home smiling, wearing her new glasses. She could now see better than she ever had before. But after one quick glance in the mirror, she didn't want to wear the glasses ever again. Now she could see her appearance and how terrible the huge, thick glasses looked on her small, six-year-old face. She also had a better view of the stubble growing on her head. She ran off to be alone and once again cried inconsolably.

Because Frances would not shrug off the taunts and join in with her classmates, the situation at school didn't improve. Frances was continuously called Baldy, Four Eyes, and other wretched names. Progress was made, however, with her studies, due to better vision provided by the glasses. Soon her test results were outstanding and she became the top student in her class. In the eyes of this timid young girl, it was clear that the only way she would earn acceptance was to make high scores. She continued to go off alone and never allowed herself to be comfortable with the other children. This situation so distressed her that she found it painful to attend social activities throughout her life.

On April 15, 1915, Maudie married Dominic Bonaventura in a joyous celebration. Everyone was happy, as both Maudie and Dominic agreed to continue their jobs at the Mascot. A special room was set up for them, and they would live at the boarding house near the family quarters.

In due time, however, Dominic had it in mind to open a grocery store next door to the Mascot, and he was working on this with his friend, John Zellitti, who agreed to be the butcher. They planned to call the store the European Market.

Dominic saw clearly that he would soon be forced to find other employment because, by the end of 1915, Colorado law stated that all establishments serving alcohol would be closed. The sale or transportation of liquor would be prohibited by passage of the Eighteenth Amendment.

Wyoming, Utah, Colorado, and Idaho were the only states putting this law into effect early, adopting the Eighteenth Amendment to the Constitution of the United States as early as 1915. It would be 1920 before the law was ratified and accepted by all states and Prohibition put into effect throughout the country.

The stress created by the coming of Prohibition was taking its toll, and John was especially disturbed. In preparation for the closing of the saloon, a family meeting was held at the Mascot.

After venting resentment and some unhappy opinions, it was obvious that Tony and Maria wanted nothing to do with any part of what would be left of the business. Maria made it quite clear that she hated the boarding house work. After discussing all the options, it was decided that John and Katie would continue to keep boarders and try to operate the saloon as a deli and soda shop. They would pay rent to Tony and Maria for half of the business and Tony would try to find another job.

With Prohibition in effect, one of the first things that needed to be done was the removal of the sign on the front of the building. Begrudging the events that were causing this enormous change, John and Tony set ladders on the balcony and painted over the letters they had so boldly and proudly placed there only eight years ago. They both felt the loss as the words SALONE ITALIANO disappeared from the building.

The new year of 1916 started off with a call of distress from Silverton. Jennie was upset, saying that her husband was seriously ill. Katie received Jennie's phone call with trepidation, noting the worried tone of her sister's voice. Jennie's cause for alarm came after Bonavida required surgery for gallstones and liver problems. During the operation his heart weakened, and doctors stopped the surgery before it was completed. Now he had taken a turn for the worse.

"*Preocupte nin, e pijan 'l treno apeine che polan.*" "Don't worry! We will come by train as soon as we can," Katie calmly told Jennie. Hanging up the phone she muttered with concern, "Why do these things always happen in January, when there is snow up to the rooftops and the train doesn't run?"

Katie and John left the children in care of Maudie and Maria and boarded the first train leaving for Silverton in early January. Winter storms had piled up mountains of snow, and the little train chugged carefully and slowly through the heavy white mass. Everyone on board let out a sigh of relief when they finally entered the mining town. There had been many bets that the little train might not make it the entire distance.

On arrival, they found a sobbing, frightened Jennie, overcome with the grief that her husband might die. Katie stayed in Silverton while John decided it was best that he return to Durango to keep things running at the Mascot. Due to Prohibition, all saloons were closed and money was tight. They now depended completely on the boarding house to keep them going financially.

While waiting for the train to return to Durango, John walked the short distance from Jennie's house to the Belleville Saloon to visit with Katie's brother, Phil. John noted that Phil appeared to be struggling to make a go of the business in a manner similar to what they were doing at the Mascot. Phil was buying pool tables and such for a type of entertainment center. However, he took John into his confidence, explaining that he was actively changing the structure of the saloon to hide a still for making "hooch." Phil was distilling liquor and storing bottling equipment in the basement of the Belleville, knowing full well that it was unlawful.

Phil Sartore, circa 1915.

The Belleville appeared to be under major construction as Phil worked to rearrange things. He was moving the bar to the other side of the building and installing a trap door behind it that would be almost impossible to detect. The stairs leading from the trap door went into a section of the basement with a false foundation. Here, the liquor was being produced for "bootlegging," or selling illegally. The other side of the basement had stairs leading to it as a separate section, and it contained no evidence of any kind. It was impossible to see that there were two distinct basement rooms, because Phil had cleverly taken pains to install separate foundations for each part.

John politely greeted Minnie, who was living there with Phil and enthusiastically taking part in the bootlegging. Her lips were painted bright red, her face was rouged and powdered, and her skirt was short, but she had a warm smile and was eager to talk with John about their plans to sell liquor, despite the laws of Prohibition.

"John," Minnie spoke after the tour of the basement was completed, "have you heard that when a secret bar is set up, they refer to it as a 'speakeasy'?" Minnie's face lit up as she continued. "When the Feds come to check, all the lights go out and the music stops and everyone stays very still and silent. It appears that there are no people inside, so the law enforcement officers go away because they don't find anything. When the police have moved on, the party resumes as usual."

John noted that, to Minnie's way of thinking, this was great fun. Perhaps she viewed it as more of a game than a crime. John made no comments but shook his head, wondering if this illegal action would come to an unfavorable ending.

As he left to catch the train, John couldn't help but think of Louis Sartore, wondering what he would have done in the face of Prohibition. Walking out of the Belleville into the cold winter air, he glanced across the street toward the Rock Saloon. He stared at the building for a few moments, then straightened his hat against the cold and walked off into the snow to catch the train to Durango.

Bonavida didn't appear to be improving, but, after consoling and helping her sister for two weeks, Katie explained that she was desperately needed at the boarding house. She returned to Durango when a train finally came through safely.

It was only a short time later that Jennie called with news that her husband was dying. Her desperate cries had Katie and John rushing to catch the first train to leave Durango.

The tracks were blocked with snow and the train didn't quite make it all the way this time. John and Katie struggled by foot, walking through deep snow for almost a mile into the town of Silverton. When they finally made it to the Bonavida residence and were greeted by her sobbing sister, Katie knew they were too late. They arrived four hours after Bonavida had passed away.

For Jennie the hard times had just begun, and she struggled to put her life into place without her husband. She had three children to support with a mine that had never produced very much. The Silver Ledge was full of gold and silver, or so Bonavida had believed. Getting the ore out of the mountain was the problem. The tunnels continued to fill up with water, making mining almost impossible. Jennie fought with all her determination to keep the mine running, but she had to fight even harder with legal problems. Bonavida's partners tried to exclude her from any part of the ownership. Jennie complained that it was difficult for a woman in a world dominated by men.

Katie listened patiently to her sister's constant cries of woe and knew that Jennie needed help. During the summer of 1916, Katie went to stay at the sagging mine shack to assist Jennie in cooking for the miners. She took young Frances, who had just turned eight, with her, while Jennie's children stayed in Silverton with Angelina.

Jennie Bonavida at the Silver Ledge Mine, circa 1916.

The mine buildings hung on the side of a mountain between the mining camps of Chattanooga and Red Mountain. It was remote by any standard, far away from civilization. The mailman came only twice a week, and Frances enjoyed following the little trail to greet him. The young girl was happy in this isolated world where she had no other children with whom to contend. She basked in the glory of attention from the miners. They were happy to see the young child because they were alone and separated from their families. The miners also valued the wonderful food that Jennie and Katie prepared for them. The two women made delicious meals in the humblest of cooking conditions.

As autumn approached and the mine prepared to shut down for the winter, Jennie found herself in a serious legal battle with the part owners of the mine. As a woman, she had limited rights, and she knew it was possible that her shares in the business would be taken over by the other shareholders. In exasperation she called on her brother, Phil, and signed over the mine rights to him. This was done with the understanding that she would continue to be in charge of the mine's operation.

In late September of 1916, the mill at the mine mysteriously burned to the ground. Of course, Jennie suspected that the business partners had set the fire, for without the mill the ore would be too expensive to process. She had no choice now, and the Silver Ledge Mine was permanently shut down.

The situation for Jennie was desperate, and she and her children were forced to move into the Belleville with Phil and Minnie. When spring finally arrived, she took a job at the Chattanooga Cookhouse in order to make ends meet. It was a job as miserable as anything around. This was an extensive area where miners came from the surrounding mines to be fed three meals daily. The work was constant, because when one meal ended it was time to start on the next. It was heavy, wretched work.

Throughout all of Jennie's hardship, Angelina helped by taking care of the children. She didn't mind, loving the feeling of being needed. She would brag that she had helped in raising Jennie's family. This task took her mind off Phil and the mess he was making of the saloon. She tried to shut her eyes to his bootlegging activities, but what bothered her the most was seeing Minnie constantly at his side. She blamed everything on Minnie and wouldn't give up the hope that someday this outlandish and indecent relationship would end.

Phil and Minnie continued to make hooch in the basement of the Belleville, feeling they were well out of the eyes of the Feds. Silverton was isolated enough that Phil figured he could be notified if the Federal agents boarded the train in Durango or Ouray. He had lookouts ready to phone him if the officers were headed in his direction. By the time the train arrived in Silverton, he could have everything hidden away.

People wanted booze and Phil was prepared to supply it. He proudly produced his own whiskey and zinfandel wine. The sink in the bar area had been reconstructed with iron bars across it, so that bottles could be quickly smashed in case of a raid. He loved to say, "They can't arrest me because they smell it!" He was busted several times, but when nothing could be detected or proven, Phil would simply make a new batch and business would continue as usual.

Minnie with Phil Sartore, circa 1924.

Prohibition made it illegal to purchase alcohol, but it didn't stop the flow of intoxicating beverages. Because winemaking was a tradition with the Italians, some of them, such as Phil Sartore, made it a profitable business. The majority of Italians did not take part in these illegal activities, but many were suspected of "wrongful doing" because of their nationality. It was yet another stigma placed on the Italian-American community.

CHAPTER XVII

The Morning Star
Mine

With Prohibition in full effect in Colorado, saloons were now closed, money was scarce, and the Baudinos were wondering what to do next. Tony went from job to job but wasn't finding anything to suit him. Their financial situation was further stressed with Maria's news that she was expecting another child.

John could see that there was no future ahead with the business as it was now. He couldn't make a living running the saloon as a soda shop and deli. Struggling with ideas, he weighed the options, realizing that all he was experienced to do was backbreaking labor.

John hadn't worked in the coal mines for almost ten years, but he had stayed in touch with mineworkers, delivering liquor to isolated areas and listening to customers at the bar before Prohibition was put into effect. He knew where opportunities could be found. Before they went any further into debt, he proposed to Tony that they do the only job in which they both had prospered—coal mining.

"E t'étö mat?" "Are you crazy?" was Tony's first reaction. He was haunted by memories of long days spent in the dark, digging into the mountains. He had put that all behind him as something never to do again.

"But it would be worthwhile if we buy our own mine," John interrupted, not wanting Tony to continue with negative thoughts. *"Ma a val la peina se la mina e la catan."*

Then it was time to weigh the other side—the fact that mining was dangerous work. Tony brought this up, reminding John of recent accidents reported in the coal mines.

"We wanted to escape that type of work," Tony argued. "That's why we opened the saloon. How many times have we seen our friends suffering with miner's consumption, their lungs eaten up by rock dust or noxious matter, or those with a hand missing from a misguided explosive? Then there are those with multiple hernias or ruptured spinal disks from the hard digging. These are the ones who lived." Tony continued. "What about the ones we know of who met their deaths working in mines? It's a terrible thing to think about the cave-ins or those who died of suffocation. All I can think of is the weight of the mountain pressing down on the tunnels, causing them to collapse when we're inside." Tony took a deep breath and looked at his brother. He had stated his case. Mining was terrible work and he wanted those days put in the past, not the future. Then he suggested, "Why don't we open up a small store in one of the mining areas? That would make more sense to me."

"There are many hazards with mine work," John stated, agreeing with Tony. "I also think it would be difficult to keep a small store supplied in a remote area, and you would be lucky to make enough money to keep yourself alive. There's a good margin of profit to be made in mining coal, because it's a commodity everyone needs.

"I see a great opportunity in a mine six miles west of Durango, in Lightner Creek Canyon," John continued. "It's close enough to town that we can continue to live here and take the horse and wagon each day. I've talked to the owners and they would allow us a lease for five years. We could see how it goes." John spoke with eagerness, not attempting to hide his excitement in this newly proposed project. But he needed his brother's approval before they took it on.

Because Tony could see no better choice, he finally nodded in agreement to a trial period of five years. Later that same week, in September of 1916, the brothers signed a lease to work the Morning Star Coal Mine.

It was decided that Tony and Maria would live in a small cabin at the mine. John and Katie would run the soda shop and deli and keep the boarding house in operation. An office would be added upstairs in the former saloon building, where John would handle the mine's financial affairs.

The short days of winter were soon upon the brothers. This meant that they would now spend every day in darkness. It was dark when John drove the horse and buggy up to the mine, and it was dark when he returned to the Mascot in the evening. It was pitch black inside the coal mine, carved deep into the mountain. Because of all this darkness, John appreciated the stars as they shone brightly in the brisk, cold Colorado sky on his daily trips to and from the mine.

There was a settlement built in the area around the Morning Star, with several cabins occupied by miners and even a school where children from the various coal mines gathered. The teacher was a friendly lady named Annie Rowe, and she also lived there in a small cabin.

Once every month, Emory Smiley, the school superintendent, would ride out with John to inspect the school. All of this activity was good for Maria, who otherwise would have been isolated. She and Tony almost never went into town, because John brought out supplies for them. Maria was suffering in her pregnancy, and not feeling well, and she was worried that she would lose another child. When work at the boarding house would allow time away, Katie often rode in the buggy out to the mine with John. She would spend the day helping Maria with some of her chores.

The mine continued in operation year around, because no matter how cold it was, deep inside the mine it was warm, and during the summer months it was cool. However, there were times during the winter that the mine was closed due to the conditions of the roads. Dirt only, with no gravel, the ruts in the roads grew deep and snow and ice made them impassable. The heavily loaded coal wagons could not operate under these conditions.

The entrance to the Morning Star was a large opening, with the tipple leaning against the mountain in front of the entrance. The tipple was where different grades of coal were separated. The mine started out in narrow tunnels that climbed slowly upward and became squares, which were large, carved-out rooms. The coal was found in veins at various heights in these squares, and in the Morning Star the coal was usually at about five to five-and-a-half feet. In order to remove the coal from the mountain, it was first necessary to use a pickaxe and cut it underneath as deep as possible. The rule on this was usually four or five feet deep. It was an exhausting job. A miner would support himself with one arm and strike the area with his free arm, a motion that might continue for several hours before the cut was deep enough.

Next, it would be time to make holes in which to place the blasting powder, and everyone had to retreat to a safe area before the fuse was lit. This required skill, because it was the only way to remove the coal from the rocks, and it had to be done without bringing down too much rock or the entire mountain. A properly fired round would remove many tons of coal and rock and advance the hole by another few feet.

After the coal was loosened by the blast, it was removed from the rock and ready to load. Then it was time to bring in the mule cart. At the Morning Star Mine they used a faithful, patient animal they all called "Jack." He worked steadily with the miners and they all shared in affection for this large mule.

To break up the monotony, the miners often made up songs as they worked. One such song included the mule and was sung to the melody of "My Sweetheart's the Man in the Moon."

> *My sweetheart's the mule in the mine.*
> *I drive her with only one line.*
> *All day I would sit and tobacco juice I spit,*
> *all over my sweethearts behind.*

The miners loved teaching this song and others to young Frances and Louis when they would visit the mine. Katie would scold all of them for this nonsense.

The work of the mule was essential to coal mining. One miner would lead Jack attached to the cart into the tunnel with only a single light on his hat to show the way. When they came to the place where others were already digging out coal, the mule would be put into place while the cart was loaded. When the cart was full of coal, they would start it on its descent down the tunnel. There were no brakes on the cart. The mule would run, full speed, while miners ran alongside, jabbing pieces of wood into the spokes of the wheels to slow it down. When the mule and the heavily loaded coal cart were safely out of the mine, the coal was separated into different grades on the tipple. It was then loaded into large bins on wagons to be delivered to a place nearby, called Franklin Junction. There it would be loaded onto the narrow gauge train and sent off to customers in Telluride, Pagosa Springs, and Aztec, New Mexico. John made it an important part of his business to supply customers all over La Plata County and the surrounding areas, as well as those in Durango.

By January 1917 it was miserably cold out in the canyon. Here, the mountains were high and came together at a deep, narrow angle, and this didn't allow for much sunlight during the winter. The mine structures were deep in shadows, and the humble little buildings were freezing cold. Maria phoned Katie to tell her that everything inside her tiny little house was frozen. During the night, the little pot-bellied stove had gone out and the meat, bread, wine, and even the eggs were frozen solid, like bricks of ice. "I had to use a pencil to write my list of supplies for John, because the ink is also frozen," Maria cried.

With Katie's insistence, Maria was bundled up and brought to the Mascot until the cold January weather passed. Maria continued to be sickly and depressed, even with Katie's loving care. She was now almost six months pregnant, and everyone worried about the fate of the baby and the mother.

Because it was Tony's job to care for the mules and horses at the mine, he couldn't stay in Durango every night, but he joined everyone at the Mascot whenever possible. He was relieved to have Maria looked after, but John also noticed that Tony was drinking heavily in Maria's absence. It was obvious that Tony did not do well living at the mine alone, so John encouraged him to come into town often.

Prohibition didn't prevent anyone from drinking, because it allowed for winemaking for personal use. It only prohibited the selling of any type of liquor. Because both John and Tony made their own wine, Tony had it readily available and seemed to require it often, "to dull the ache in his heart." John could only hope that with the birth of this child, Tony and Maria would find the family happiness they both desired and life would improve for them.

Springtime in the Rocky Mountains brought both warmth and hope to the family. On May 12, 1917, Tony and Maria became the parents of a beautiful baby boy. They named him Giovanni and affectionately called him Giani, or Johnny. They returned to live at the mine both ecstatically happy with their healthy bundle of joy.

Things were prospering both with the business and in their personal lives. With a hopeful outlook toward the future, John and Tony talked of buying the mine outright and doing away with the lease. It was hard, miserable work, but after less than a year, it was proving to be profitable.

"Will it be possible for you and Maria to continue to live at the mine?" John asked Tony. "We need to have someone looking after the animals, supervising the equipment, and watching over everything in general."

"We can manage it now that Maria is happy with the baby. If we fix up the house a little, things would be better," Tony answered.

They looked at one another for the answer, and soon both nodded in agreement, smiling but serious about the decision they had made. In July of 1917, the Baudino brothers legally purchased the Morning Star Coal Mine.

Both John and Tony realized the importance of having hardworking, responsible men laboring beside them. They hired John Boggio with his wealth of experience from working in the copper mines of Calumet. They were also fortunate that the Crotta brothers had come to the mine looking for work. They were reliable and dependable and worked up to the standards set by the Baudinos. John had laughed at their soft white hands when he first met them. Louis, Evasio, and Maggiore Crotta had worked as waiters in the dining room of the Waldorf Astoria in New York City when they first came to America. John told them that working with coal would turn them black from head to toe and their hands would never be soft and white again. But the Crottas were eager to purchase farmland and accepted the challenge of heavy labor.

Things at the mine fell into a routine, and the summer weather made it more pleasant. However, Maria continued to have problems with weak health conditions that led to depression. She often took the baby to the Mascot, where Katie would help look after little Giani. It was a worry that Maria had a serious illness that would not improve.

After many months of hard work, they were approaching year's end. The days were getting shorter, making it difficult to get the coal out of the mine and delivered as quickly. There was always a bit of anxiety with the mine work because they all knew the dangers involved. John prided himself with a record of safety and was cautious, allowing no one but himself to handle the explosives.

But he had a habit of pushing the men beyond what was required. This day, he wanted to get one more load of coal out of the mountain before he started home in the evening. The others grumbled in having to put in longer hours, but John argued that it was warmer inside the mine, and the November evening was dark and cold outside. He talked them into getting this one more load out so he could make a delivery the following morning.

They all pitched in loading the cart with coal, and finally the mule and the loaded coal cart started moving down the track. The mule was set into motion and running, with John and the others running beside the heavily loaded cart. The first large piece of wood that was shoved into the wheel spokes was weak and it broke. The speed of the cart was not reduced at all and the miners shouted words of warning as the crisis was realized. John was seized with alarm as the cart moved too quickly behind the mule. He ran to insert another stick in hopes of slowing the cart, but in his haste he jabbed his arm in the spokes along with the piece of wood. He pulled back before it was able to break like a twig, but his hand and arm were cut with open wounds—gnarled and gashed. John ignored the pain and the blood gushing out of the torn flesh on his arm and the throbbing of his crushed fingers. He was shouting and running, calling for someone to hurry and slow down the cart.

John couldn't see the disaster that transpired in the darkness of the mine, but he knew from the horrible sound that the coal cart had crashed into the back of the mule. John swore to himself, angry that he had allowed this to happen, and his anger was mixed with fear as to what he would find at the site of this calamity. His arm hung weak and mangled, but he pushed the others out of the way and ran to see what had happened to Jack.

It took the help of all the miners to push the coal cart away from the back of the fallen mule. It was determined that both of Jack's legs were broken and the poor animal was badly cut and bleeding. John looked into the eyes of this beloved mule and saw fear along with the understanding of what was to come. Tears poured from John's eyes, and he talked softly to Jack as he pulled out a revolver. He begged forgiveness for what he was about to do. John stood there, crying openly, as the other miners stood back. John put the gun to the head of the mule and pulled the trigger.

John insisted that Jack be removed from the mine that evening. No one argued, and the mule was loaded onto a coal cart and taken outside. Tony tried to care for John's arm, because John was holding on to it, supporting it with his good hand. John allowed Tony to wrap a piece of cloth around his arm and to bind up his hand, and then he continued to see to Jack. They all gathered to dig a giant grave in the rock-hard, frozen ground, so they could bury their fallen companion. Jack was finally laid to rest at the end of a very long and terrible day.

"I'm not going to allow you to drive yourself home it that condition," Tony shouted as John attempted to harness and attach the horse to the buggy for the trip back to Durango. It was as though John heard nothing and he continued with the harness, swearing because he could only work with one arm, and it was almost frozen from the cold.

Tony watched his brother, but he understood that this display of stubbornness meant that John was very angry with himself. John took the blame for the accident and he was now ready to punish himself for being at fault. Tony knew there was no use trying to talk to his brother; he simply helped prepare the buggy for the trip to Durango. But when John climbed into the seat, ready to leave, Tony also climbed aboard, taking the reins in hand.

"I will see you home tonight. The others will care for the animals."

John didn't reply but moved over to make room for his brother. As the horse moved slowly toward home the two men fell silent. In the stillness of the frigid night air, the stars lit up the sky and the clip-clop of Billy, the horse, fell into a pleasant rhythm. John continued to berate himself and swore over and over again under his breath. Each time he muttered, his breath hung milky-like steam in the cold air. Now that the trauma of the accident was behind them, John began to grimace in pain from his injured and bloodied wounds. Tony said nothing, but he noted John's suffering.

"Why did this happen? How could I have been so stupid to push everyone until it caused this misfortune? I am a fool!"

Tony said nothing. John made a sobbing sound, and Tony realized that tears were flowing from his brother's eyes once again. Tony remained silent, knowing that nothing anyone could say would take away the guilt John was inflicting on himself. Now, in the suffering of this moment, all the recent sadness came to the surface and John began to talk.

"I was stupid to think we could make the mine successful. What good will come of it if we are maimed and crippled?" Then John's thoughts moved to the problem that hurt him most of all. "Having to close the saloon was the worst thing that could've happened." He let out a long shuddering breath. "It isn't fair that life has taken such a turn, causing us to work like slaves and break our backs inside this damnable mine. What can we do, Tony? What else can we do to make a good life? With all that has happened, it would be better if we had not come to this country. We start to do well and something comes along and puts a stop to it, like Prohibition. Next, the unions will come and make demands at the mine. Can we stay ahead of all this? Perhaps this country hasn't been right for us all along."

Tony knew that John was searching. He could see that he needed to reassure his brother before John would continue with the mine work.

"What would we be doing in Italy?" Tony finally responded. John said nothing. "Here, we're the owners of a beautiful building on the main street of Durango, and we also own a mine that has a wealth of coal." John remained silent as Tony continued. "You have a wonderful wife who runs the boarding house by herself and two healthy, bright children. If you had remained in Italy, you would not have been able to marry such a wife. The class system is too strong."

"But there are complications in our relationship," John muttered solemnly. "You know all this, so you know my life is far from perfect. I try to do this for my wife and family, but the love isn't there. For that reason, nothing is worthwhile."

"What is meant by a perfect life?" Tony stated in anger. "My wife loves me and I love her, but the doctor tells us that because we are first cousins, the blood of our children isn't strong. My wife has not been the same since she heard this news. Don't complain to me that your life isn't perfect!"

As they were approaching Durango, Tony mentioned that they should first find a doctor to administer care to John's injuries.

"No!" came John's emphatic words. He held his teeth rigid against the pain as he spoke. "Just take me home. I'll be all right!"

As they drove into town, light from the moon seemed to illuminate the former saloon building and John let out a sigh of reminiscence. His eyes traveled up to the top of the building where the words SALONE ITALIANO had once stood out in bold letters. John couldn't hold back the words as he spoke: "The spirit remains, but the dream has ended. We were doing well with the saloon, Tony. Why did things have to change?"

"Change is a part of life," Tony said, in his casual manner. "In fact, I think that change and life walk hand-in-hand. We are constantly challenged and tested. Sometimes we don't handle either change or life very well, but we have to keep on and do the best we can."

John had nothing more to say about this. The loss of the saloon due to Prohibition was a blow from which he had yet to recover.

It was almost midnight when the two weary men drove the little horse and buggy into the alley behind the Mascot. Katie and Maria were waiting up, knowing something was wrong. They had been counting the hours, watching the clock, as the time grew later and later. They looked up from their mending and both wore shocked expressions when Tony staggered in, trying to support John, as they entered the house. John had grown weaker now from loss of blood, his arm and hand still wrapped with the original bloodied pieces of cloth. Both men had a greyness of color and looked tired and dirty, still covered in coal dust.

The women jumped to their feet: Maria put her hand to her mouth to stifle a cry. Katie ran to her husband and guided him to a wooden stool in the kitchen. She gently unwrapped the damaged arm, and she and Maria examined it carefully. "What shall we do, Katie?"

Maria asked, her eyes not wanting to look at the skin hanging loose on John's bloody arm or his mangled fingers. Katie instructed her to boil some water and asked Tony to go to the horse barn where they kept a large pot of pine tar. The dark viscous pitch was obtained from distillation of the wood of pine trees, and it was often used in the treatment of skin ailments. When these two requests were granted, Katie quietly told Maria and Tony to go to bed: She would see to John's arm alone.

Katie carefully removed John's torn shirt. She then took some of the warmed water from the stove that was not yet ready to boil and began to carefully wash the black coal dust from her husband's face, working on his hair and down his back. She then moved gently to clean his battered arm and hand. The warm water soothed John's tensed body, but his mind was still in pain.

"The accident was my fault," he told her. "I worked everyone too hard and we were all tired." His tears flowed once again as he told her the story of the fallen mule that he had to destroy.

"You're like my father in that way," Katie said softly as she gently tried to shape the broken mass of skin and flesh together on his arm. "He always pushed everyone to do more."

John listened to her words intently, because to him it was an honor to be compared to Louis Sartore.

"But you're different from him in other ways," Katie continued, keeping him distracted as she carefully cleaned the damaged skin on his hand, checking for broken bones. "You're a much better father. You are gentle and loving to our children and give them much attention." She continued as he jumped up with the sharp burning pain. "My father was remote from us, perhaps because he was away from us for so many years. He loved us but seldom showed affection. Perhaps it was a different time, because most fathers seemed removed from their families when I was a child. I'm happy that you're not like that." She murmured this last part softly, carefully prying the flesh apart on his arm. Uncorking a bottle of whiskey she poured the liquor liberally over the deep slashes as a disinfectant. When John flinched she stopped and poured him a glass, which he downed in one gulp. John sat motionless as she applied the pitch to the arm to bind the skin together, distracted and moved by her words.

"By the way, this is the last of our whiskey," she added.

John didn't say anything, but he swore under his breath against the pain as Katie worked to straighten his fingers and bind the gashes on his hand with pine tar. He tried not to complain, because he knew his wife was working as gently as possible. His mind moved to thinking about where he would get more whiskey now with Prohibition in effect.

"Phil will find whiskey," John said, his voice hoarse with pain.

"Oh, yes," Katie gave a soft laugh. "My brother knows about liquor. I wonder if he'll be able to stay ahead of the law much longer? He called today," she said as she pulled the skin of his arm together and applied the sticky pitch. "He had a serious run-in with the pro-hies—you know that's what he calls the prohibition officers. He was tipped off that they were riding the train up to Silverton to physically destroy his bar in the same way that they used axes to chop up some of the expensive, artistically decorated wooden bars in Durango. Phil hired some extra hands, and when the revenue men walked through the front door of the Belleville with their axes, the barroom didn't have a stick of furniture in it. They had worked all night to carefully dismantle the bar and hide it. Minnie is treating the episode as a great triumph!"

John gestured with a nod and a sigh. "It will be a miracle if Phil survives in his bootlegging activities without suffering penalties." Minnie was even more of a problem, but John didn't want to discuss this with his wife.

Katie studied him as she worked to wrap his damaged arm. John fretted more about life in general than the damage he had inflicted on his body. He made a comment that he had to deliver coal tomorrow, and she chided him for even thinking of such a thing.

"You're strong minded but also stupid," Katie remarked. She knew he probably would deliver coal tomorrow morning, because he had decided it was necessary. This stubborn determination was part of his character, but this time she viewed it as a force that could impair his health. She knew he had promised the coal and would keep his word, regardless. He used little sense in such matters.

For a moment he looked up and their eyes met. It hurt her to see his usually blue eyes clouded and grey. Wounded pride now wreathed his features, and he felt beaten down by life. He was looking to her for an opinion, because it mattered to him how she viewed their future. Should he give up the mine work, and along with that give up his desire to make a better life?

"I have almost saved enough money to buy property for a house," he muttered. "If we quit the mine, I'll have to give up that part of the dream." He wanted a real house, not the apartment in the saloon building. He wanted a home on Durango's Third Avenue.

Her heart warmed as he expressed these thoughts and fretted about a new house. She realized how badly he wanted to be worthwhile in her eyes—to make her happy. As he spoke of his disappointments, of Prohibition, and the mine accident, she sensed his vulnerability and fear of failure. As he sat there in this dishevelled, miserable state, she felt drawn to him in an unusual way. She was suddenly keenly aware that her indifference to their relationship had hurt him in the past, but she now inwardly admitted that she had grown in love for this man. Respect for him had opened her heart. She lovingly reached to hold his head with both hands, waiting for him to look up at her. She wanted to ease the ache inside of him and also to heal the guilt she carried.

John with Daisy the mule at the Morning Star Mine in 1922. The Baudino brothers continued to run the mine until they sold the rights in 1935.

"Listen to me, John," Katie began to speak in tones that meant a lecture was to follow. "It's true that I married you because my mother wished it, and this caused me to hold back my feelings. You see, some sins go beyond forgiving, and I didn't want to give my mother any satisfaction after what she did...to Peter." Katie's voice trembled softly as she spoke the name she had kept hidden inside. "None of that was your fault, and now I see how I've hurt you." Katie continued, as John reached for her hand and brought it to his lips. "I'm blessed with a husband who only wants the best for me and his family and I'm proud to be your wife! You have given me the strength to look toward the future, and I want to be there with you and our children."

In one clear moment they could both see their entire history, way back to the beginning. Through it all, they'd created a balance that made life comfortable. During their ten-year marriage, they'd built a secure relationship with familiarities that each quietly accepted and understood. Perhaps they would now be able to bridge the gap that in the past had kept them from being whole.

He reached to embrace her with his one good arm. After a brief moment, she helped him to his feet and led him from the kitchen. "We have to get some sleep," she teased, trying to make light the emotion her words had stirred in both of them. "You have coal to deliver tomorrow."

EPILOGUE

The building in the center is the former "Salone Italiano," located at 552 Main Avenue in Durango. The first floor houses a restaurant, and on the second floor are the offices of the Durango & Silverton Narrow Gauge Railroad. John Baudino sold the building in 1948.

The old Belleview Saloon at 1260 Blair Street, Silverton, Colorado, 2002.

Author in the tunnel leading from the basement of the Belleview Saloon in Silverton, Colorado, 2002.

The author at right, with her grandmother, Katie Baudino, at the cabin of Louis Baudino, at Electra Lake in 1952.

In this story we have uncovered only a small part of the history and events held secret in the letters, but we will now look into what the future held for some of our favorite characters.

The Eighteenth Amendment to the Constitution of the United States, known as Prohibition, was repealed in 1933, but the Mascot Saloon was never reopened. The years that followed the closing of the saloon in 1916 were filled with many painful moments. The Spanish flu epidemic of 1918 claimed four family members, leaving heartache in its wake. It is said that soldiers returning home from World War I spread this killer disease quickly around the world. The terrible influenza preyed first on the very old, the very weak, and the very young.

Angelina Sartore was considered one of the first victims of the flu in Silverton, and her beloved fifteen-year-old granddaughter, Lina Bonavida, followed her "Nonna" in death only a few months later. The next victim of the terrible epidemic was Maria Baudino, who was already suffering from depression. This left her bereaved husband, Tony, to care for their young child Johnny. In 1919, when it seemed that everyone was safe from the horrible virus, baby Giovanni, Katie and John's third child, was stricken and died at age six months.

In 1920, Katie gave birth to a baby girl, naming her Angelina or Lena, and in 1922 John completed his dream home at 531 Third Avenue.

Above is the Baudino's rock home, with young Lena standing on the front steps in 1928. On the pillar is a sign advertising coal for sale from the Morning Star Mine. The home remained in the family until 1998.

When John Baudino's friend, Colombatti, was killed in a mining accident, John stepped forward to pay for his funeral. Because most of the Italian miners came to America without family, they had only fellow countrymen to turn to at times of distress. John and Katie joined

Top photo, founding members of the men's Italian Lodge #172, From left to right: Frank Gresenti, Frank Cardone, Evasio Crotta, Otto Seroni, and John Baudino.
In the bottom photo, founding members of the women's Italian Lodge #29, From left to right: Adelina Crotta, Katie Baudino, Catherine Leonardelli, Rose Fanto, and Concetta Zellitti.

with other Italians in forming the Cristoforo Colombo Italian Lodge in 1924. It was to be a society of mutual benefit, bringing them together socially and offering help in times of need.

Following the death of Maria Baudino in 1918, Katie and John helped Tony with his young son, Johnny. When Tony died in 1934 of emphysema, or possibly miner's consumption, John and Katie legally adopted Johnny, raising him as their own.

Johnny met and married Mildred Vonderheid while in the army, stationed in Wyoming during World War II. They moved to Farmington, New Mexico, where he owned and operated a hardware store. He eventually sold the business and was hired as manager of the Farmington Elks Club. The club had a full-time bartender, but he enjoyed stepping behind the bar to help out on special occasions. Johnny and Mildred had

Young Johnny and "la piccolo Lena." Circa 1924.

two children, Rick and Mary. Johnny died in 1984, at age sixty-seven, and is buried in the Durango Hillcrest Cemetery near his parents.

In 1925 Durango faced problems from the Ku Klux Klan, as this group of local citizens terrorized the area. With immigrants as the intended victims, they used fear tactics to drive the "non-Americans" out of the community. Cross burnings on Smelter Mountain were a common sight and a fearful reminder to those who were being stalked and provoked. Sacred Heart Catholic Church, a gathering place for immigrants, was burned to the ground. Prohibition was used as an excuse to harass innocent people, and because it was the Italians who were capable of making wine, their homes were often attacked and raided by the hooded accusers.

The following is a translation of a portion of a letter written by Tony to his brother and sister in Italy. It describes the day the KKK pushed their way into the Baudino home, trashing everything in sight, looking for evidence of bootlegging.

Letter no.76
From Tony Baudino to Carlo and Camilla.
Durango, Colo., June 29, 1925
These days you see all sorts of things never seen before in these States. There is a set of vandals that came out, called the Ku Klux Klan. At the head of it are many rich people who, first of all, hate foreigners, then the Christian religion, and try with every means to get rid of us. They are at the head of every administration in the county and the towns, like judges, sheriffs, police, and do terrible massacres. Even if you are innocent they sentence you mercilessly, and don't consider right or wrong.

A few weeks ago they went to John's house. They threw everything upside down, as if he were a criminal. They found some wine that he keeps for his family use, and he had to go to court for justice. Because of the good reputation that he has always had in this town, he got away with a fine of $150 and court fees. With the lawyers' fees, it cost him quite a bit. One loses credit. This is disgusting for everybody. John stayed out of jail, but was innocent and has never had any dealings with the court before. The other people got three months in jail and a $250 fine, without knowing why. They had businesses and nine of them were Italian. It's frightening. We have to drink water, even if it's bad, and coffee. It's scary. It's all them KKK in power and they do as they please. This is the American freedom.

Frances Baudino was a student at Durango High School when members of the Ku Klux Klan visited the school. Under the guise of so-called "patriotic citizens," they attempted to intimidate those of Irish, Italian, and Hispanic descent. They stood at the school grounds handing out small American flags, refusing to give them to those from immigrant families. Frances was one of the students denied a flag, and this was humiliating to this shy young girl who was already sensitive about being Italian. When the school superintendent, Emory Smiley, was informed of this narrow-minded bigotry, he called an assembly and spoke out against it, but much harm had been done in the selection and separating of students.

Frances continued to struggle, but she couldn't shed the feeling of not being suitable. She attempted to change her name from Baudino to Bodine before she entered Colorado Teacher's College in Greeley, Colorado, thinking that it would make her sound less Italian. An understanding teacher convinced her not to do so, but the scars from many discriminatory incidents remained.

Frances Baudino in front of Park School where she taught, 1937-1947.

Frances ultimately became a country school teacher, finding employment in the areas outside of Durango: Florida School, 1927—1928; Thompson School, 1928—1930; Upper Spring Creek, 1930—1932; Oxford School in 1934; and Cottonwood School, 1934—1937. While employed at Cottonwood School, she met and fell in love with a very nice young man. They became engaged and Frances blossomed with happiness. It is ironic to note that her mother, Katie, did not approve of the fiancé. Frances finally gave in to the pressure inflicted by her mother and broke off the engagement. At age 40, Frances married John Wegher, who owned a grocery store with his brother, Charles. After their marriage in 1948, Frances did the bookkeeping for Wegher's Food Store, located on the corner of Sixth Street and Fifth Avenue in Durango. John Wegher was of Tyrolean descent.

The Baudino's second child, Louis, became an outstanding student with seemingly little effort. His Uncle Tony wrote in a letter, "He works with wood and can build anything, but he seldom studies." Louis was class valedictorian and received a scholarship to the University of Colorado in Boulder to study engineering.

At the university, Louis was extremely popular, and because of his many social activities, he lost his scholarship his freshman year. His father struggled to keep up the payments necessary to keep Louis in college, but during his junior year, in 1931, Louis eloped with Ouray native Dorothy Stough, in a civil ceremony.

John was furious and pulled his son out of college putting him to work at the coal mine. Katie cried over the marriage and refused to take Dorothy into the family. However, when the young couple moved out to one of the mine cabins, their relationship with John and Katie improved, and the family eventually warmed to Dorothy's accepting and loving ways. In primitive conditions she made a comfortable home, taking care of Uncle Tony and giving him a happier and better quality of life. She later pleased the family further when she married Louis in the Catholic church.

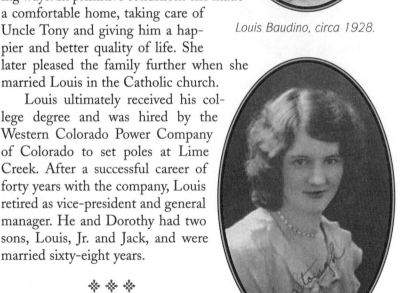

Louis Baudino, circa 1928.

Louis ultimately received his college degree and was hired by the Western Colorado Power Company of Colorado to set poles at Lime Creek. After a successful career of forty years with the company, Louis retired as vice-president and general manager. He and Dorothy had two sons, Louis, Jr. and Jack, and were married sixty-eight years.

❖ ❖ ❖

Katie and John Baudino's youngest daughter, Lena, loved to sing. From the time she was a little girl, she would accompany her father on his rounds of chores in downtown Durango. Lena would sing little songs

Dorothy Stough Baudino, circa 1928.

and the merchants would give her candy. She continued her singing as a young woman, winning local contests, and her teachers encouraged her to make music a career. She begged her parents to send her to Lamont School of Music in Denver, but Katie and John thought this was a frivolous career for a woman. Lena had excelled in typing and shorthand in high school, and her parents wanted her to attend a business college. Lena finally accepted the idea and was enrolled at Woodbury Business College in California.

Lena Baudino in 1937 at age 16, ready for high school graduation.

But this dream was also shattered when her mother, Katie, was diagnosed with cancer of the uterus. When John asked his daughter to stay and help care for her mother, Lena couldn't refuse. She took a job at the First National Bank in Durango to be near her parents. Katie successfully battled the disease and lived to be eighty-eight years old. John preceded his wife in death at age 85—he died on his birthday in 1960.

Lena still sings at age eighty-four and has been a member of the St. Columba's Catholic Church choir in Durango since she was eleven years old—more than seventy years.

Lena married Peter Babey in 1940. They have two daughters—Kay, the author of this book, and Carla, the artist and illustrator.

The oldest child of Domenica Baudino and Michele Naretto was Giuseppe, known to the family as "Peppino." His uncle Dominic Naretto, a priest, offered to pay for boarding school in Ivrea with the hope that Peppino would develop the desire to become a priest. But when it became time for Peppino to make a choice, life pulled him in a new direction and he left the seminary. He was drafted into the army in 1917, and served for two years, defending Italy in the

Trentino region. He was discharged in 1920, and in 1927 he married Angela Perona: they had eleven children.

Peppino worked as a banker: First at *banka Canavesana*, and later *banka di Novara*. But he spent the last 34 years of his life following his vocation for painting. He was primarily an artist at heart and examples of his artwork are featured at the beginning of Chapter 7.

When his parents died, Peppino and his sisters shared the management of the bank accounts for the family members in America, and also cared for the Sartore house in Pasquaro. The house was never

Angela and Giuseppe (Peppino) Naretto circa 1927.

Peppino Naretto at work in his studio in Italy in 1967.

rented; it was occupied only by family members on visits from America and by the Boggio family until 1921. During World War II, a family from a bombed-out area in Torino, was allowed to occupy the house. In 1970 Phil Sartore sold the Pasquaro house to Peppino's daughter, Quinta Naretto Carruozzo, so the property remains in the family to this day. The original house has been for the most part, torn down and rebuilt.

The Sartore's legal papers, letters, and photos were originally stored in the old house but were moved during World War II. Peppino's oldest son, Michele—or Lino—found them in the attic of his father's home in Rivarolo Canavese. The family bond and correspondence across the ocean has never ceased and continues to this day.

Original house in Pasquaro, Italy, in disrepair, circa 1960.

In 1922, Peppino's brother, Giovanni Naretto, arrived from Italy. This brought the American relatives even closer to those in the Old Country. It's due to Giovanni's expressive letters that much of the information on coal mining could be explained in the story.

Giovanni, or John, was the youngest son of Dominica Baudino and Michele Naretto and a nephew of the Baudinos. He begged his uncles to give him a job in the mine and borrowed the money to come to America to change his course in life. He was warned by his Uncle Tony, "You will waste your youth working heavy labor in the darkness of the mine."

John Naretto worked in the Morning Star Mine for four years, living the life of a hermit in order to save every penny. With only a fourth-grade education, he took advantage of every opportunity, walking the six miles into Durango for the free English night classes offered to immigrants. He

Giovanni (John) Naretto, circa 1922.

would have to walk back to the mine in the dark of night and start work early in the morning.

He left Durango in 1926 and headed east, finding work digging the tunnels for the New York Subway. In a letter to his mother, he said he was now closer to Italy but, sadly, he wasn't coming home. He wisely invested his entire savings, buying an entire block of buildings in New Haven, Connecticut. He rented out most of the buildings but opened a bar as part owner and ran a business he called The French Bakery. He was still intent upon saving money and only allowed himself one passion: He attended the opera once a month.

At age thirty-five he married Mary Dagostino. They eventually moved to Florida with their two children, Jeanette and Johnny, where Mary's parents were living. With talents that allowed him to develop many skills, John became a realtor and building contractor, settling into a successful career in Miami.

When Anna Bonavida turned fourteen, she was finished with all the schooling that Silverton had to offer. Worried about her future, her uncle, John Baudino, insisted she come live with them in Durango so she could attend a business college. Anna was always very grateful for this opportunity and proved to be a good student. After graduation she was hired to work at the First National Bank in Durango, where she was employed for the next fifty-four years.

Emilio Bonavida was driven away from home by the tyrannical moods of his mother, and Jennie's oldest daughter, Lina, had died of the flu in 1918. This left only young Anna to take care of her mother. Because

Anna Bonavida, circa 1918.

Anna had a good job, John helped her buy a house. This made it possible for Jennie to leave Silverton and move to Durango and into Anna's life. Jennie immediately took control, refusing to let Anna date or attend social activities where she might meet men. Jennie selfishly thought that if Anna married, she would be left on her own.

But Anna was beautiful and had a warm personality so, it wasn't a surprise when she began a friendship with a young man who had a business on Durango's Main Avenue. This blossomed into romance and when the news reached her mother's ears, Jennie inflicted strict conditions that Anna was not to see him again. Because of this, Anna suffered a nervous breakdown. When she recovered, life continued as before, with her mother in charge. Anna gave up the man she loved: Her life consisted only of working at the bank and taking care of her mama. Katie often tried to intervene on Anna's behalf, but the arguments had no effect.

Because Jennie Bonavida lived to the age of ninety-two and controlled her daughter's life, Anna never married. The love of Anna's life, the man who continued to run a business on Durango's Main Avenue, never married either.

❖ ❖ ❖

Tony and Freda Boggio, 1912.

When Maudie and her father, Boggio, left Italy in 1910 to join the family in Durango, Tony Boggio joined them for part of the journey. Tony, Margherita's firstborn, had decided to return to Calumet, Michigan, where he had lived as a young boy. He stopped off first in Rockford, Illinois, taking a temporary job. There he met a beautiful young Swedish girl, Freda Johnson, and they married. Tony later took Freda to live in Durango along with their two young daughters and son, Ted.

Tony had great athletic ability and became the star player on the Durango baseball team. He was also an avid boxer and was chosen to spar with famous boxing champion, Max Baer.

Tony Boggio, on the fender, being honored in a Durango parade in 1923.

Tony opened his own athletic club in Durango and it was successful, but he eventually moved his family back to Illinois so Freda could be near her relatives. There he was employed by WF&John Barnes, selling heavy machinery to countries all over the world.

From left to right, front row: Daisy the mule, Maggiore Crotta, Ella Crotta, Frances Baudino holding Lena, Louis Baudino, Johnny Baudino, with Anna Bonavida between them. Next to Johnny is Eddie Crotta, Katy Boggio Crotta, Margherita Boggio, John Baudino and Giovanni Boggio. In the back row, left to right: behind Frances is Louis Crotta with Tony Baudino behind him, Evasio Crotta, and Adalina Crotta, 1922.

In 1921, Margherita Boggio finally left Italy with her daughter, Katy, to join her husband and family in Durango. Through the family, Katy met Maggiore Crotta and they married on September 21, 1922. The young couple moved to a cabin at the Morning Star Mine and, for a time Katy cooked for the miners. The Crottas eventually bought a farm outside Durango on Florida Mesa. They were the parents of one daughter, naming her Margaret, after her grandmother.

In 1927, Maudie Boggio Bonaventura tragically died at age thirty-three while undergoing surgery of the throat. A huge funeral followed, because she was much loved by all of Durango. She left behind six children and a bereaved husband. Katie took care of the children for a month until permanent arrangements could be made.

Madeline, Nick, John, Margaret, and Concetta Bonaventura in 1926.
These are five of Maudie and Dominic's children. Frank, the youngest was
only sixteen months old at the time of Maudie's death and is not pictured.

Because Dominic couldn't take care of six young children alone, the grandparents, Margherita and John Boggio, offered to help provide loving care for Maudie's children. They moved into a larger house so all of them could live together. John Boggio died of miner's consumption in 1933 and Margherita lived until 1938. Dominic Bonaventura never remarried.

Phil Sartore married Minnie Meyhew Heberling in 1924. They were apart from each other only when Phil was finally charged, and found guilty, of bootlegging and spent a year in prison. Phil moved Minnie to Durango in 1930 so she could be near family members during his prison term.

Minnie lived alone in the large brick home on Fourth Avenue while Phil was away, but because she was thrifty and

Phil and Minnie Sartore, Circa 1940.

Phil and Minnie at home, circa 1930.

needed income, she turned the house into several apartments. Ten-year-old Lena Baudino was often sent to spend the night with her "aunt" who lived only two blocks from the Baudino home. Aunt Minnie was thrilled to have the companionship of the young girl. And because Minnie was eager to please, she often served Lena chocolate cake for breakfast before sending her off to school.

Minnie suffered with a weak heart condition and died in 1948 at the age of sixty-two. Phil never remarried. He sold the Belleview Saloon on May 13, 1948, shortly after Minnie's passing.

In the early 1940s, Phil was asked to bartend in the Elks Club facilities in Durango while the regular bartender was gone for two weeks. After approximately thirty years of faithful service, he was still their "temporary," and dearly loved employee. In the following photo from the *Durango Herald*, Phil is shown being honored in a special ceremony by the Elks in the early 1970s.

Phil Sartore died in Durango at age ninety-four in 1980.

PHIL SARTORE (seated, center front) was recently honored by the Durango Elks Lodge for his long and faithful service to their club. Mr. Sartore came to Durango from Silverton in the early 1940's. While in Durango he was asked to bartend in the Elks Club facilities while the regular bartender was gone for two weeks. After approximately 30 years of faithful service, he is still their "temporary" employee. This special class of initiates was dedicated to Mr. Sartore by the officers and members of Durango Lodge No. 507 B.P.O.E. In the photo are (back row left to right) John Wegher, Dick Byler, Floyd Harris, John Nesbith, Danny Huntsman, Glenn Chapman, Robert Sherman, Le-Roy Schumacher, Herbert Siegele, Fred Horvat and Dew Peden (all officers) and (front row left to right) Bill Pugh, John Barry, Roger MacDougall, Tony Sarver, George Sterk, Michael Amato, Ronald Martin, Rick Gold, David Woodard and Don Walton (all new initiates.)

Like so many others of his day, Joseph Sartore succumbed to asthma and miner's consumption in 1916. He had been a well-known and respected long-time Silverton resident. His wife, Angelina Dighera, lived until 1931. Both are buried in the Sartore-Vota plot at Hillside Cemetery in Silverton.

Their daughter, Mary, and her husband, Ludwig Vota, had one son they affectionately named Joseph. Prohibition was in effect when Ludwig died in 1926 of a heart attack at age fifty-eight. After Ludwig's death, Mary and her brother, "Little Phil," sold the rights to Ludwig's Dance Hall and set up a bottling works operation in the Orella Saloon building in Silverton. They legally produced a foul tasting non-alcoholic liquid, but they were also bottling illegal "likker." It was well known that genuine whiskey was being served in Mary's Parlor. When convicted and found guilty of bootlegging, Mary took the rap for her brother, Phil, and served a short prison term.

Kate Nigra was the one her mother, Catlina, relied on at a very young age to help with the younger children. Because of this, Kate missed so much school that she was forced to drop out at age twelve in 1903. To help with the financial struggle of the Nigra family, she then took jobs scrubbing floors for fifty cents. She soon learned that if she didn't take all of the allotted time to scrub floors, she

Wedding of Kate Nigra and Paul Trione in 1915. Margaret Nigra and Charles Trione are standing behind them. They married in 1917.

would be expected to do other chores, such as pluck chickens—one of her least favorite.

Kate was fifteen when she met seventeen-year-old Paul Trione. They dated for seven years under the strict eye of her father, and finally married in 1915. Two years later, Kate's sister, Margaret, married Paul's brother, Charlie Trione.

Paul Trione started working in the mines of Calumet at a very young age. His mother, wanting a different life for her son, offered him as a delivery boy at Vertin's Department Store. Paul worked hard and was well liked by the store's owners. After a short time, he became the Italian clerk for the store where he continued to prosper, eventually becoming part owner. Because of this, Kate's life was greatly improved. The couple had two children, Genevieve and Gordon, and cared for Kate's parents in their old age. Catlina suffered a stroke and died in 1936 and Kate's moody father, Antonio, lived with them until he died in 1939.

❖ ❖ ❖

Baudino Golden wedding anniversary,
celebrating fifty years of marriage in 1957.

Durango Herald News:

Mr. and Mrs. John Baudino observed their Golden anniversary Sunday at a reception at the Baudino home at 531 Third Avenue. More than 300 persons called between 2 and 6 p.m. Among the guests were Mr. And Mrs. Paul Trione and Mr. And Mrs. John Nigra, all of Calumet, Michigan. They are cousins of Mrs. Baudino whom she hadn't seen since 1901. Mr. And Mrs. Maggiore Crotta of Grand Junction, formerly of Durango, also were present for the observance. The Baudino wedding picture can be seen here on the wall over their heads.

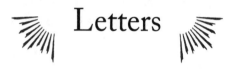

Letters

Following are copies of actual letters showing the letterheads of the family businesses. Katie Baudino is the author of the first two letters and Jennie Bonavida writes the third letter.

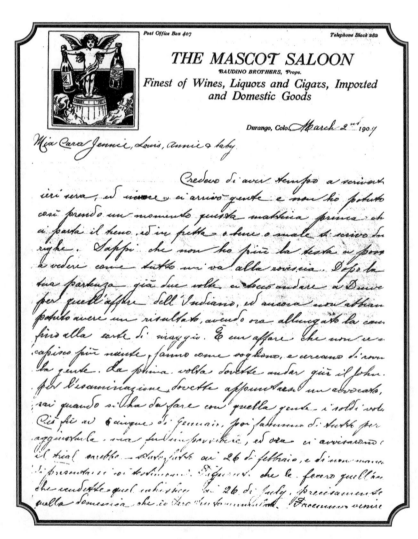

Post Office Box 407   Telephone Block 282

THE MASCOT SALOON
BAUDINO BROTHERS, Props.

Finest of Wines, Liquors and Cigars, Imported and Domestic Goods

Durango, Colo. March 2nd 1909

PHONE DURANGO 28 J-2   P. O. BOX 434

THE MORNING STAR MINE
BAUDINO & COMPANY

DURANGO, COLO., *Dec. 15th* 1917

Carissimi Cognati e Famiglia

Essendo vicinissimi le fest
del Natale e Capo d'Anno, se anche un po' in ritar
non possiamo tralasciare senza augurarvele bei
sebbene sappiamo purtroppo che l'allegria non può reg
ora nelle nostre case, ma coll'aiuto di Dio speriamo
passarle tutti in salute, e concordia. — L'affetto che no
vi portiamo è troppo grande, perché possiamo trascurar
in queste ricorrenze. È vero che non vi scriviamo tan
sovente; ma ciò non vuol dire che vi dimentichiamo, son
le troppe occupazioni, che c'impediscono molte volte di
scrivere. Scusateci, e accettate i miseri auguri che vi
mandiamo, di un prospero e buon Natale, e buon fine
e miglior principio d'anno. Voglia il novello anno porta
sempre buona fortuna, e Gesù Bambino, che ora siam
lo preghiamo, voglia proteggerci i cari nipoti da questo
fratello Si..lia, e ricongiungeli suoi nell..... on
alt.. ora una ...amiciano, e sono cert... che .....
.... le nostre ; e ....
quelle .... che ci consuma è vi sia ... nel ...
.......a .... va ...., pensa per i tuoi figli

Belleville House
1260 Blair Street
P. O. Box 415   Telephone
Philip Sartore, Proprietor

Questo è firma indirizzo

Sig. Luigi Bonavida Silverton Colo Box 415 North America

Silverton, Colorado, March 10th 1920

Signor Carlo Baudino

Rivara Canavese

Caro Amico,

Sarà con sorpresa e forse trover
strano, nel vedervi giungere in mio scritto, piove
-fido nella vostra bontà memore della vita an
in tempi passati e migliori ed è per questo che mi
prendo tanta libertà nell'inviarvi la presente mia
Sempre volevo scrivervi molto tempo prima, poi
le disgrazie successe le une alle altre, che al so
pensarvi mi fa tremare, e giunsi fino ora,
Dunque scusatemi tanto il mio ardire e sopratu
accordatemi il favore che sto per chiedervi.
In questo massimo tempo che scrivo a voi scrivo
pure al Signor Grivetto S. Orsega il quale tiene
nelle sue mani il mio libretto della Cassa di Risp
mio unito a uno di posta della mia povera Lina.
Per certi affari che a voi rivelerò più decisi di leva
il tutto dalle sue mani e consegnare il tutto a voi
avrete tanto cortese da volerli accettare, siccome tenete già
gli affari di mio fratello e sorella, così potete anche aver
miei che son sicura saranno in mani giuste e sicure

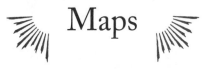

Maps

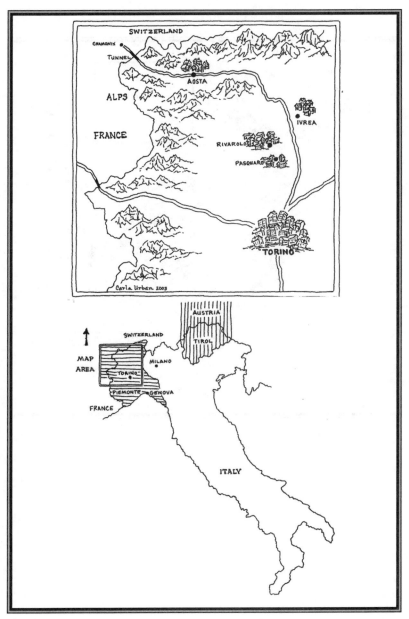

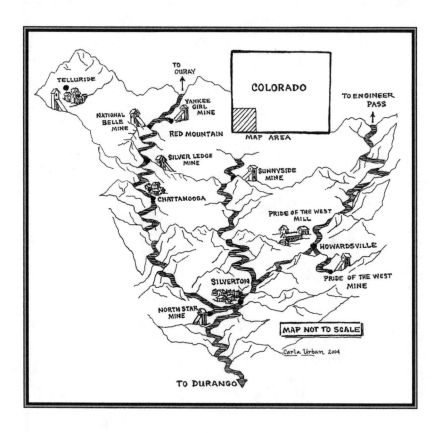

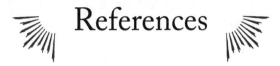

APPENDIX C

References

Bird, Allan G. *Bordellos of Blair Street.* Pierson, MI: Advertising, Publications, and Consultants, 1993.

"Colorado, San Juan County," *Twelfth Census of the United States 1900.* February 27, 2003. www.genealogy.com

"Colorado, San Juan County," *Thirteenth Census of the United States 1910.* June 18, 2003. www.genealogy.com

Durango and Silverton Directory, 1903. Durango, CO Householders Directory, 1911-1912, and 1921.

El Saadawi, Nawal. *The Hidden Faces of Eve.* London and New York: Zed Books, Ltd., 1980.

Engel, Dave and Gerry Mantel. *Copper Country Metropolis 1898–1913.* Rudolph, WI: River Cities Memoirs-Maki, 2002.

Lindgren, Waldemar. *Mineral Deposits.* New York and London: McGraw-Hill Book Company, 1933.

Myres, Sandra L. *Westering Women and the Frontier Experience.* Albuquerque: University of New Mexico Press, 1982.

Osterwald, Doris B. *Cinders and Smoke.* Hugo, CO: Western Guideways, Ltd., 2001.

Peterson, Freda Carley. *The Story of Hillside Cemetery.* Vol. 1-2. Silverton, CO: Freda Carley Peterson, 1996.

Reyher, Ken. *Silver and Sawdust, Life In the San Juans.* Montrose, CO: Western Reflections, 2002.

Sacconier, Franco. *Rivarolo la mia citta. [Rivarolo, My Town.]* Torino, Italia: Collana Memoria, 1992.

Seyfarth, Jill. "Durango, Colorado AKA 'Smelter City'," *Historic Durango 1999*. Vol. VI, p. 15. Durango, CO: La Plata County Historical Society, May 14, 2000.

Smith, Duane A. *Guide to Durango and Silverton*. Evergreen, CO: Cordillera Press, Inc., 1988.

Smith, Duane A. *Rocky Mountain Boom Town*. Niwot, CO: University Press of Colorado, 1980.

ACKNOWLEDGEMENTS

I give endless thanks to my friends and family for making this book possible. The journey has taken me many places and introduced special people into my life. But the spirit and soul of this story belongs to the characters whose lives unfolded as I wrote. I was aware of their guidance every step of the way.

Thanks to the Naretto and Peila families in Italy for staying in touch with me throughout the many years. The letters and photos from Lino Naretto were the basis for most of the story, and they came alive through the translations of our cousin, Angela Peila Sundquist. Thanks to Alberto Naretto for scanning the many photos and to Quinta Naretto Carruozzo for sending her favorite recipes.

What I needed to know about Silverton was discovered in a collection of biographies called *The Story of Hillside Cemetery* by Freda Carley Peterson. Making contact with Freda and her husband, Brison Gooch, proved to be significant, and I value the friendship that developed through this common interest. It was their suggestion that, rather than simply publishing the letters, I should develop the characters so we might better understand the letters. So, the story was written.

My mother, Lena Baudino Babey, overcame her apprehension for the project and searched her memory for answers to my endless questions. My daughter, Stephanie, and my sons, Brad and Chris, were there at the very beginning of what would become "my obsession with the past." My husband, Jon, guided me, helped with his computer skills, and listened to my incessant chatter as my excitement for the project developed. It all came to life when my sister, Carla Urban, offered her artwork in doing the illustrations.

I started this project while Jon and I were living in Sydney, Australia, so when I needed a reaction, I called on my local friends to read and give me feedback. Sue Lewis, Sharon Pink, Leslie MacKintosh, Dale Schrivener, Dal and Wynn Swain, Carlo Colpani, Wendy and John O'Brien, Ruth Hamilton, Lyn Roseby, and Susanna Gillings offered encouragement as they read through those early chapters. Dal Swain, MSc PhD, even researched information I needed on minerals and ores. I hope they are all able to visit Colorado one of these days when we can explore together the unique places of Silverton and Durango.

The Animas Museum in Durango was one of my first sources and I thank Charles DiFerdinando, Robert McDaniel, and Henry

Ninde for their interest in the project and for helping me find needed information.

Phone conversations with those in Colorado connected me with Margaret Crotta Morris and JoAnn Vota. As we chatted, they came up with intriguing answers to many difficult questions.

Connie Bonaventura Trontel provided me with wonderful stories, photos, and addresses so we could connect the family once again. Her daughter, Mary Ann, along with Sandy and Silvia Bonaventura, offered interest and support. Also, Connie's brother, Frank, in Alaska, wrote to me, expressing his excitement in the project. Through Connie, I also found Genevieve Trioni Robinson and daughter, Dee Cleary, and brother, Gordon Trione, and his wife, Joyce. With their help, we pulled together the families of the three Giordano sisters—the connecting factor and basis for the story. Dee studied old census pages, sending valuable bits of information over the Internet. She and her Uncle Gordon both sent books, making it possible for me to insert historical information about Calumet, Michigan. It was a wonderful bonus when Dee and her husband, Mike, came for a visit all the way from Jefferson City, Missouri, to Sydney, Australia.

On visits to Silverton, I met Joe and Teddie Todeschi and Gerald Swanson. They were able to give me first-hand opinions on historical happenings. Marvin Payoff, a former owner of the Belleview Saloon, gave us a thorough tour of the old building so I could visualize the story there.

I thank the members of the Sydney Mandolin Orchestra for performing the music I wrote that was inspired by the story, and special thanks to my mentor and former music professor, John Kincaid and his wife Georgia, in Gunnison, Colorado. They gave me constant encouragement and assistance with the story and the music. The piano magic of Lino's daughter, lovely Anna Naretto, as she recorded my music in Italy, connected us in a significant way, bringing tears to my eyes.

Many thanks to my editor, Bonnie Beach. With her amazing editing style she broadened the scope of the story. Her enthusiasm and encouragement to see the story through helped guide me to publication—and she made it fun.

To each of you, my heartfelt thanks. I could not have done this alone.

—K. A. Niemann

About the Author

Kay Niemann was born in Durango, Colorado, but began her life abroad in 1967 when she was hired as a teacher by the United States Department of Defense. She taught music to American dependent children in Okinawa, Japan, and later transferred to Incerlik Air Base in Turkey. There, she met Jon Niemann, and they married in Durango in 1972.

Kay and Jon continued their life together as corporate gypsies, moving to seven different states and two foreign countries within thirty years. Kay received news of the letters found in Italy and was inspired to write *Salone Italiano* while living in Sydney, Australia. She and Jon now live near Los Angeles, California.

The author with the roulette wheel from the old Belleview Saloon. The photo taken in the old jail, now the San Juan County Historical Museum, in Silverton, Colorado, 2002.

If you enjoyed *Salone Italiano*, you may like reading these other titles from Western Reflections Publishing Co.:

Swanee's Silverton: A Firsthand Account of Silverton, Colorado from the 1930s to the Millennium

Colorado Mining Stories: Hazards, Heroics, and Humor

Silver & Sawdust: Life in the San Juans

Mountains of Silver: Life in Colorado's Red Mountain Mining District

Ida: Her Labor of Love

A Brief History of Silverton

Colorado Mountain Women: Tales from the Mining Camps

Maggie's Way: The Story of a Defiant Pioneer Woman

Bess: A Woman's Life in the Early 1900s

Father Struck It Rich: Story of the Thomas Walsh Family

To find out more about these titles and others, visit our web site at www.westernreflectionspub.com or call for a free catalog at 1-800-993-4490.